BS Stands for Blacksmith
Dale's Tales of Growing Up in Hetland, SD

By Dale M. (Mory) Andersen

Copyright © 2007
Dale Andersen

ALL RIGHTS RESERVED

This work may not be used in any form,
or reproduced by any means,
in whole or in part,
without written permission
from the author.

ISBN: 978-1-57579-365-8

Library of Congress Control Number: 2007937892

Thank you to Greg Latza/ Peoplescape Publishing
for providing the cover photograph.

For additional copies contact:
Virgil Andersen
2805 W. Delrich Drive
Sioux Falls, SD 57107
bs-blacksmith@hotmail.com

Printed in the United States of America

PINE HILL PRESS
4000 West 57th Street
Sioux Falls, SD 57106

Dedication

This book is dedicated to my Dear, Loving and Caring wife, EVA and to our kids, Myrna, Virgil and Vi, through whose labor of Love this book became a reality. THANKS, "Kids."

Eva & Dale with Myrna, Vi, Virg, Elaine and Melanie

Table of Contents

Dedication v
Foreword ix
Preface xi

1. Nicknames 1
2. Growing Up in Hetland 5
3. The King has Abdicated 25
4. Married with Children 35
5. Family *Matters* 53
6. Hetland in War 67
7. A-Hunting We Will Go 73
8. All Creatures Great and Small 93
9. Just for Fun 107
10. Characters of All Kinds 117
11. Have You Heard About... (Town stories) 127
12. In the BS Shop 153
13. Life Along the Railroad 163
14. Tall Tales 169
15. Faithful Living (Church stories) 175
16. Reading, Writing, and Arithmetic 185
17. Team Efforts (Sport stories) 201
18. Fraternal Ties 209
19. Dale's E-mails 217
20. Epilogue 241

viii BS Stands for Blacksmith

Top: Main Street, east side, from south
Middle: West side of Main Street looking north, 1908 (postcard labeled wrong)
Bottom: West side of south Main Street, looking north, ca 1908

Foreword

In 1862, the Homestead Act offered 160 acres of free land to people who would live on the land for 5 years or plant 10 acres of trees and keep them alive for 8 years. In 1878, Dakota Territory was opened to homesteaders. Many who settled in east central South Dakota were immigrants from northern Europe — Scandinavia and northern Germany. They came seeking economic opportunity and freedom.

To speed development, railroads were built into the new territory. By 1881, the Chicago and North Western Railroad had extended to Pierre, SD. The railroads platted town sites every 7 to 10 miles to provide coal and water needed for their steam locomotives. The towns provided population centers for trade and created markets for the goods the trains brought in. Elevators and stockyards provided places for farmers to sell their grain and livestock to be shipped by rail.

In 1888, Asa Felton and his wife founded a town on the Chicago and Northwestern Railroad line in east central South Dakota, about 45 miles west of the Minnesota border. Believe it or not, they named this town Felton. Some time later it was discovered there was another Felton, SD in the records. The town's name was changed to HETLAND to honor the memory of John Hetland, an area homesteader who had been murdered in 1878 while returning home from Sioux Falls. As far as we know, it is the only town named Hetland in the nation.

Hetland, the locale for most of Dale's stories, is located in Kingsbury County a mile north of US Highway 14. The county seat is DeSmet, the "Little Town on the Prairie" of Laura Ingalls Wilder fame. The railway now belongs to the Dakota, Minnesota and Eastern Railroad. Two larger lakes are located in close proximity to the town. Lake Whitewood lies to the southwest and Lake Preston to the west, each about 7 miles long. On the southeast edge of the town is Lake Ole, perhaps 100 acres in size. These lakes and numerous sloughs provide excellent habitat for pheasant, duck and goose hunting. The land is gently rolling and the rich soil produces excellent crops.

The road into Hetland from Highway 14 becomes Main Street. The railroad tracks divide the town into two distinct halves. The north half is fairly level and the business district, church, school, etc. were all located here. The M. Andersen and Son Blacksmith Shop was located one-half block west of Main Street, on the south side of North Street, kitty-corner from the back of Starksen's Store. Morris and Ruby Andersen lived in the house west of the shop. Dale and Eva Andersen were across the street, north of them. The south half of town slopes from the railroad tracks down toward a small creek. Grain elevators dominate the area near the railroad tracks. Most of the remaining area is residential.

Morris Andersen came to America in 1899, at the ripe age of 23. His first choice was to go to sea, but he said, "Ma raised so much HELL about it that I decided to apprentice to be a blacksmith." He went to Copenhagen to learn the trade, and after that joined the Danish Army for his obligatory service. The few photos he brought with him showed him as a handsome, dashing, athletic figure.

He told stories of sailing on the fjord in north Jutland near Vestervig, Denmark. His love of boating (especially when there were lots of white-capped waves) and his appetite for fish - fresh, pickled, dried, salted or canned - were holdovers from his boyhood. He landed in Halifax, Nova Scotia and traveled by train via Chicago to Bryant, SD where he stayed with his aunt and uncle to work, learn English and become Americanized. He then moved to Hetland where he built a small shop near the church. He lived in a room over the shop, then later bought Lynn Barber's blacksmith shop located across the street from where he had purchased a home. He moved the shop building to the east of his home and turned it around to face the north, adding a couple rooms to it. He lived and worked in that location until his death in 1972 at the age of 96. In 1909 he married Ruby Clark, a schoolteacher who would be his partner as they raised a family of four sons. The example they set of honesty, hard work, integrity, community service and faith was a legacy for their children and grandchildren to emulate.

Their first son, Dale, was born in January of 1914. During the 1930s prolonged drought dried up the lakes. Grasshopper infestations and little rain led to crop failures for farmers. Drought and the national depression meant hard times for all. Money was always tight, since blacksmiths plied their trade for struggling farmers with little to spend. During WWII, Dale stayed home to work in the vital blacksmith trade while his younger brothers, Homer, Clayton and Elden served in the military. The war brought shortages and price controls. The end of hostilities promised a brighter future.

But the technological revolution caught up to agriculture. Gasoline and diesel tractors replaced horses and steam engines. The REA electrified the farms. Plows, disc harrows and cultivators that were all the bread and butter of the blacksmith trade were replaced by throwaway components and new farming practices. Steel wheels and rubber tires replaced wooden wagon wheels. Farms grew from small acreages to a thousand acres or more with their own repair shops. Small family farms that were the lifeblood of the blacksmith and the rural community disappeared.

Many of the stories Dale tells are set in the depression era. Everyone was poor and had to get by on as little as possible. People with so very little still helped people with even less. Entertainment was up to you, and fun was what you did to make it. A nickel went a long way, a quarter was a fortune, and a dollar made you rich! Everything was saved for reuse. Baked and canned goods were homemade. Tools were made when needed, since there was no money to buy them. Gardens were for subsistence. Indoor plumbing was a luxury and refrigeration was often not affordable. Many homes had a cellar as the only place where produce and dairy products could be kept cool.

When Eva Guptill came to Hetland to teach school, Dale entered the world of romance, marriage and family responsibility. Together they made a significant impact in their community, and reached out to cultivate lifelong friendships with so many people. When Eva was in a nursing home and after her death in 2000, Dale was faced with long evenings alone. Always a gregarious storyteller, he responded to our request that he write down stories and recollections of his life experiences. This book is a compilation of some of those stories. They are a precious part of our family history that we would like to share with you. We hope you will find them both entertaining and informative.

- Myrna, Virgil and Vi Andersen

Preface

REMEMBER WHEN IN HETLAND?
Dale (Mory) Andersen

Tales and facts about growing up and living in Hetland, SD, the "BEST" and only place that I have ever called "HOME!"
- *Dale M. (Mory) Andersen*

This is no "bull" even though it might not be always judged that way by some of my readers.

I don't remember anything about being born, but my folks, Morris and Ruby (Clark) Andersen said I was born on January 16, 1914. Don't know the exact time of my arrival so I don't know if I was on schedule or not.

I was the first of four boys born to this union. Homer, Clayton and Elden came to round out our family.

As a family we didn't have much of the world's goods, but we had a lot of love and a happy life together. Our Ma was never in good health but never complained and always saw to it that her family was well taken care of.

Our folks always instilled in us the difference between right and wrong and to stand up for what was right. They also taught us to be kind and loving and I like to think that what they taught us through the years has "rubbed off" on each of us boys and our families.

Dale, 1915

I have been blessed with a loving and caring wife, Eva (Guptill), who put up with me from June 24, 1937 when we were married near Springfield, SD, until she went Home in November of 2000. We have two loving and caring children, Myrna and Virgil, both of whom we are proud to call our kids. We lost our firstborn, a boy named Wendall, at birth. We have a loving and caring daughter-in law, Vi (Davis), who came into our lives when she married Virgil. He couldn't have picked out a nicer girl to be a part of us. Besides that, we have two granddaughters and two great-grandsons, all of whom have enriched our lives.

We have had a wonderful relationship with our in-laws and all of their families. We have loving nieces and nephews of whom we are very proud and whom we enjoy as a vital part of our family.

The Lord has richly blessed us and our cup runneth over! Thanks to all of you for being so good to us. We love you.

Now–this Epistle has no rhyme or reason to it. It is in no particular order, as you will come to realize, but came as I thought about events that took place while living in Hetland.

Hetland in 1907 from schoolhouse. Dale's house in foreground.

Chapter 1
Nicknames

Sign on east side of Main Street,
north of railroad tracks

Morris and Ruby (Clark) Andersen with sons Dale, Homer, Clayton and Elden

Chapter 2
Growing Up in Hetland

Left: Morris Andersen in Danish Army, 1897
Middle: Morris Andersen and Ruby Clark wedding photo, September 4, 1909
Right: Ruby Clark Andersen

Spot (C. L. Laymon)
Springs (Richard Olson)
Starkey (Donald Starksen)
Streel (Mervin Nelson)
Three Horse (Delbert Johnson)
Tillie (Mildren Sherkenback)

Tommy (Floyd Thompson)
Toodle (Wayne Johnson)
Toot (Philo Bishop)
Woodrow (Roy Wilson)
Zib (Ed Melstad)

Nicknames

I don't think I know of any other community where more people had nicknames than we had in Hetland. Some were pretty nice, and some were not so nice. A list of some that come to mind include:

August (Herman Nelson)
Barney, Charley (Charles Johnson)
Boober, Bruce (Leon Melstad)
Bubs (Benjamin Nelson)
Buck (Russell Buckley)
Buckskin (Emil Johnson)
Bumpy (Billy Bishop)
Cal (Art Calvet)
Cap (Donald Sorenson)
Charlie (Charles Ballou)
Charlie (Charles Cleveland)
Chuck (Charles H. Starksen)
Cleve (Lloyd Cleveland)
Count (Kenwood Cleveland)
Dane (Elden Andersen)
Debs (Charles Starksen)
Del (Delbert Barber)
Doc (Clair Warne)
Dorie, Bunny (Darlene Starksen)
Duck (Guy Dutcher)
Dutch (Verle Dutcher)
Flop (Phil Johnson)
Gub (Wilbur Stangland)
Gunder (Ralph Mauch)
Guptill (Eva Andersen)
Gus (Russell Eidsmoe)
Hans (Milford Tande)
Happy (Melvin Larson)
Happy (Harold Nelson)
Hilda (Telmar Pederson)
Hiram (Harrison Ballou)
Hobo, Emil (Homer Andersen)
Huber, Baldy (Howard Crandall)
Jack (Otto Krueger)
Jerry (J. N. Bundy)
Jiggs (Stanley Nelson)
K. V. (Kenneth Hesby)
Knock 'em stiff (Fred Buckley)
L. A. or Diddle (Lewis Crandall)
Mel (Melvin Peterson)
Moon (Gale Dutcher)
Morrie, Admiral (Maurice Matson)
Mory (Dale Andersen)
Mose (Darcy Melstad)
Nasty (Gerald Dutcher)
Nip (Harold C. Nelson)
Obbie (Orris Melstad)
Old Mory (Morris Andersen)
Opal (Oval Stangland)
Oz (Oscar Pederson)
Pewee (Carl Scherkenback)
Pete (Harold Mauch)
Pete (Clifford Nelson)
Pick (Eileen Johnson)
Red (Eider Stangland)
Scots (Myrum Matson)
Scott (Gordon Lovell)
Scrub (Harry Russett)
Shrimp (Lyle Cleveland)
Sig (Carl Peterson)
Skinny (Clayton Andersen)
Skip (Stanley Farness)
Skipper (Alvin Pederson)
Slug (Joe Johnson)
Snort (Ludolf Buhn)
Snowball (Howard Melstad)
Sonny (Leon Melstad Jr.)

Growing Up in Hetland

When Pa left the old country, his Ma was crying and told him that she would never see him again. Pa told her he would be back, but he never had enough money to make the trip back to Denmark. After I was born, his mother often wrote that she would sure like to see little Dale. She never had any grandkids, except the four of us. I didn't even get to know what a grandpa or grandma was like, so I can see now what the Andersen boys missed, but at the time we didn't know the difference.

One time we were in Vermillion to see Virg, Vi and the grandkids. Before church I went downstairs to get the little ones from Sunday school. One of them saw me and said, "There's Grandpa." A little boy looked up at me and said, "What's a grandpa?" It hit me right between the eyes that the little boy didn't have any grandpa to call his own, and would be like us, never to have the excitement of having loving grandparents to cuddle up to.

Eva was fortunate to have grandparents on both sides of her family. She was an only child, and I used to feel sorry for her that she didn't have a brother or a sister. She always said she would have had a good time loving one or the other. The way it was, a doll had to take the place of a next of kin. She told about one time the Congregational preacher was coming to visit them. Her mom told her daughter to hurry up and get some clothes on her doll before Reverend Warner showed up. Maybe Grandma Guptill figured the preacher had never seen a naked doll. Who knows? But we would get a good laugh out of that.

When we had a preacher over for dinner, we never checked to see if our grandkids' dolls were presentable or not. Times have changed, I suppose. They used to ask us if they could sit by the guest. We were always ready to oblige, and the Man of God enjoyed being their friend, as well as ours. John Johnston, one of our ministers, always ate Sunday dinner with us. We always called him Father John. Our little granddaughters knew that they could sit on his lap before we ate dinner. They always sat beside the guest, and after the first time sitting by John, they took it for granted that they would sit on either side of him.

When Pa first came to town he met a fellow on the street who asked him if he was the new blacksmith in town. Pa told him he was and just then this fellow (who happened to be a Norwegian) reached up with his open hand and dug his fingernails into Pa's face and said "You are a nice man." BOOM, just like that this Norske was flat on his back, as a Dane newcomer wasn't about to let anyone scratch his face like that. Then this guy took off his hat and showed his bald head. Nels Petersen, a Dane who ran the livery stable came over to the shop and said, "Morris, what's going on? You can't come to the U.S. and knock people down like that!" Pa wanted to know what kind of damn people lived over here to pull something like that on a newcomer. Nels had a good laugh about it but Pa didn't think it was funny.

When our folks were married in 1909, they bought a round dining room table and six chairs. It could be lengthened out to be a big table, as it would accommodate several leaves. When one of the Andersen boys was going to do bodily harm to one of his brothers, the table would come in handy. The one who was to get "worked over" would get on one side of the table and the avenger on the other. Then we would try to settle the differences over the tabletop. Most of the time, that didn't work, so - around and around the table we would go. If the one being the aggressor stopped, the other one did too. More talk and more chasing. Finally, by mutual agreement or decision that this was a waste of time, the feud was ended, thanks to the table separating the two adversaries.

Virg and Vi have the table and chairs now, but I have never heard that their girls, Melanie and Elaine, ever used the table for any other purpose than what it was made for, to eat off from. Underneath the table in big bold numbers is listed the price of this now antique table and chairs - $24 to be exact. That would indeed be a bargain if purchased today.

The folks told the story that after they were married, Pa complained that our Ma's rye bread wasn't as good as what his Ma baked in Denmark. One day he was exasperated enough that he told her he would show his new bride how his Ma baked bread. He proceeded to do so. After the so-called "good" bread had cooled, they used it to hold down the covers on the pickle crocks in the cellar where they were placed to keep cool. Guess they were hard as rocks, and Pa never baked any more bread. Ma had the reputation of baking the best rye bread in the country, and I can vouch for that. We ate lots of it, as that was about as cheap as any food we could eat.

When some of our little friends came to visit us, they didn't go away hungry, as Ma always let them eat as much bread as they desired. Mamie Petersen would tell her kids, "Now don't eat all of Ruby's bread." That admonition always fell on deaf ears.

Our Ma, (and Pa should be included in this), had 4 boys in 5 years, so she had her work cut out for her. She used to say, "We have the

Dale, Homer Clayton and Elden

worst kids in town," until she would visit some one else with kids, and then she decided her kids were not so bad after all. By the way, when we were up to some deviltry, (which happened occasionally) I, being the elder one of the foursome, seemed to be the designated leader. We always seemed to get home in time to enjoy a delicious meal after our shenanigans, what ever they might be.

When we were kids we had a fence around our yard. I would open the gate, occasionally, and let my brother Homer out. He would amble up toward Main Street. When he got just about there I would run into the house and tell Ma, in a surprised voice "Homer is out and already uptown!" Ma, being a schoolteacher, must have figured out how her son had escaped from the yard.

Ole Stangland had a dog that could bite. One time he was over to the shop with the dog

Marion Phinney, Homer and Dale at "The Gate"

and Homer and I were out in front pestering the darn dog. The dog took after us. I could run faster than Homer, so I got through the gate and shut the gate on Homer. The dumb dog bit him. Homer was madder than hops and said, "What did you do that for? Why didn't you let me in too?" I told him it was better that one got bit than two. That didn't help his frame of mind at all. Oh golly, he was MAD!

The folks used to tell that when I was a little guy, I would imitate Pa talking to Ed Farness on the phone. It went like this, according to them: "Ding a ling, Hello - no, I can't shoe your horses, I don't have time. No, I can't shoe your horses!" Bang, the receiver was up. "Who was that?" (That's what Ma would ask Pa after the call.) My reply, "It was that damn

Dale and Homer

Ed Farness." End of my big ears listening in, or rather eavesdropping on an interesting connection.

When I was a little squirt, I would be over to the shop to watch Pa shoe horses. I guess I was a big nuisance. One time a horse wouldn't come into the shop and somehow he came through the big door and nearly fell on me. After that I was scared of horses, and didn't get in their way anymore.

We used to have a leather couch with one end higher than the rest, so if you lay down on it, there would be a place to rest your skull. Well, I would lead the pack, climb up on the low end and march across to the other end and jump off. I, being the eldest of the lot, naturally had to be in command, and little Elden brought up the rear. When I got tired of these shenanigans, we all quit, and I was the boss. What a pity the other three loving brothers had to put up with me. But otherwise we grew up anyway, and seemed to have a lot in common, with a good mother and father to keep us in line.

Sometimes after Ma got all four of us boys all cleaned up and ready to go someplace, we would go up to Starksen's store. Debs would be so kind to us that he would give us black licorice to chew on. When we got home, Ma would need to clean us up again. Ma used to say she had a hard time deciding whether she should get dressed first or dress us first. One time she dressed us up. While she was changing her clothes we got out into mud or something. When she saw us, she took off her good clothes, put on her work clothes and none of us went anywhere. I don't ever remember her giving us heck for it. But, I think she could have choked Debs for giving us the candy.

Ma used to make the best homemade beef soup, and money couldn't buy that kind of soup. Our old Dane friend, Pete Larsen, the butcher in Lake Preston, would give us beef bones, free of charge. Now the stores charge a fortune for bones. Ma would cook it with what little meat she could afford to buy. Boy, it was good! Eva did a good job making beef soup as do her kids, Myrna and Virgil. I'm no culinary expert.

For years Virg brought various kinds of homemade soup to Mom and me. It tickled our gullets. He still does the same for me, and let me tell you that any soup he brings can't be bought in any store. At times, I scratch my head as to the contents!

Ma would make pie crusts and cut them into little pieces, put one piece on top of the other and make a hole in the top crust to put jelly in. She would bake these, and they were delicious. She sent my brother Skinny (Clayton) over to our neighbor, Jessie Hurd, with a whole pie pan of the little morsels. Jessie wasn't home at the time, but he was welcome anyway, as the door wasn't locked. As he was going into the house he tripped over the threshold, and down he went, pie pan and all. He wasn't too big, so he proceeded to sit his butt on the floor, and started to put all the broken pie crust pieces back together like a jigsaw puzzle, I suppose. He didn't come back for quite a while, and Ma was getting worried about him. When he finally came home, she wanted to know what took him so long. He filled her in as to how hard it was to fit those broken pieces together in the right places. What a great guy! A few days later, Ma told Jessie about it, and she said, "I wondered what happened to the crust, as there were so many pieces." They had a good laugh out of it, and I'll bet the pieces tasted all right, even after being laid out on the floor, probably catching some dust, too. Who knows?

By the way, we preferred pure apple jelly to complement the pie crust, although other kinds of jelly tasted OK if pure apple jelly was not available. Plum preserves were another delicious treat, even if eaten without pie crust or bread.

When Ma would cook mutton, and we were ready to sit down to eat, Skinny would lift his head up like a scenting bird dog and say, "Mutton!" That was it, and we wouldn't touch it. Why, I don't know, but Ma would be disgusted with us kids for not even trying it.

Pete Larsen, the butcher, made rolapuls out of mutton and we thought it was great. Now, Virg makes rolapuls out of beef flank or pork loin, and that is delicious too. If you have never eaten rolapuls, you don't know what you are missing! It is even better than lutefisk! I can hear some comment on that observation from you non-lutefisk eaters!

Clayton, Dale, Elden and Homer

Ma used to churn butter with an old crock and a wooden paddle in order to save as much money as she could. When we got older we would help out pushing the paddle up and down until we had butter made. Then, when it came to getting the butter out of the churn, we little squirts wanted her to leave little pieces of butter on top of the buttermilk, as that made the buttermilk taste better. The buttermilk was delicious, and I like it to this day, but this cultured (imitation) stuff isn't like the real stuff.

When we had margarine in the early days, our "big wigs" out in Pierre were mostly farmers in the legislature. They passed a law that the only margarine sold had to be white, in order to protect the dairy industry. People would know it was margarine, and not real butter. If you wanted to color it, there were little capsules full of yellow color to mix with the margarine to make the "ole" look like the real stuff. What a mess, when we got this chore done. Finally the poor people who couldn't afford butter got the law repealed so that today it comes colored.

When the Co-op Creamery was operating in Arlington, before going "belly up," they had buttermilk that looked pretty blue, as there was no butter left in it. We could buy it for a nickel a gallon, and if we let it ferment awhile, it tasted pretty good. Now we pay a buck or more for a quart of so-called cultured buttermilk. I still enjoy drinking the stuff!

My folks were married in 1909 and had a rough time of it for several years after their marriage. Everything Pa made, and that wasn't very much, went to pay hospital and doctor bills for Ma. However, in the late 20s, Pa had scraped together enough money that he decided we could get a radio, so we weren't always way behind the Joneses. Dakota Iron Store in Sioux Falls had the agency for Atwater Kent, so we got a small, inexpensive set, and got it wholesale at that. Boy, was that great. We used to play an old Edison phonograph, one that had records that were made like a tube. We kids had about worn out the "Stars and Stripes Forever" march, and Virg and Myrna spent many hours upstairs in Grandpa and Grandma's home playing the old phonograph, too. They enjoyed good music then and still do. The machine still works, and Myrna has it, as she conned her Grandpa into letting her have it.

We couldn't get many stations on the radio, but some that we could get were good programs. Not a lot of "smut" like we hear nowadays. One station we got a kick out of hearing was the announcer saying "This is station W-H-O," and then he would ask "Who? Des Moines." It sounded just like someone asking the question, "Who?" as if they didn't know what it was all about. When the news was about to come on, the announcer would holler, "Take it away, Foster May," and Foster May would know that was his cue, and would "take it away" with fresh news right out of the speaker.

When we were growing up, if someone offered a couple of us a nickel to mow their yard, we would jump at the chance to earn all that money. Two of us would furnish the reel-type push mower and get the job done in a hurry to get the money. We would get five pennies in change and each of us would take two cents, so we had a penny left to divide between us. We would flip a penny to see who would get to decide what kind of candy we could get or else see who would get a chance to hit the penny in a machine at Spot's drug store to see if we could get a nickel for the penny. This outfit had a bunch of pegs in it and the idea was to knock the penny across the pegs and get it into a slot on the other side. We had to hit the penny pretty hard, or else it would meander through the pegs and go down into the money chamber where Spot would collect his winnings. Most of the time we used to go into Starksen's Store to study for about five minutes what kind of candy to buy for that lucky penny. Debs would stand patiently on the other side of the glass counter while we deliberated what candy to buy. I don't see how he could stand there and wait, but he did, as it meant a sale, even though he wasn't going to get rich on this big sale.

Another way we tried to make money was to go out along the roads and pick up pop bottles. This wasn't a very lucrative deal, as we could only get a penny apiece for them. We had more exercise walking than bringing in any loot. The state didn't put up any signs letting people know who was keeping the ditches clean. We didn't need to get credit for what we did and we had to furnish our own gunnysacks, besides. Big deal, but it helped keep us out of mischief.

When we were kids, if Pa had 50 cents left on Sunday after paying his bills, he would give it to me to go up to Spot Laymon's drug store to get a quart of maple nut ice cream. We didn't want any other kind. The four of us little stairsteps would go together to get such a delicious treat. I can remember standing with our heads looking over the ice cream counter while Spot ladled out the ice cream in a tall round cardboard container. We were watching to see how hard he pushed the ice cream down into the container. Seems like he always managed to have some "air holes" below the top, but he always smoothed out the top so the ice cream was nice and flat. The only reason he did that was to make it look like we had "full measure." That was a bunch of baloney, because we had watched real close, and told the folks that we didn't get full measure. Anyway, what we had to eat was a special treat, and one that we didn't have very often. I still like maple nut ice cream, but it is hard to come by, and it also costs a "mint."

When we were kids we all wore short-leg pants. I remember well the time I got my first pair of long pants. I didn't want to get caught out with them on. Anyway, Ma put them on me to go to Sunday School. I can still see us going over to the church, and by the time I got to the front door I was moving at a snail's pace. Got inside and leaned against the big door so I wouldn't be too conspicuous, as nobody could see my long pants from behind. Some of the kids came up and pinched my legs and said, "You've got long pants on." I know my folks had to skimp in order to buy me those first long-legged pants, as money in our family didn't grow on trees. Ma always managed to have something for all of us to eat, even though she was in very frail health. She didn't complain, and was always thankful for her family and the love we all had for each other.

Edgar "Spot" and Mable Laymon

We saw many of the men rolling their own cigarettes, and some did a good job of it. We would experiment and try to roll our own, using pieces of newspaper and roll corn silk in it. We were generally on the west side of the house when we proceeded to try out our corn silk cigarettes. We would get the things lit, then peek around the corner of the house to be sure Pa wouldn't be coming. However, if he happened to look out the window of the shop and see us kids checking on him, he would know something was going on and more than once came out and caught us smoking corn silk. I can't recall what this smoking tasted like, but I never got addicted to it or tobacco either, for which I'm thankful.

When we were kids at home, Pa would get a big tame goose, and take the breast off of it. Then he would mix up some kind of brine, and soak the breast for several days. After that, he would take it to Pete Larsen's butcher shop in Lake Preston, where Pete would smoke it to perfection. When we were little, Pa would give us one slice, and it was thin, and that was it. As we got older, we wanted more, so a goose didn't last long. Ma would melt up the fat from the goose, and we would spread that on a slice of bread and put a piece of dried beef on it. Boy, was that good! Today - ???

The first year after we were married, I came home with a nice, big goose and proceeded to take the breast off like Pa did. There wasn't much left of the goose with the breast gone, so my bride put the kibosh to that forever. What a shame, as smoked goose breast was a special Danish treat. Even us part-Danes like it.

Our neighbors, the Costers, had a daughter named Aletha Mae. Why they named her that I don't know. Her Ma would stand outside the house and holler as loud as she could (the old girl had a shrill voice, too) so the kid would be able to hear when she was to come home. "Aletha Mae, Aletha Mae, Aletha Mae." When we heard this static a few times, we would join in the chorus as shrill sopranos to help the mother out to get the kid home. We changed the ritual, and would holler, "Al-leak-a-May, Al-leak-a-May, Al-leak-a-May," and drag it out. After our "cat calls" the old girl would get back into the house and let us giggle at how frustrated she was. The kid must have come home sometimes, as she was with the family when they moved away from living beside us. We must have helped out in getting her home, even though we changed her name to Al-leak-a. Maybe we had a hard time saying this, but on the other hand, maybe we thought she was out of water due to a leak. Who knows?

Dr. Grove came to Hetland and gave all of us kids smallpox scratches. It hurt, and I told the folks I'd get him for that. The Doctor used to laugh about that. When he first started his medical practice here in town he had to grow a beard because he looked so young. After he was older, he moved to Arlington and didn't need the beard.

You may not believe this, but Dr. Grove came to our home to give us the scratch. We were playing outdoors and I can see him yet, coming to the south side of our house, and we let him do to our arm, what he was getting paid to do. He used something sharp to scratch our "hide," and we didn't get smallpox, thanks to him and that little scratch.

Our Ma never had good health but she always took good care of her family even with all her frailties. Pa would never eat lunch between meals while in the shop and afternoons she would watch when she could see me and rap on the window that she had lunch ready and it was time for me to "come and get it." She always had something I would like and I appreciated it too. She was a loving and caring mother.

That was always a special time I spent with my Ma, as she never could eat a big meal after having most of her stomach taken out. She would have to nibble on some snacks between meals in order to keep going, so she would eat with me. After all, she was the mother of four boys coming into this world in five years. That would be a job in itself, as those four boys were half Dane,

Ruby and Dale

which could be a big problem. I shudder to think what we would have been like, if we were genuine lutefisk eaters instead of amateurs.

We never could afford running water and had a cistern for water. Every Sunday night, year in, year out, we would take the copper boiler and put it on a wagon or sled and go up to the pump house and fill it with water so Ma could wash clothes on Monday morning. Pa would get the cookstove going to heat the water. In later years, we had a three-burner kerosene stove for heating it. We didn't have enough money for a change of clothes every day like kids do now, but ours had to last the week or we were in trouble. In the winter Ma hung the clothes on a clothes rack in the house and in summer they were hung outside on the clothesline.

Not having any running water inside, we had an outdoor toilet with 2 holes in it. I have seen 3 holers, but that wasn't for the average family. It seemed as though the colder the weather the more I had to go out and sit on one of those holes with my bare butt exposed to the elements. I think the other hole was to keep the air circulating if no one sat on it. Anyway, I was scared to go out to that outdoor toilet in the dark, so Ma would light the kerosene lantern and we would proceed out to the "can," rain, sleet or snow, it made no difference. I never was too "speedy" doing whatever I did sitting on the toilet and for me it was no place to go when in a hurry. It must have been exasperating for Ma, as I would look at the nice glowing lamp and profoundly say, "We've got a lamp haven't we, Ma." She would say, "Yes, we have a lamp but hurry up!" Speed wasn't my middle name and this dialogue would go on several times before nature decreed I was finished and we would head for the house. Ma never complained, but if she had been like some mothers I know, she probably would have "hung me up to dry." I know she loved me and I loved her too, as did my three brothers.

Pa was on the town board when one night after supper the town cop came to our house and told Pa that one of the town's citizens had consumed too much "hooch" and had hit a farmer on the head with a hammer. The liquored-up guy was sitting in his house with a big butcher knife and was going to kill anyone who came in to get him. The cop said he was scared to go in. Pa said he would go and see about this. We four kids followed along, scared of what might happen. It looked like half the town was standing outside the house door, and there the fellow sat at the kitchen table with the knife in his hand, really spouting off—probably about like Goliath when he berated David back in Bible times. People were yelling at Pa not to go in. Pa didn't miss a step when he walked through the door. The guy got up with his arm drawn back with the knife at the "ready" and told Pa to get back or he would kill him. Pa kept going and said "give me the knife" but that just made the drunk madder and he moved the knife to commit murder when, bang, Pa had the knife and the guy under control all at the same time. Don't know how he did it but his four boys were glad we still had a Pa, and Ma still had a husband.

The drunk's wife said she would file papers, to have him put in the "clink" but she had a change of heart and took him back into their abode, so he could take another "slug" of firewater at a later day. Love knows no bounds, after all, the twosome had five kids to show for their life together. Pretty well-behaved kids too. Norskes, of course.

Dale, Homer, Clayton and Elden, ca 1928

One afternoon, a Dane up by Badger called and asked Pa if he would meet the evening passenger train, and meet a Danish girl from the old country. Jens Petersen couldn't get there in time to meet her. We little tykes asked Pa how he would know which girl she was. He assured us that he wouldn't have any trouble picking out a Dane girl. He must have thought that he was a connoisseur of women, but we found out that wasn't the case. Of the six people getting off the train, four were women. We were there with him, and we wanted to know which one of the girls we were to take home with us. He didn't know! Can you imagine his not knowing a female from across the water that should look like a Dane? Finally, there was only one girl left. She was it, and didn't look any different than the "native" girls. I can remember her in our home talking good English and telling us so proudly that she could drive a "Ford wagon." Evidently, they had Ford cars in Denmark too.

As we were part Dane, the four of us brothers used to argue a little. I know some of our relatives would think that was, or is, an understatement. Sometimes it was three against one, other times it was two against two, and then maybe we would decide to change sides in the argument. One Sunday after church, Skinny and I were doing dishes. He washed and I dried them. I still had my vest and tie on with a chain and watch hanging across from one pocket to the other. For some strange reason, he hit me over the pocket where the watch was. He must have really been mad, as he broke the crystal and smashed the balance wheel and most of the inside parts. Took the jeweler in Lake Preston a year to get it fixed and then it quit before I got home. I took the watch back and the old Norwegian traded me a new one for two bucks to boot. I still have that watch and I think it would still run.

Pa and his four boys really liked honey. Ma didn't care too much for it, but we could eat it three times a day or more. There was a farmer who lived up northwest in the Holy Land, and lived right close to the Holy City, who raised bees and sold honey. Pa would take us kids along with him and buy a case of honey, six gallons for a dollar a gallon. This was supposed to last us through the year until the next harvest. I don't know what six gallons would cost now, but I think it would take a bank loan to finance the purchase.

Pa finally got tired of buying honey so he bought two swarms of bees for himself. He bought extra supers, and an extractor to spin the honey out of the combs, so he had quite a lot of stuff to take care of his two swarms of bees. Like everything else he did, Pa did a good job of tending his bees. After supper, he would sit near the hives by the hour and watch those bees bring in the nectar, landing in front of the hive like they were sent for and were in a hurry to get in. Then they would unload their nectar and take off for the clover field, which might be several miles away. He watched like a hawk, and the bees would produce 200 or 300 pounds of honey a year. Boy, was it good! Nice and clear, and no water added to it.

Pa would furnish the honey in new gallon cans, furnish the gas and the old Model T, and Homer and Skinny would go around the country selling honey for a dollar a gallon. That wasn't the worst of it. Pa let them keep the money, so he was a beekeeper who wasn't figuring out how to make money by getting stung.

About the first time he was taking off supers full of honey to extract, he wanted me to lift off the supers. When those little devils stung me, I swelled up like a balloon and was sick right away. But I was brave for once and knew Pa needed help. I tied up my pant legs and shirt sleeves and buttoned up my shirt at the neck, had a bee veil over my head and wore gloves, too. Pa had a veil but no gloves, and when he got stung, he just brushed the stinger off.

Everything was going just fine, or at least I thought it was. All at once I could feel big claws or feet or whatever bees used to crawl with, climbing up the back of my thigh, heading for my butt or higher. Why that little creature wanted to climb my frame I'll never know, but he was doing just that. I could feel him inching his way up to

Morris with bees

wherever he was going, and I feared what might happen. He was going to nail me, or maybe I should say sting me, even though I wasn't bothering him. I was holding a super full of honey, and I told Pa that there was a bee climbing up my leg. "Don't drop the super," he told me. "He's still climbing," I told him. It was time for me to put the super down and put an end to that formidable bee. I drew back my hand and let him have it through my overalls. But, I was too late - he let me have it in my leg before he went to his happy hunting ground. Talk about hurt! It did, and my leg swelled up like a tight drum. That little devil had the last laugh, and I was the sucker. At least I survived and he didn't.

Another time, a bee stung me on the forehead and I had to go to school with a bump as big as an egg on my head. Unfortunately this time I didn't get to finish the bee off, as he blitzed me and took off.

One time our neighbor, Cach Coster, brought his daughter, Aletha Mae, to show Pa where one of his bees had stung her. He told Pa that he took her to the doctor and spent two bucks for the call, and thought he should be reimbursed. Pa wanted to know why the guy thought he owned the stinger bee. It must be one of the Andersen's bees, as he didn't know anyone else who had bees. Pa gave him two bucks. A few days later brother Homer came into the shop to complain that a bee had let him have it. He wanted two bucks too, but alas, Pa wasn't about to pay his own kids for a bee sting.

When we four boys were growing up, we all slept in one bedroom above the living room. At Christmas, we didn't get much of anything for Christmas except lots of love, for which we were thankful. Pa, being a blacksmith, was too soft-hearted to charge a living wage. If he did have any extra money, it would go to pay Ma's doctor bills, as she didn't have very good health. She nearly died from a botched appendicitis operation. She had gangrene in the open sore for a month, and she finally went to the Mayo Clinic in Rochester where they finished what was supposed to have been done before.

We generally would get some socks or something else to wear that Ma (Santa Claus) would get to put in our hung-up sock. We would be wide awake early, waiting to "hit the stairs" to see what might be awaiting our arrival. We had orders to stay up there until the folks were up. We would hear Pa shake down the hard coal heater and dump in a bucket of coal in the top of the stove. The coal would feed down into the fire when needed. The stove had isinglass so we could see the red coals with a nice blue flame throwing out the much-needed heat. Incidentally, the room we slept in didn't have any heat in it, but the stovepipe came up through the floor into the chimney. The room was cold, but we didn't mind that. We got dressed in a hurry so we didn't freeze our butts off. I don't recall that the excess water we got rid of ever froze in the pot, which we had to empty every morning in the outdoor toilet.

Anyway, now that we knew the folks were up, it was time to hit the deck, or in this case the floor, and four pairs of little feet did just that, going down the stairs at breakneck speed to relieve our expectations and see what Santa had left us. Whatever was there, we were thankful for. We knew that our folks would have liked to give us more, but we knew too that they had sacrificed to give us what they had to make a good Christmas for their four little offspring. We never complained about our gifts, even though we knew that some of our more affluent friends would have looked down their noses at the presents we had received from Santa. We thought we were truly blessed, and we were.

Morris and Ruby's home, rear view from the south

To show you how naïve the Andersen boys were, we didn't know much about the birds and the bees. We were out in the back room of the blacksmith shop doing a lot of pounding when Pa came back and wanted to know what was going on. I proceeded to tell him, as I was the oldest and supposedly the smartest at that stage of life, that we were building a home for old Tom, as he was going to have kittens. We didn't realize that old Tom must have enjoyed Ma's cooking, and was just fat, not pregnant. Kids today would have had this figured out, but not us. We didn't know the facts of life, I guess.

If it has wheels —

When Pa got his first Model T Ford Ma wouldn't ride with him until he could stop in front of the house right where the sidewalk quit. He couldn't do it—either went by or stopped beforehand. Finally, one time he got lucky and made it. He killed the engine when the car was just at the right place, so she got in and rode with him. Seems to me he paid around $480 for the new Model T. When he got rid of a couple of Ford cars, Myrum Matson bought them from the Ford dealer.

The only time I ever knew Pa ran out of gas was up on the county line, coming from Hayti. Back in those days every farmer didn't have gas. Pa walked over to this farm where there were some Danes living and wanted to know if they had any gas, as he was out of fuel. The woman said they didn't have any gas. Then Pa started talking Dane to her and said he had been up to a funeral of his brother-in-law, George Clark, in Hayti. Then the woman wanted to know who he was and he said he was Morris Andersen. She said, "Oh, the blacksmith from Hetland?" She said Valda Clark, my cousin, had taught in their school, up by the Dane cemetery. She continued: "Oh yeah, we've got some high-test gas." He always said if he hadn't been able to talk Dane he would never have gotten the gas. I had the measles so couldn't go to the funeral but enjoyed hearing Pa tell about it.

We were visiting Ma's brother, George Clark and his family in Hayti and they wanted us to stay for supper. Pa said we had to get home before it got dark. They talked us into staying, so we started out late. We got to Lake Norden and the lights went out. Pa drove into the garage and the guy put in a new bulb. We started out for home, went a block and the light went out again. There was another garage there and we stopped at that garage. Pa wanted to know how far it was to the next garage. He said he had stopped at the one just north of here and had put in a new bulb. The guy put in a bulb and that bulb lasted long enough for us to get home. The next morning he took the car up to Nels Nelson's garage and it wasn't the bulb at all. It was a loose wire that caused the bulb to flicker. We were lucky to get home without any more trouble.

Henry Mauch, the banker, would get his son Ralph to drive out into the country to look over the crops. I would sometimes go along. Henry would sit on the back seat and "Gunder" and I in front. If we got up to 25 miles per hour, Henry would tell Gunder, "Better slow down." We discovered we could get up to 35 miles an hour if I would cross my legs to have my foot conveniently covering the speedometer. Henry would move his head, and my foot would automatically move over the speedometer so that he couldn't see how fast we were going. I don't know if he knew how it happened that my foot moved when his eyes tried to focus on the speed indicator. This was one way to get the car speeding along.

I used to go up to the Boyd farm when I was a kid to help out with the early morning chores. George and Nels were not married at this time, so had to do their own cooking. I would get up there early enough so I could get in on another breakfast. They did the chores first, and then went in and made breakfast. They didn't just have cereal. They had potatoes, creamed gravy and salt pork, and that was their first meal of the day. I thought that was a good deal – to eat out, even though I had just had a good meal at home. Today? Nay, nay on that stuff! Today, I start out the day with 12 or more pills, half a slice of toasted homemade bread, with cheese or peanut butter for protein. Then a glass of orange juice to wash down the pills, and that's it. What a comedown from spuds, gravy and salt pork.

We used to mix up wheat, oats and barley in a barrel and then pour water into the barrel to make what the farmers called succotash. The mixture would ferment or do something to the grain so that the pigs would eat and get fat for market. There was no buying high-priced feed from some scalper in those days. We made our own and beat out the middleman and the big feed companies. One morning George told me to take a couple of pails and slop the barrows. I thought he said barrels. I took the two pails of feed around the other side of the hog house, looking for barrels to put the feed into. There were no barrels in sight, but there were lots of pigs crowding around me, looking for a handout. No doubt they could smell the treats that I was carrying in the pails. So, as I couldn't find any barrels to put the feed into, I went back and told friend George that there weren't any barrels to get rid of the feed. "You darn fool, I told you to slop the barrows (pigs), not barrels!"

I was too naïve to know that this herd of pigs, at one time, were gentleman pigs, before some slap-happy guy got busy with a sharp knife and proceeded to take away their masculinity, They were no longer gentlemen pigs, but now went by the name of barrows. They didn't have a very happy future to look forward to, meat on somebody's table. Probably salt pork or bacon. The kids nowadays would know what this was all about, but I had lived a sheltered life and wasn't onto the fine points of raising pigs, male or female.

Dale on the farm

George Boyd had a white bull that seemed to enjoy raising the devil here in town. George and Nels Boyd lived on the Boyd farm up on the hill behind the church. Every so often, their bull would just seem to enjoy himself when he could get out of the pasture, and onto our streets he would come. Just taking his time, walking up one street and down another, at the same time letting out a continuous string of bull bellers. He sounded like he had it in for the rest of the world, and wanted us to know it. We didn't dare to go after him, but George wasn't afraid of him. One time when I was up there, George sent me out to get the cows home. This old bull saw me coming and headed for me with all four feet leaving the ground. I took off the opposite way, picking 'em up and laying 'em down as fast as my feet would go. I was far enough away from this mad animal so that I lived to see another day. When I told George about this narrow escape, he grabbed a pitchfork, and out to the pasture he went on a dead run. The old bull looked cross-eyed at him, but not for long. George met him head on and circled to the old boy's behind and stuck the tines into his rump. I don't know how deep the times penetrated, but that old bull wasn't mad now. He took off for points unknown with blood running out of him. As for me, I really enjoyed this. The old creature had been waylaid by a sharp pitchfork. No more bull to put up with, at least for that day.

I used to work out at Myrum Matson's when I was growing up. I got 25 cents a day for pulling mustard plants out of Myrum's white sweet clover, which he sold for seed. Then I might be turning shocks of grain so the bundles could dry out for the bundle haulers to take into the threshing machine. Myrum had a Fordson tractor that didn't want to start. We would pour ether into it and then crank it some more. I never knew why he thought ether would help start the outfit, because that was what the doctor used to put people to sleep!

Myrum had the cleanest white dwarf sweet clover in the country as we did a good job of cleaning out the mustard. Myrum's two kids, Maurice and Art, used to pick on me, or maybe I picked on them. I was older and bigger than they were, so even though it was two against one, they knew who was the boss. They found out they had better behave, or else something else might happen. Don't recall if I ever paddled them or not. In spite of their frivolous antics, they grew up to be good kids, and are still good friends of mine, even though I did "ride herd" on them. I didn't think of this before, but maybe it was part of my job to keep these two young squirts toeing the line. In spite of me, they turned out OK, and must have learned something along the line, as they are well-behaved now. At their age, they should be!

We picked bushels and bushels of spuds out at Matson's, as this was good potato country at that time. Seventy or eighty carloads of potatoes would be shipped out of Hetland in a year, and we always had to get 16 bushels to put in our cellar. Pa would go down to the loading chute and see some spuds that looked OK. He would tell the old Dane boss, Nels Jepsen that they were the ones he wanted for winter. Nels always told him he would pick out the best ones and send them up to our house. When the better spuds came in, our Danish friend saw to it that we had 16 bushels for winter. I might add that in the spring we would haul out four or five bushels of rotten potatoes, but that made no difference. The next year we got 16 bushels again.

When we were kids, we had a couple of places where we went fishing for bullheads, one in Myrum Matson's pasture, and another out by a bridge where Karbans live at the present time. Matson had a bull that seemed like he was always mad. Mad at what, I never knew. He chased me out of the pasture more than once. One day Verle Dutcher was sitting on the bridge over the creek, fishing for bullheads. He had his shoes off as the day was hot, when all at once he heard a beller behind him. Here came the bull, full speed ahead, aiming for Dutch. He left fish pole and shoes, and headed for the fence and for town. The mad animal stopped when he hit the fence and proceeded to tear up the ground with his front feet, just like a spoiled kid. Dutch didn't dare to go back for his stuff until nearly dark.

We would walk out north of town with our cane poles to the bridge by Karban's and try to catch fish. There was a hole north of the bridge that had water in it after the spring runoff. The fish would come upstream from Lake Badger or Preston, and some of them never made it back to the lake. We didn't have much luck catching anything, but we were like Huckleberry Finn - we tried. What few fish we caught were pretty scrawny, as the puddle got pretty hot and there wasn't a lot of food for them to get fat on. But we enjoyed the outing and the good fellowship.

Gub Stangland and I were trappers – at least that's what we called ourselves. We had a couple of traps and a book that showed pictures of wild animal tracks. We would be down in Lake Ole, see a track in the snow, and get out our book and check to see if it was a mountain lion or what. We never checked out any elephant tracks. We set a trap in an old culvert that was plugged on one end. Went down the next morning before school, and lo and behold, the trap was gone. We looked into the open end of the culvert but it was too dark to see. I got a flashlight and Gub got down and looked in. A striped skunk was in the other end of the culvert, and he and Gub were eyeing each other out.

How would we retrieve the skunk and trap was a problem. Our trapping book didn't have any directions on how to solve it. Then we had a brainstorm. It was Gub's idea, and not mine. Get a strand of barbed wire and feed it into the culvert and see what happened. Gub shoved the wire through and got the skunk tangled up in it. He began to pull the varmint out. Since it didn't take two kids to handle that little skunk, I stayed back while he pulled the creature out far enough to clobber him on the head and send him to its maker. It was nearly time for school, so we put the skunk in Stangland's barn and headed for school. We were all in our seats and all at once the teacher looked up and began to sniff the air. Reminded me of a bird dog testing the scent to see if there was a bird in the bush. She came down the aisle and I thought oh-oh, we're in trouble. She got to Gub and stopped and raised her snoot little higher and said, "Wilbur, go home and get a bath and different clothes." I lucked out – whew!

When we were kids, we had a great time trapping gophers. We didn't use regular traps, except on rare occasions. When we wanted to catch a gray gopher or ground squirrel, then we would use a trap. Out along the railroad by the Dago pond and in the pasture by the dump ground was gopher heaven, or at least it seemed like it, as there were lots of the rodents out there. Generally, we would use a snare and put it in the hole, and then back up a few feet and wait to see if the gopher would stick his head up. If he did have his head in the noose, sometimes we would catch him by the neck and finish him off. We would let him run on the end of the string, and then yank him over on his back before we sent him to his happy hunting grounds. If they wouldn't come up out of the hole we would whistle, pretending we were giving the mating call. Sometimes their curiosity got the better of them, and that was a mistake.

Sometimes, when nothing else worked, we would get a pail of water and drown the varmint out. They didn't like water, and when they came tearing out of the hole we would try to club them. Sometimes they got away into another hole, and then the same procedure was repeated until we nailed him or gave up for something easier. There was a time for a year or so that the county would pay a bounty for gopher tails, the whole sum of a nickel, I think it was, but we had to get them to DeSmet in order to get any money. I don't know what they did with the tails, maybe they pickled them. Who knows, but the "wheels" finally decided it was a losing proposition, so they quit paying the bounty.

My brother Homer (Hobo Emil) was lucky one day and found a five-dollar bill out in the alley by the blacksmith shop. He came tearing into the shop all excited to show us the bill. He wondered who might have lost it. Pa told him to wait a few days and see if anyone came looking for it. Nobody said anything about losing anything, but that five bucks was burning a hole in Homer's pocket. He came into the shop one day and proudly showed us a dollar bill, and said that he had found out who lost the five. I might add that he did a good job to locate the owner of the lost five bucks. Our wise brother asked one of the town businessmen if he had lost a five-dollar bill. I need to tell you that this guy was "on the rocks" and he was flat broke. He soon went out of business. Yes, he said he had lost the bill, and asked where Homer found it. "In the alley by the shop." Yes, that's just where he lost it. Boy, Homer was glad when he conveyed this message to Pa and me. Then he proceeded to tell us the new owner of the bill told him to take it over to the bank and get five one dollar bills, and he would give Homer one of them. That's what happened, and our brother was happy as a lark with one buck in his pocket instead of the five. He never did live down such a way to give five bucks for one. At least he wanted to be honest and find the loser of the money. We figured the other four bucks found a pocket that never had seen the five-dollar bill.

I can still see Pa, as though it was yesterday, at 5:45 PM in the wintertime, sitting in his chair in the southwest corner of our living room, always leaning forward to hear what came out of the radio on a table beside him. This was the time when Lowell Thomas, the top news reporter, came on to give us the news of the world. So be it, if one of us decided we wanted to talk, BOOM! we were out of there into the kitchen in a hurry if we wanted to talk over something important. The radio was scratchy anyway, and silence was needed to hear what was going on. Thomas' famous slogan when the news was done was "So long until tomorrow." He had an excellent speaking voice and I suppose Eva would pick him out as a bass.

After supper we would have some other programs that all six of us would enjoy. Fibber McGee and Molly, Amos and Andy, Baron Munchausen and Time Marches On. The funny ones were put on in front of live audiences because we could hear the crowd laugh when we did.

Amos and Andy was our favorite, and boy I would have liked to have seen those clowns on TV. They had another character named Kingfish, and occasionally Mrs. Kingfish would add to the comedy. Anyway, these three clowns were all brothers (fraternal), belonging to the same lodge, "The Knights of the Mystic Sea." Don't know if this was a forerunner of the Knights of Columbus or not. When these three got going, it was hilarious all through the show. The Kingfish was the secretary of the lodge, and evidently had charge of the finances. Sometimes he would come up short on his bookkeeping and finances. I presume he might have had his finger in the pie or the till. These guys would get to arguing sometimes about something that went on in their Mystic Sea Lodge meeting. The old Kingfisher, as he was sometimes called, would get out his minute book and proceed to get ready to read the gospel truth as recorded by said Kingfish. He would clear his throat several times, and I would presume, adjust his tie, and then get going. Some of the time he couldn't read his own writing, and then there would be more of the same, clearing his throat while he tried to figure out what went on during the meeting. We would about split at the dialogue of these characters.

Kingfish, when he couldn't read what he was supposed to, would then kill time by clearing his throat some more. That reminds me of Joe (Slug) Johnson. He would be telling us a tall story and then his mind would be going faster than his talking, so he would decide that he had to spit out some of his tobacco. Then he would take his time to do it, then wipe his mouth to take more time so he could figure out how to keep going on his "tall tale."

We would get an old hen from Peenie Peterson and a bunch of eggs, and let the old girl (hen) sit on them for some time. I don't know how long it was before there were about dozen or so little chickens gathered around the mother hen. We had an old gravel truck box tipped upside down that served as a chicken coop. All of these chicks had names, of course. I remember one was named Buffy, as she was light colored, and was a Buff Orphingten strain of chicken. One time we had a red one, but I don't recall the name. It was a Rhode Island Red. I never hear of these kinds of chickens now, as the Leghorn chickens seem to have taken over as laying hens. Those chickens were spoiled from day one of their lives, and had plenty to eat and drink and were nice and big. The folks would suggest we were going to have a chicken dinner. Wait a minute! We were not about to eat one of our friends, and I remember us telling Ma, "You don't think that we would eat old Buffy, do you?"

They never got to kill any of our chickens, but when winter started, we would take them up to Starksen's store, as Debs bought chickens as well as eggs. We didn't get much for each bird, but we knew that someone would have a few good chicken dinners, but it definitely wasn't going to take place in the Andersen abode! That was final! Maybe the four of us didn't always agree, but in this case, there was absolutely no disagreement, so I can see where Virg got the same idea, that he wasn't about to eat his feathered chicken friends. He got this from his Dad and his uncles. All blood relatives, too. I doubt if our folks would have wanted to knock our chickens in the head, either.

We had a new girl who came to school and it soon became known that she had a reputation for being "fast." She didn't seem to be so nimble on her feet so I assumed that word meant something else. She would try to cozy up to me, why, I don't know, as I wasn't the cuddly type, or at least I didn't think so. One day she told me if she could get me out she would get my clothes off. Maybe she didn't know that I had undressed myself for several years. I was a green boy having grown up with three brothers so I wasn't sure what this was all about.

I found out later from one of the boys that he had been out with her and she helped him take her clothes off. Don't know if he got "stripped" by himself or if he had help from the girl. Didn't find out any more details as to why the clothes had to be "ditched." It must have been a noble experience. I'm glad she looked around before trying out her extra "wares" on me. Don't doubt my word on this, as our folks always told us to be honest and tell the truth, so please don't doubt my integrity. I was naïve even then. I'm still gullible and probably always will be.

George Pettis had a son named Emmett who had several swarms of bees. He made enough money selling honey to pay for his college education as well as paying to put him through med school. When he was home for his mother's funeral, he wanted to meet Eva to see what kind of a girl would marry me. He had already met her. I told him I thought the same about him, how anyone that was sick ever expected to get well having him for a doctor. Needless to say, some of the people that didn't know us that well were shocked, to say the least, to hear two friends who talked about each other in such a derogatory manner.

Way back when, there wasn't much expensive equipment to open the roads in the wintertime. To help out the farmers and to bring business to town, we would take a whole load of men with scoop shovels, load them into Barber and Johnson's old International truck and proceed out into the country to shovel snow. Can you imagine the backbreaking job of shoveling out drifts several feet deep in order to let a car go through? Some days we didn't get much done but we would enjoy the fellowship and doing something worthwhile to help out our farmer friends. After all, they patronized us so we could keep our business going.

On one occasion that I remember, the roads were blocked and we had a call from a Norske up in the North Preston area, asking if we could get a crew out from here to shovel out the roads north of town, as they were out of grub. They would have a crew meet us. That sounded good so we started shoveling and we opened nearly four miles of road, north and west of town, and no one from the Streel country was in sight. Then we saw Max Neilson and George Tolzin come down the mile line west of us, with a team of horses pulling a bobsled with a walking plow tied on to the side of the sled, plowing out one side of the road. Some invention? We gave up the shoveling and headed the old truck for town. Lo and behold, we met the chief planner from the Holy Land, out at the corner north of the cemetery. We had the road blocked, as it was only one way traffic. He had gotten out on a county road, gone to Arlington and the back seat of the car was loaded with groceries from Arlington merchants who were not out shoveling snow. I don't know if you might say he caught "Hell" or not, but we certainly let the old boy know what we thought of the whole deal! He got home the shortest way after the road was plowed out, or I should say, shoveled out by Hetland people. We had been snookered by a Norske, at that. It didn't happen again, I assure you. We had learned our lesson the hard way, shoveling SNOW!!!

Grandpa Barber had a no-good dog named Jocko. All he wanted to do was bark and nip at peoples' heels. Someone asked Lynn what the dog barked for. He replied "the dog had barks in him and he had to get them out, it was as simple as that." Anyway, luckily the dumb dog finally died. The old man prepared a final rite for Jocko to be buried out north of the home. The big event arrived with half of the kids in town gathered around the hole in the ground and the dog wrapped in a gunnysack. Barber put on his specs and opened the Bible and started to read some passage of scripture suitable for a dog burial. He was having trouble reading from the sacred book as I think his white mustache got into his line of vision. Finally in disgust, he slammed the Bible shut and in a loud and vehement voice exclaimed, "The hell with it." He kicked the dog in the hole and started shoveling dirt. Needless to say, we kids were impressed.

Ma had a "hen party" for a bunch of women. For you who don't know the meaning of that term, it is a time when a bunch of women get together to gossip, eat and drink coffee, all in that order. I have heard via the grapevine that some of the ladies got to the party early, before some one could gossip about them. It's a possibility. Well, one time when Ma entertained the gossip club, I needed some money from the house for making change. Being in a hurry, I barged right though the assembled gossip club, saying, "Hello everybody," and went into the bedroom to get my money, and headed out. Annie Starksen hollered at me, "You don't need to be in such a FART." Annie, seeing the surprised look on Mable Johnson's face and as if to calm Mable down a bit, sagely remarked for all to hear, "That means hurry in Norwegian." Could be? I didn't ever pursue the meaning of a Norwegian FART. To those of us who are Danes, there was a Smell or distinct ODOR connected to the above mentioned FART. So be it for now. If some of you want to do some research on this in your spare time, you have my permission to do so, but it might be best to keep your findings to yourself and your next of kin.

Chapter 3
The King has Abdicated

Eva and Dale's wedding photo

The King has Abdicated

The first time that I got married, or hitched to the hitching post, was in the schoolhouse during a school carnival. This time I was the bride! You may think some of these voluptuous blondes are really endowed, but you would change your mind in a hurry after looking us over. I had pillows in front and behind, and everywhere that women have their curves when they walk and shake their behinds. I came, or I should say we, as Shrimp Cleveland was my father, to where Telmer (Hilda) Peterson was waiting at the altar to get hitched when the preacher performed his duty. All the time we were coming down the aisle, Superintendent Eidsmoe was singing the wedding march, or maybe I should say, wedding dirge. It went like this, and it sounded great! "Here comes the bride, big, fat and wide, and see her father a-marching by her side." When the preacher asked all the questions and wanted my answer, I said "Ah does!" and so the knot finally got tied. Didn't have any honeymoon with Hilda Peterson, so we both got the short end of the deal. The room was packed with people who paid a nickel to see how the nuptials were performed. The next time around, I was more refined and when the preacher asked the same questions, I said, "I do."

I always seemed to be a timid individual, and don't think I've changed much as I've gotten older. (HA HA – Myrna, Virg & Vi) Anyway, after debating all the pros and cons and family consequences, I finally decided to ask the new teacher, Eva Guptill, if she wanted to go to a good show in Arlington. I knew that she must be older than me, and more experienced in the ways of life, but, what the heck, she seemed to be a pretty nice "chick" so what did I have to lose? She could turn me down, or decide to check me out. Lo and behold, she thought the show would be good and she would go along with me.

Now my cautious nature got the best of me. What was I getting into, going out with a girl who I had just known for a few months? Boy, this was risky business. I began to have second thoughts about my daring adventure. But I was a man of my word, or at least I thought I was, and couldn't back out now, after offering to spend money to take Eva to a show. I was in a dilemma as to how to cope with this situation. I hadn't ever been a party to anything like this before. Then a brilliant idea hit me. (Once in a while that happens, but rarely.) Eva roomed in the Oanes home. I thought that Orville Oanes might be interested in seeing this show that was ballyhooed as being so good. Boy, he would be glad to go along, as he thought that would be a good outing. I forgot, or maybe I should say neglected, to tell him that we

Dale and Eva at the depot

had a female passenger, Eva, who was also going along. You should have seen the look on his face when Eva came along too.

I didn't have a car, so Pa let me use his Model T. I don't remember anything about the show, but I do remember that the old Ford wouldn't start when we were ready to go home. Luckily I had a good friend in Arlington who ran a garage, and I got him to get the car started so we could get home. I can just hear the sly remarks if I had kept the teacher out all night! So - you can see that my foresight was pretty good as I had Orville along to back up my claim as to what really happened. My mechanic friend didn't mind that I called him after hours. Oh, incidentally Eva didn't complain either, and she didn't know if the car not starting was planned or not. She must have trusted me as she went in the Model T several times after that.

When Eva and I - or I should say she - set the wedding date for June 24, 1937, lo and behold, that was my mom's birthday, too. Neither one of us thought about that, I suppose, because we were excited then about getting "hitched." I didn't have a car and had used the folks' old 1926 Model T Ford 4-door passenger car, with windows in it, too, as Pa didn't drive any more. This Ford had what they called balloon tires on it. In other words, they were fatter than the old style cord tires, and so it was a better riding car.

Anyway, the folks didn't have a car to get to the wedding, and if they did, I wouldn't have one to get there either. Harry Starksen, the postmaster, heard about the dilemma, and offered the folks his Model A to go to Springfield for the big whing-ding. That was OK. Pa didn't know how to drive a shift car, but Homer, Skinny and Elden did. Then there was a "monkey wrench" thrown into the whole deal. Pa wasn't going to the wedding because he couldn't lock up the shop, in case some farmer had a breakdown and needed to get fixed up. How is that for dedication? He meant it, and he wasn't going to go, but Skinny, bless his heart, volunteered to stay home and run the shop. That took care of a bad situation, but Skinny had to hear all about the ceremony after it was all over. I don't suppose it would have worked if I had stayed home and had a "stand in." Elden was my stand up best man, so he needed to go to give me moral support, as he probably figured I needed it. Don't know what he did, besides stand beside me, but whatever he did, he did a good job, as he always did.

I took off for Springfield the day before, because I knew there would probably be plenty of work laid out for the prospective bridegroom. There was plenty to do. However - I being in a hurry to get to the place where I was going - got the idea of taking a short cut to save time, as well as miles. It ended up as a bad mistake. I got lost and didn't have any idea of where I was, except I figured I was still in South Dakota someplace south of Oldham. After driving around looking for something, I don't know what, my eyes got a glimpse of a water tower. Hot dog! I was in luck, as I finally got closer to the landmark, and it was Howard, and I was still in South Dakota, and knew how to get to where I was going. Eva and I both were never any good about directions, except up and down, and we were not too sure about that, either! Even now I doubt what the compass says, but I know it is right, so I'd better follow what it says, or I'd be lost again.

The big day - June 24, 1937 - finally came along for our wedding. Seems like it took a long time to get here after we had decided on the date. In England, if a king had died, his loyal subjects used to chant "The King is dead, long live the King!" My loyal subjects, my loving brothers, had a different version. "The King has abdicated, long live the King!" I suppose Homer took over after I left the nest, but I didn't hear of any swearing-in ceremony. They probably kept it low key.

Well, anyway - the folks and Elden took off in Harry Starksen's borrowed car with Homer at the wheel, heading due south to Springfield, SD for the big event, the first of three more for the Andersen clan. Ma had fixed a delicious dinner for them, as there wasn't enough money to go to a restaurant and eat, as well as buying gas for a long trip, about 150 miles. There was a schoolhouse between here and Yankton, located by Highway 81. They saw this well-kept yard, and decided they better stop and eat. They had the blanket all spread out on the ground and ready to eat, when Pa said, "Wouldn't it be nice if we had some fried chicken, too?" Lo and behold, no sooner said than executed! Eva's high school singers drove in and they had dinner along with them. Anna Kvinge had fried scads of chicken for them to eat, so the kids shared their chicken, and everyone had plenty to eat. Anna was a good cook, and she wasn't going to let Jeanette, Betty and the rest of the kids go hungry. I didn't find out about this until later. Another example of Hetland hospitality.

It was 105° in the shade when Eva and I got hitched, as the hillbillies would say. We had to have at least two or more candles in front of us to make more heat in the prospective bride's living room in the Guptill home. I suppose that was the proper protocol for such a festive occasion. The preacher, Dr. Warner, of the Springfield Congregational Church, was a short little bald headed Englishman. He was standing in front of the two of us, between the candles and us. Thank goodness for that! He was a devout man of God with a good sense of humor, a down-to-earth minister. Nothing high toned about him, and he could preach "make sense" sermons. Anyway, before we said the final I do's, the sweat was running off from his bald head, and I was fascinated to see the course the water took down the sides of his face. I could have been burned at the stake for being a heretic but my mind was still on the business at hand, getting married to my lovely girlfriend who was about to change her name from Guptill to Andersen.

When the service was over, I stepped out of my new Nunn Bush shoes and put on my old shoes. My feet were killing me. I don't know why I thought I needed to spend hard-earned money for new shoes when nobody, as far as I knew, had any interest in looking at my feet. They were too busy ooh-ing and aah-ing about how lovely the new bride looked. They couldn't say that about me, the groom. I was just there. After the wedding of course, we had to have a different program. Eva's girls and boys from high school sang to cheer us on. Don't know what they sang, but let me tell you that these kids didn't take the back seat for anyone, and had the trophies to prove it. One of Eva's friends played a solo on an old saw. Another read "The Village Blacksmith" and used the original version, "his arms were strong as iron bands" and not like some of my friends' version "his arms were strong as rubber bands." There was lots of other "stuff" that went on before we finished up the whole shebang by having scads of food to eat.

Dale and Eva on their wedding day

It was a joyous occasion, and we "hung in there" for 63 years – a long time to live with a stubborn Dane. We both felt that our sojourn through life together, holding on to each other for support and sharing our joys and our sorrows together, was a wonderful experience. It wouldn't have been possible if we hadn't found each other and had God's blessing to uphold us.

I probably need to add a postscript to our getting married. I hadn't taken any girl out on a date until Eva came along. They tell the story about women trying on all kinds of dresses (I can vouch for that) before deciding to go back and get the first one they saw. I didn't do much of that, even though I'm a born procrastinator. I would see something to wear, and didn't spend time looking for something else that might be better. Eva caught my eye, I guess, and whether she slowed down so I could catch her or I slowed down so she could catch me, we never decided. Anyway, I'm glad that I didn't check out any other "chicks." She was wonderful for me.

We spent the first night after being married in a hotel in Yankton. The Model T was pretty noisy with all the clanging of stuff put on the car by some of the wedding guests. The last I knew this hotel had been turned into a nursing home. Don't know if we helped out in its demise. The second night, after we had gone back to Springfield to get some of the loot we had left behind the night before, we took off for Hetland. We were burning up the road even though it was a really dark night. What do you suppose? At 3 AM we were barreling along, coming into Arlington, just a short way from home, when the old Ford must have decided that it was time to give up the ghost. The car stopped on a hill right by the Arlington cemetery. Well, the newlyweds just curled up to wait for morning. Had no more than settled down than here came a cop to disturb our tranquility. He decided we were probably law-abiding citizens, and then told us there would be a lot of traffic from the north as a dance at Lake Poinsett had just ended. No sleep, as the road was narrow, and we were as close to the ditch as we could get. Here those cars would come, roaring at us, and Eva and I didn't know if a drunk was behind the wheel or not! We survived, and the next morning I caught a ride into town and my friendly mechanic came out and put on a new piece and we finally made it home.

That night as we were getting ready to hit the hay, I sat down on the edge of the bed when "bang!" the whole bed fell to the floor. My loving brothers – Eva's new brothers-in-law – had sabotaged our bed. However, being a blacksmith, I was able to salvage the faulty bed. It was luck that the trigger was set to go off too easily, or we would both have been down in the middle of the bed, resting on the floor. I don't remember if we got any sleep or not, but at least my bride had an idea as to what her new relatives were capable of doing, not only to their brother, but also to their new sister. She learned to love them in spite of their tricks.

It's lucky that Myrna and Virgil ever had a mom and dad. After we were married we went to Big Stone Lake for our honeymoon, I guess that was what it was called, as I have never been on one before and haven't been on one since. Of course, Eva, being of the fairer sex, needed someone to show her how to fish and row a boat. As this was my first experience in showing my new bride how good I was in those categories we proceeded to go out into the lake, which, by the way, was as smooth as glass. In fact, there was a north wind blowing a gentle breeze. Just enough so that the fish didn't want to bite. Wanting to show off, "Lover Boy" decided the fishing must be better on the Minnesota side of the lake. All we had done on the South Dakota side was give a minnow a bath.

Anyway, being young and undoubtedly more foolish than I am now, I advised my girlfriend we were going across the lake to get fish. What a laugh! The further out into the lake we got, the bigger the waves and the stronger the wind was blowing from the north. Being of Viking stock and probably being related in a roundabout way to Leif Erickson, I foolishly persisted in heading for Minnesota. Finally, when we could hardly see the opposite shore over the waves, I somehow got the brilliant idea that we should perhaps turn around and head back to South Dakota. Being a landlubber and not too fond of water, I wondered how to get the boat turned around without sinking the ship. The Lord had to have had a hand in this hair-raising maneuver, as we made it and headed for the South Dakota shore. I told Eva to hang on and indeed she did. I'm sure she was as scared as I was, but she didn't say so and she must have had faith in me that we would get back to shore. I had blisters on my hands when we finally hit dry land.

It was a harrowing experience and showed that at least one Dane should have had better sense and probably needed more "between his ears." If we could have walked on the water or parted it, the going would have been easier. I found out afterwards that Big Stone Lake was noted for rapid wind changes. I'm glad the Lord was with us as He always has been, and gave us a chance to be parents of such loving and nice kids as Myrna and Virgil. Our cup runneth over.

Not long after we were married, I found out that being a husband included more than just trying to eke out a living. My new bride: "Honeeeeyy, would you pleeeease come in here?" Me: "Yes, dear." She was in the bedroom, which was also our dressing room, as being newly married, we couldn't afford one of each. I might add that we were getting ready to go someplace, and needed to dress up. She was standing there with not much on, which was OK as long as we were married. I think the preacher said that this was permissible. What was the problem? I knew it must have been something big, the way she stressed the honey and please so much, and I knew that it probably would be testing my scientific mentality to solve whatever was wrong. "Honey, would you see if my seams are straight?" What a letdown, although my "blacksmith eye" carried me through. I sized up the situation and told her the seams on her stockings were OK. I don't know how my bride got along in a situation like this before I came into her life.

Another treat that came with me when I brought my new bride home was to put sugar on fried eggs. Hard to believe? Pa did, so I, being the eldest, followed in his footsteps - or maybe I should say - eating pattern. I can't believe it tasted good. It took a while before Eva talked me out of wasting sugar on eggs.

We hadn't been married too long when we had some good friends over for supper. There were no toothpicks on the table. Don't know why not. I had more teeth than I have now, and noting that the table wasn't completely set, I proceeded to get the box of toothpicks and passed it around the table. Seems like all who needed one took one. After our friends had left, my new bride informed me I should have put the toothpicks in a toothpick holder. I was probably short on brains when they were passed out, so I was glad to find out about this delicate matter early in our married life. However, in order to make amends after my perilous adventure, I told my bride that after all, these were good friends, and that I was sure that they knew - or should have known - that toothpicks come in boxes before getting put into holders, and before that they were a part of a tree. Now, I'm old enough, and don't have teeth enough, so toothpick vendors won't get rich off of me, but I learned a little bit about how a toothpick should be dispensed!

As I look back over the years, I suspect there might have been a little "devil" in me. Let me hasten to add that I'm sure some of you think the little guy never left me. That is a matter of opinion, and even though I like to argue, we won't pursue this any farther.

After we had been married for a few months, Eileen "Pick" Johnson came to visit us. As was customary, she and I got into an argument over something. I don't recall what it was. In the course of the conversation, she told me she could do anything a man could do. I told her that I'd bet she couldn't! "What can't I do that you can?" she asked. Eva, being the fine musician that she is, had a piano and also a piano bench to complement the keyboard instrument. I proceeded to show "Pick" that the piano bench could be used for something besides sitting on to "tickle the keys." I got down on the floor on all fours beside the piano bench. (By the way, I wouldn't try that now, as I'd probably still be there on the floor.) I asked Pick if she could do that. "Of course I can," was her quick retort. Then I raised my leg up against the aforementioned bench, and politely asked her if she could do that. Of course she could.

Eileen Johnson and Orville Oanes

I got up and told her "Let's see you do it!" Lo and behold, she could do all this, including lifting her leg. "See, I told you I could do that," she told me. I told her she did a good job of lifting her leg too, and then I told her, "Now bark!" Boy, did she let her leg down in a quick hurry. My "pride and joy," Eva, was embarrassed that I would pull this on our friend. After all, she stood up with us at our wedding. As I look back I realize that "Pick" was pretty versatile to complete this harrowing maneuver.

Eva made up a big batch of "slumgullion," I call it, made of spuds, meat, carrots, etc. She was to be gone, so made this up in an old black frying pan (black on the outside) so that I wouldn't have to make dinner, it was all ready. She always saw to it that her family wouldn't go hungry. Noon came, and one of our favorite salesmen, Walt Hallan, was at the shop and ready to leave. I asked him to come over for dinner. No, he couldn't, and didn't want to put Eva out. I let him know that dinner was all ready and that Eva was gone, so he could just as well eat with me. OK, then he would come.

I, being very meticulous, put the old black frying pan (which by the way, had cooked many a good meal, by the looks of it) on a hot pad on the table, and we two Masonic brothers proceeded to fill our plates from the tough looking pan. Boy, it was good, and Walt and I wolfed down all we wanted to eat. I told him that Eva would "hit the roof" if she knew I had served him in such a grand way.

At suppertime (my girlfriend was home by that time), I told Eva that Walt Hallan had eaten dinner with me, and it was extra special. "I hope you didn't put that old skillet on the table," was her response. I'm like George Washington, and couldn't tell a lie, so I told her that was what happened, and that Walt appreciated a good hot meal.

When we were first married, it was during the drought years. Several of us had big gardens up in the north end of town, and I mean BIG, about 50 feet wide and 150 feet long.

We were just like the farmers, we gambled on putting in our crop, and were hoping for rain and good weather. It was really dry, and we had scads, no, millions of grasshoppers that moved in and ate up what little crop there was. Our beans were looking good in spite of no rainfall, but the hoppers were having a field day chomping up the beans. Something had to be done to stop this carnage! Wait a minute – even though poison didn't deter these hungry hordes, I stumbled onto a solution after careful study and prolonged thinking, racking my brain. After all, I had gotten out of Hetland High School with a signed diploma, so there was absolutely no reason that those little creatures were going to gorge themselves on our beans.

We had some screen windows off of the house, and I proceeded to get ready to cover the beans with the screen. I flushed out thousands of these bean eaters, knowing that there were still lots of them hiding in the bushes, and proceeded to spend a lot of time seeing to it that no more hoppers would get into our bean patch. When I finished the job, it was a marvel to behold. I was really patting myself on the back, the way I had outfoxed these critters. Maybe I could even get a patent on this ingenious brainstorm, which I knew in my mind's eye, had never been thought of before. What luck. Boy, oh boy, we would have beans after all, if the rains should come, and we had hopes that they would.

I brought my new bride over to the garden and showed her how smart her husband was. Guess she never had one before, or anyway none that I knew of. She put her arm around me and with that loving look in her eyes told me it looked great. I also suspected by that loving look she thought she had married a genius, to outsmart these hungry hoppers. I was inclined to agree with the genius look, but it didn't have anything to do with grasshoppers. I thought, and still do, that I was a genius when I was nimble enough to get her to come into my life, not knowing then, that it would last for 63 years of wedded bliss until she went Home.

OK, we had that problem solved. However, in a few days I checked on my project. Lo and behold, the beans were still getting eaten up, worse than before. What was wrong? I finally found out the problem. These little devils that were on the inside must have called all of their relatives to come and eat beans. They got inside the screens through a hole, and couldn't find their way out, and probably didn't want to. All they had to do to pass the time was to gorge themselves on our beans! No more thought of a patent. My high school diploma didn't help me, after all. Enough of this fiasco? The grasshoppers had it – the last word, or should I say the last bite. What an ending. I hope the hoppers enjoyed their menu. Maybe they should have had some "Beano" to help them not to pass gas, but I think these were the wrong kind of beans, and were not the gas passing type. Who knows? "Let's pass gas" was probably their motto, after being stuffed with beans.

One year Obbie Melstad and I had put beans in real early. They were about three inches high when the dumb weather man reported frost. Three nights in a row he predicted that big calamity. Three nights in a row, Obbie and I covered our several rows of beans. The next morning we proceeded to uncover our beans. The fourth night, our paid weatherman gleefully reported, "No frost." Boy, that was a big relief to us two Luther Burbank disciples. That day, I was over to Henry Mauch's and he was just putting in his beans. Of course, I had to tell him how high our beans were, and how did he expect to raise a crop, putting them in this late. "Dale, it's pretty early, and it might freeze," he told me. Baloney on that, as we had heard the news report for no frost. Do you know what? The weather man must have had his head in the sand, and made a mistake. He must have given the weather report for South America. It froze and froze hard! Our beans were completely gone, and we had to replant them. Before Henry Mauch opened the bank, he ambled down the street to the BS shop. I expected something and I wasn't disappointed. "How are the beans this morning, Dale?" Then he gave that little chuckle for which he was noted. I had a retort all lined up for him. He had beans before we did. If it hadn't been for the frost that night, we could have given him some of ours.

Byron Foss and I used to plant our gardens with the main issue being to see who was to get produce from the garden first. Our gardens were doing pretty good, so one afternoon I went up to Starksen's store and bought a bunch of fresh radishes. Now, don't ask me what for. I'll tell you. I got them all cleaned and ready to eat, and then proceeded to amble over to Foss' so they could have fresh produce for supper. I knew that would be a treat. I might add we didn't keep any for ourselves, as they liked radishes better than we did. I brought them into their home and showed them that they had more supper to eat than Carolyn had planned. "Where did you get them?" Byron asked. "Where do you suppose I got them? You don't think I would go uptown and buy them, do you?" "I wouldn't put it by you," was his retort. Eva and I had finished supper and here came Foss. "Let's go up to your garden and look at your radishes, and see how big they are." Of course I obliged him, and we proceeded up to the garden. He started looking for radishes, and couldn't find any big enough. I asked him how he expected to find any big ones now, as they couldn't grow that fast if I had cleaned them out. (You notice I didn't say I had picked them, as I said "IF," so that way I wasn't stretching the truth.) I finally told him what had transpired, so he didn't think his garden was too bad, after all. "I figured you had done something like that," was his retort, after I filled him in on all of the details.

When we cut down on the size of our garden plot, we hauled in a pickup load of old rotten sheep manure from Howard Karban's. We put it on about six inches deep. Some of my "know-it-all" farmer friends and would-be gardeners told me that all that manure would kill the plants. I told them if it did, I would go up and get my garden produce from Obbie, as he would have plenty of it, and that I had been kind enough to furnish some of the seed.

We had sheep manure pretty deep all over the garden, and it turned out great. The soil wasn't all lumpy for several years, and we had bumper crops of all kinds of vegetables. My friends that were feeling sorry for me, with my garden being full of dung, hadn't read the right book on gardening. I didn't read the book either, but panned out lucky, with help from above, with rain when we needed it. End of a long tale about free fertilizer, right from the sheep. In one end (feed) and out the other (fertilizer). Not a bad trade.

Obbie was a good gardener, too. Even planted spuds in the snow on Good Friday, so he could brag about his early potatoes. I don't know if they winter killed or not. He came to the shop one day with a pail of spuds and informed me that the "old girl" (his sister, Fern) wanted some "small" spuds to go with new peas, as that was a delicious treat. New potatoes and fresh peas. I let him know he wouldn't have any trouble finding small spuds, as that was all he had anyway. Then he dipped his hand in the pail and out it came with a potato about an inch across. "Look at that big devil!" Every time he brought his hand out, it was the same great big devil. I was on to his shenanigans, as I hadn't lived next door neighbor to him all of my life, without being on to his tricks.

Chapter 4
Married with Children

Eva and Dale with Virgil and Myrna, 1944

Married with Children

When our first baby was born, little Wendall Neil, Eva was in labor for a solid week. We went to Volga to see Dr. Peeke when we thought the baby was coming. This was at nine months. He told us to go home and expect to come back shortly. Nothing happened. Two weeks later, we went to see Peeke, and he was frustrated, as the baby had turned over, and was sitting for a breech delivery. He tried everything to turn the baby, but to no avail. At ten months, the water broke on a Saturday night, so we tore over to Volga. A week later, on Saturday morning, Drs. Peeke and Hopkins had to take the baby. When they finally brought him out, he had one hand behind his head, and the cord was around his neck, besides being born breech. They couldn't save the sweet looking little boy.

Peeke told me they were more worried about saving Eva than the baby. She never did get over the ordeal, as her pelvis was wrecked, and out of kilter. I was the lone heartbroken pallbearer for our little Wendall, the little boy that his Mom never got to cuddle. He was laid to rest in 1940 in the Hetland cemetery, and now his Mom is with him in heaven. Now she can love him there, as she did when she was with us on earth, even though he had gone Home. Jeanette Kvinge took care of the committal services, and did a commendable job for me and for her ex-teacher.

Mom always said God made up for our loss by giving us a girl, Myrna, first, and then a son like Virgil, to take Wendall's place. Our cup runneth over, even when adversity hits.

She doctored and doctored for a long time with problems connected with her back and pelvis, to no avail. Finally, I took her to Dr. Tieszen, a rub doctor in Marion. He pulled her sideways, etc., and she felt some better. We were over to see Dr. Peeke later on for some ailment. He wanted to know how she was feeling. Eva said, "Lots better, but no thanks to you." Then she told him that we had been to see Tieszen. He told her, "Good for you," but he never would have told her to see a so-called doctor who most of the medical profession classed as "quacks."

When Myrna was just a baby, her Mom took her down to Springfield, SD to show her little prize to all of the Guptill relations. When Virg came to add to our treasures, she took both of them to show off, leaving me at home to keep the home fires burning. This first time when Eva and Myrna were down south, they had been on the go all day, visiting. When they got back to grandpa and grandma Guptill's, she laid her little bundle of joy in her crib to call it a day. Mom said, "Myrna let out a little squeal, kicking her legs in the air, and then snuggled down in her mattress, put her thumb in her mouth, and had the most pleasant smile, as if to say, enough is enough. I'm going to sleep," which she did. When little Virgil came to bless our lives, then she had two little ones to show off to her relatives. Virg would sing himself to sleep. He didn't need to have the cradle rocked to know it was time for sleep.

Mom used to cover Myrna up good and tight in the crib in order to be sure that she wouldn't be cold. She would no more than get the blankets tucked in, when Myrna kicked them off. She was too hot. Dr. Peeke told us not to wor-

Myrna, 1942

ry, as this little tyke knew when it was too hot for blankets.

I had to make an extension to make the crib about 18 inches higher, as Virg wanted to crawl out. One day, I heard him making all kinds of commotion and, lo and behold, here he was, standing up and shaking the high rise extension. All at once, KA-BOOM! Out he went, head first, before I could catch him. He and the supposed protector went end over end onto the floor. After a brief cry, he was all right, and wasn't hurt, for which we were thankful.

I was always taught when I might be walking down the sidewalk with a girl, I should be on the outside of the walk, next to the street. I suppose that was to protect the fair sex in case some errant driver might lose control of his car and jump up on the walk. This way the man would protect the lady from any damage that might approach them. One Saturday night I took our daughter Myrna downtown to see the sights. Probably I had another reason, too – I'd get to show off our little girl. Anyway, we ambled along at her speed, as she wasn't too big, and was wobbly on her feet. When we came to Hazel Rottum's ice cream store I took her in and we both had ice cream cones. This was her first cone, and she enjoyed it to the last "drip." The next Saturday we had the same schedule worked out. When we came to the front of Hazel's store, lo and behold, this little tyke, being on the inside holding onto my hand, stopped and started pulling me into the store. Of course, I had no idea what this was all about. Inside, Myrna waltzed us over to the ice cream counter, and Dad paid for more ice cream cones. Mom had her dressed up so cute, and I was proud as a peacock to think that after being in that store only once, she knew how to work me to get another cone. She still likes ice cream but she can't seem to tolerate it.

Myrna

We have a cute baby picture of Virgil without many clothes on. A big framed copy of the picture was on display in the window of the photography shop in Brookings where the picture was taken. Boy, he looked pretty sharp then, as well as now.

Virgil, 1944

Eva took the kids over to Dr. Grove to get some of their "shots." When he laid Myrna on the table and gave her the shot she let out a "beller." Must have hurt! He gave Virg the same dosage and he just took it in stride. No big deal! When their Mom took them for their next shot, that was something else. As soon as Myrna hit the table, she let out a roar, and Dr. Grove and her Mom had to hold her down to get the job done. Virg? It didn't bother him at all. Dr. Grove told him that his heart was beating. Then came the profound statement, "I know, it even beats when I eat." Their Mom had to fill me in on this.

When I was a kid, we went to Dr. Grove for our physicals in order to play basketball. Doc told me my heart was beating faster when I came into the office than it was after I had done the exercises, supposedly to reach over and touch my toes. I don't ever recall my back bending except to do that. Touching my knees was more in order.

When Myrna was small, she was scared of lightning, and thunder, too. But if she could get into bed and curl up next to her Dad, she figured she was safe and went right to sleep. I was always glad she felt protected, even though there wasn't anything I could do about the storm. Myrna would look at her little brother sound asleep, oblivious of any bad weather. Myrna would say, "Look at him. He's not afraid at all!"

When Myrna was a baby she had colic, I think they called it, so every night we had to rock her to sleep in the cradle, which had wheels on it. She would go to sleep, and I was pooped out from the rocking spree, so I would stop moving the cradle. Bang! Just like that, our little sweetheart would wake up and start to bawl, so we started from scratch, and kept the wheels rolling. I told her Mom afterwards that if I had to do the same thing again I would have put a motor on the cradle and let electricity do the manpower.

After Myrna got older, we still had to rock her to sleep. Finally one night her Mom said, "This is it. We are putting her upstairs, and if she bawls, let her bawl until she goes to sleep!" Boy, I thought, this doesn't sound like that sweet mother that I was used to hearing cooing around our little girl. Upstairs the two of them went, and I dreaded what was going to transpire. Sure enough, Eva hadn't gotten downstairs before there was a loud wail. Myrna wasn't used to being alone, even with the light on, and she was letting us know what she thought of it. It finally got so bad that I was afraid she would choke, as she was just panting for more air. I told her Mom I couldn't stand any more of this, and that I was going up to rock our little one. "No, you don't!" The disciplinarian ex-teacher told me. We had been married a few years, so I knew that my girlfriend meant business. I just settled down in my chair and covered my ears. Every so often I'd listen, and finally it was safe, and no more crying. Her Mom had weaned her little one away from crying without any help from father. I must have been a softy!

Luckily, when our sweet little boy came into our lives, he didn't need to be rocked. He could sing himself to sleep, but I doubt if he knew the words to whatever he was singing. His Great Aunt Gertie Guptill asked Eva one time if she could hold him as she liked to hear him sing. Our little boy is still singing, as is his older sister.

When Virg was a little boy he didn't seem to have time to go to the toilet to dispense some water. His Mom finally told him she was out of dry pants, and if he wet the ones he had on, she would have to put a dress on him. He didn't listen, so she put a long dress on her little boy. He looked cute, too, as he ambled over to the BS shop. George Wolfe saw him and said, "Hello, Susie?" and Virg said, "Hello," too. George gave him or her a nickel, and told him to go uptown to get some candy. Our little "girl" did just that. It didn't bother him a bit to wear the dress, so his Mom didn't try that tactic again. He must have gotten the no "spray" from his Dad, as my Ma said I would stand out in the yard with my knees together to keep from getting rid of hot water. She would rap on the kitchen window to let me know that it was time for me to empty my bladder. She was a smart mother.

We took the kids with us whenever we could. We didn't leave them at home if we were going to something that they would enjoy. On one occasion, we went somewhere and left

Myrna, approx. 9 months, 1942

them at home in the care of their uncle Elden, who we knew would be a good babysitter. When we came home, our faith in my youngest brother was not well founded. He was sound asleep in the chair, Myrna was busy doing some coloring, and where do you suppose our little boy was? He was on top of the piano, having a good time. He wasn't old enough to read music, so I suppose the next best thing was to see how high in the air he could climb, and the top of the piano was the next closest to the ceiling. Our babysitter woke up after all the commotion had disturbed his rest. We of course thanked him, but he didn't get any salary for watching his little niece and nephew. After all, we had him under contract to watch the kids, and we weren't paying him to sleep on the job. Incidentally, before he was married, he would let us know in no uncertain terms that if they were his kids (Myrna and Virgil) he would tell them to sit down, and they would sit down. After he and Shirley were married, and they had Donna, Rhonda and Terri, I would let him know that if they were my kids I'd tell them to sit down or else. Guess the chickens came home to roost.

Myrna and Virgil 1944

One year when Myrna and Virgil were little tykes, their Grandpa Guptill was giving them a hard luck story about his being broke. He was all out of money, and he didn't know how he was going to live without any money. He didn't even have anything to buy Bull Durham Tobacco to roll his own cigarettes. Little Virgil left and went upstairs. When he came back he had his little bank in his hands, and went over to his grandpa and gave the bank to him and said, "Here, Grandpa, this is all the money that I have, but you take it because you need it." He wasn't going to let his grandpa go hungry if he could help out. What an example our little boy set for all of us. Grandpa told Eva afterwards that Virg wasn't the one he was gunning for. Maybe Myrna was broke too, but then who knows?

Virgil and Myrna with Grandpa Clyde Guptill

I went uptown to mail a letter one winter afternoon, and noticed that the plate glass window in the store was broken. When I got inside, Dale Boyd had to tell me the gory details of the broken window. Our little boy, Virgil, and some other kids were having a snowball fight out in the street in front of the store. Virg had a big fat snowball, and wound up to throw it at one of the kids in the middle of the road. Instead, he held on to it and somehow turned around and threw it though the store window. Dale said the other kids all ran away, but not our Virgil. He came into the store as big as you please, and told the owner, Harry Starksen, in a loud voice, "Well, Harry, I broke your window, but my Dad will pay for it." That was easy, he had faith in his Dad even then. Don't know what it cost, but I didn't have any insurance to cover the loss. Harry put cardboard over the hole, and when Virg saw that he came back into the store and profoundly told Harry, "Well, Harry, I see you've got the window fixed." Dale Boyd was laughing all the time he was telling me about how systematically Virg handled a tough situation. He still has all of those qualifications today. Myrna does, too.

When Virgil was a little tyke, (yes, he used to be little) and found out what a spoon and fork were used for, he started to branch out, and really grew up. I tell him that he stayed green longer than I did, that's why he is so tall. When he and his Mom came home from the hospital, and his grandma Ruby Andersen saw him, she of course thought he was really a good-looking lad, but then she commented, "But he is pretty small." He was born 15 minutes before his grandpa Morris' birthday. His grandpa asked Eva why she didn't wait a few minutes longer, so they could both celebrate the same day. Her reply, "I waited nine months, and that was long enough!" No give and take there! I suppose that Virg had been "cooped up" long enough, and wanted to see what the world had to offer.

Morris and Virgil on Virgil's birthday, August 29, 1948

When Myrna and Virg were growing up, and bigger than they were the first time Eva first took them to Springfield, they returned to see the grandparents and other relatives. Their cousin Clark Thomas was taking the three of them back to the old homestead when disaster struck! Mom and the kids were in the back seat, and Clark was moving along at 30 or 35 miles an hour when our little daredevil, Virg, stood up, grabbed the door handle and out he went, head first onto the gravel road. The back doors of Clark's four-door sedan opened from the front, not from the back like the cars do now. Clark got the car stopped, and Virg was really whooping it up, as he had a right to. He was split open on his head, and was full of gravel. Mom asked him if he was hurt. (She must have figured he was.) Virg wailed, "I thought you were going to leave me." After all, that was a good answer. Who would want to be out on a strange road after dark, in a strange county, with blood running down his face, and no way to get to a doctor?

They got him into Doc Blasik, an old Bohemian, and he got him fixed up as good as new. When I went to bring my precious family home, the first thing I heard about was all about the gory details. He was lucky he didn't get killed! Someone was looking out for our little boy, and we can thank the Lord for it. His great uncle Marvin Spurrel was really laughing about the whole deal. I didn't think it was a laughing matter, but at the time it probably was. After all it was over, and our little boy survived.

Virg used to go around and visit the older folks in town. I'm sure they enjoyed him, and probably had a cookie for him so he would feel welcome again. He couldn't say Mrs. York, and one time when we asked him where he had been, he said he had been to see Mrs. Lork. Don't think Myrna did as much of this type of visiting, as she was probably home baking or helping her Mom. This exposure to older people has sure influenced their lives, and they have always benefited from having the wisdom that the "oldsters" gave them.

Virg liked to go over to our neighbors, the Melstads, especially when Fern was cooking koomla, which he really liked. When she made this stuff, she had a giant kettle to cook it in, and then told all of the Melstad tribe to come to supper. Our little boy would stand and sniff the fragrant smell and then probably comment to Fern how good it smelled. She knew what this little neighbor boy was thinking, and always wanted to know if he wanted to eat supper with them. That was all he wanted to know, and he was heading home full speed to ask his Mom if it was all right for him to eat out. Of course it was, as she knew Fern had koomla. This is some kind of dumpling, I guess. (Norwegian potato dumplings, a combination of raw grated potatoes, flour and a little salt, affectionately known to some as "belly bricks." – ed.)

When we were growing up, every home had a cellar, a hole in the ground, under the home or dug in the ground outside, for safety, to be used in case of a tornado. Then everyone would head for the cellar. There were cyclone cellars, root cellars, and just plain cellars, a dug-out hole under the house. When Virg got a little older, his Mom heard him doing something downstairs in the cellar. She went down and asked him, "What in the world are you doing?" We had gotten him a little play pail, and a little two-inch shovel to play with. What do you suppose that little tyke was doing? "I'm digging out the basement," was the answer to his Mom's question. She must have figured with that big modern equipment that our little boy would be an old man before the digging was done. She used to comment in later years she probably should have let him keep on digging, as she would rather be caught dead upstairs in the house, rather than in that hole, if a tornado happened to hit us. That might not have been a bad idea, when I come to think about it. The wind could have blown us all of the way to the pearly gates, and we could have waved to our neighbors while flying by.

One night a bunch of us were shooting the breeze in the hardware store with Nasty (Gerald) Dutcher and Dennis, one of his boys, who were here from Sioux Falls to go hunting the next day. We were giving Nasty a pretty rough time and his kid was wide-eyed, the way we were overhauling his Dad. When they got over to Dutcher's house after the confab, this young fellow was telling his Mom and grandparents how all of us had picked on his Dad. Then he told them that Mory meant it, too! He didn't know much about the friends his Dad had to put up with when he was growing up.

Nasty, Adeline Oanes (his date and later his wife) and Eva and I used to double date. We would get Adeline all flustered when we would all get to singing "Sweet Adeline, For You I Pine." We had good times together, and sang lots of other songs besides Sweet Adeline in falsetto.

Dale and Eva's home, ca 1990

Adeline and Gerald Dutcher

One night at the supper table when our kids were growing up, we had a surprise from our little son, Virgil. All at once out of a clear blue sky, he said, "Dad, do you know something?" Of course I didn't know something. "What?" I replied. "If there was a mad stampede to get television sets, do you know who would be last?" Of course I didn't know anything about stampedes, not having ever been in one – "Who?" "You!!!" Mom and I looked at each other and grinned, and after that decided maybe we should get a TV, if we were to be the last ones on the totem pole. After all, it was a mark of prestige to look up on the roof of a home and see a TV antenna. Maybe there wasn't a TV in the home, but who knew the difference?

Besides being glad that I grew up in Hetland, it was so nice that our kids, Myrna and Virgil, had a chance to spend the formative years of their lives living here, with Eva guiding them along the right path and helping to mold their lives as only she could do.

Pa used to say he hoped that he would live long enough to see Virgil grow up so he could handle his big sister. Grandpa Morris must have felt sorry for him, as I presume he thought Myrna was "browbeating" him. They always got along with each other, even after Virg got older and could probably have turned the tables on his sister.

We had a car that didn't want to run part of the time. It would jump and buck around. One time Eva, Myrna and Virgil were in Arlington for piano lessons. As they left Ruth Maxwell's house the car started to act up, jumping around and bucking. Eva said, "Jump, you jumping jackass!" When they got home, the kids came running over to the shop laughing and all excited and told me what their Mom had said. They had never heard her say anything that bad before. If it had been me, I probably would have said worse. We finally did get it fixed so it didn't do that.

I bought an old Maytag wringer washing machine for a buck on an auction sale. We had it outside in the yard, and used it to wash clothes when we didn't care to go to the laundromat. I told Eva that every time we washed in the Maytag we saved a lot of money using that dollar machine. We had a well to do neighbor who would drive by and "rubber" at us washing in the old outfit, as she had a real modern washer. I used to bask in the thought that she must have been thinking, "That poor Eva, Mory couldn't even afford a better washer than that old one." But it washed clothes cleaner than most new ones. On occasion, I would strip down and take my shorts and undershirts and put them into the tub. Eva was embarrassed, but I didn't ever hear of anyone seeing me outside with nothing on but my shoes and socks. She sometimes remarked that I should be in a nudist colony. I didn't go along with that, as I wouldn't know how to act. Besides, I would have to have my shoes on, as my feet weren't made to travel without shoes. After all, I'm wearing a leather deal on each foot that holds up my toes so I won't be so likely to revert back to my ancestors and start climbing trees. I don't like high places, either!

Eva worked for years on genealogy on her side of the fence and mine, too. She put the Clark name, my Ma's name, into a computer listing. We heard from a woman in California that said she and I were related. When we called her, she was excited that we were blood relatives. She said we got related in 1640 and that I was the 10th generation of the Gaylords in the US. Wow, what an honor! Our distant relative, Gaylord, had come to the US with a patent from the king of England, showing he was a deacon in the Congregational Church. Seems as though from Eva's research that this distant relative was a non-conformist and a free thinking maverick. Maybe that's who I have been taking after, even though I never knew him in person. I thought I was probably related to Christopher Columbus or Leif Ericson who, according to the Danes, discovered America. I think I'm leaning toward old Leif instead of Columbus. I'm still a Congregationalist, so I didn't stray far from the religion fold.

The next day, I strode up to the bank building, where several of the whiz kid elite were in serious discussion. During a pause in their discourse, I calmly announced they were looking at the 10th generation of the Gaylords in the US. I knew that they would - or should be - elated over my disclosure, as they were friends of mine, and didn't realize I had other connections in the world besides being a Dane. Alas, my high expectations were shattered. One of my so-called "friends" didn't even crack a smile and remarked, "Who the Hell cares?" Boy, was I devastated! I could have cried in my beer if I had any. I knew I would get some response, but after this remark, nobody had even smiled. So I decided I would just have to live up to the lineage of being of good Danish blood and to be thankful I didn't have any relatives that had come from Norway, as most of those so-called friends were descendants of Streels or other Norske clans.

Eva found out in her genealogy that I am eligible to be a member of the Sons of the American Revolution, and of course Virgil could be, too, as we had relatives who fought in the Revolutionary War, in order to get the colonies away from John Bull (England). One of my cousins told me she was sure I always wanted to belong to the Sons of the American Revolution. She knew I had no inclination to join that elite group. When Myrna and her Mom were in Salt Lake City looking up dead relatives, they heard a guy start hollering and thought he must be hurting something awful, or even dying. Do you know what? He had just located a relative who had fought in the revolution, and now he could belong to the SAR. He had been looking for this "veteran" for many years. Here we are, with several relatives in the war, and decide not to pursue going into this select group of people. What a pity.

If there ever was a busy gal, it was Eva, my sweetheart. As I think back, I don't see how she got everything done each day in only 24 hours. She had 60, yes 60, piano students a week, and finally charged $1.50 a lesson. Before that it was $1 or less. Besides, for some of the kids whose folks couldn't afford it, she gave them lessons for free.

She preached in the Hetland and Badger Congregational Churches for years, directed the choir in the Badger church, did all of the calling on sick people, funerals - you name it. She was a go-getter in the Ladies' Aid and did her share in baking food and serving lunches after funerals, after having preached the funeral service and taken care of lining up the music, etc. Then she chaired the Kingsbury County School Board and started and directed the big Easter Intercommunity Choir. She always had an office in the Order of Eastern Star, and was the Chapter musician for many years.

She never seemed to want to turn down a job that needed to be done. Besides, she managed to keep her family together and we never went hungry. Many a time, at 1 AM she would start canning a bushel of tomatoes, or whatever else needed to be done. We always had canned stuff from the garden that she had put up. Jams and jellies were always a treat, as most of the Andersens had a sweet tooth.

One night, after her last student left at about 6:30, I told the kid's mother that Eva didn't know it but there were 40 people coming for supper. Wow! These were church friends, and it was supposed to be a surprise on both of us, as they were bringing all of the food. Finally, someone decided that I should be told about it. Probably they figured I might look out to see if there were any conspicuous cobwebs that needed to be disposed of. I doubt I even looked for dust, because I knew that our friends were coming, not to look for dust in the home, but rather to show that they loved us, as indeed they did.

Oh, incidentally, after Eva had a heart attack and was back to see the doctor, he told her she could go home and do anything she wanted to. So she changed clothes and was out in the garden using the hoe, killing weeds. Her sisters-in-law were flabbergasted, and said that was the last thing for a Doctor to tell Eva, "Go home and do what you want to." I used to tell her, when she was up most of the night getting sermons or doing something else, that she had her days and nights turned around. It must have rubbed off on me, too. Pa used to say he could look over here at midnight and we were lit up like a hotel.

I came home from work one night and Eva told me that Bonnie Quinn (she lived in Arlington) had called, and wanted her to be chairman for something in the county Red Cross. For once my girlfriend turned Bonnie down. She told her she just didn't have the time to do it. Bonnie said, "Well, I always wondered what you people did with your time when you lived in a small town?" I wonder too. Arlington must be big! Eva was the wrong person to ask such a question, but she took it in stride, and didn't lip off to Bonnie. After all, they were friends and sisters in Eastern Star. Enough said!

One time Eva substituted and taught for a few days in the Arlington school. One boy wanted to know how it felt to teach in a "big" school. She told him she hadn't noticed, and didn't realize that she was in a big school.

As I look back I don't know from whom I inherited some of my harebrained schemes. My Ma wouldn't have passed it on as she was so sweet and loving and wouldn't have even thought up some of the stuff that I tried to get by with. Pa was too busy trying to make ends meet and support his family. Maybe - just maybe - it was still that "devil" in me.

Eva chaired the county school board when the schools were getting reorganized. I took her to Erwin one night for a citizens' meeting. She always said the people would smile at me and look down their noses at her. Incidentally, when the "powers that be" were picking out board members for each commissioner district, they told me it was Eva or me for the job. I put thumbs down on my being on the board. She was more qualified than I was. Getting back to the meeting. A fellow came up to me and in a gruff voice wanted to know if I was the Superintendent there. I hasten to add this character looked like he had come out of the hog lot, and was pretty dirty. Maybe he didn't have water to even wash his hands and face, or didn't have time to wash up. I probably looked seedy too, but at least I had cleaned up, and didn't wear my work clothes (no suit and tie, either). I told him I wasn't the superintendent, but was the blacksmith from Hetland. His retort, "You don't look like one!" I told him that once in a while I cleaned up. I never did find out if he found the "head honcho."

Eva, Margaret Wonsbeck and Fern Melstad were all the same age, with only a couple of months separating their birthdays. When spring came, and the birthday season was here, I would take the three of them and their friend, Louise Christensen, to McDonald's in Brookings for a birthday party. We all had a great time, and I think the management enjoyed it as much as anyone. They gave the girls, as I called them, hats, balloons, etc., and even gave all of us ice cream sundaes free of charge. People would go by the window and smile and wave at the birthday gals. Our bunch wasn't as noisy as some of the kids' parties are. Then I would take them for a ride around the countryside to take in the sights. We did this for over ten tears, and I think they were all 87 years old when old age took over and put an end to a great time.

When Hank Lund came to the shop one day to get something fixed, I told him I'd better get him fixed up right away as I was going to take a couple of chicks to the doctor. He wanted to know how old the chicks were. "80," was my answer. "Oh – that's all right – then," he said. I never did figure out what he meant by "then."

Virg built one super duper (BIG) free flight plane that was a "dilly." Boy did he have a good time, zooming that thing around up above the town and countryside. One day something went KAPUT with it, and refused to start. Virg put more fuel in, and when it finally started, the plane seemed to thumb its nose at him, and took off to an altitude much higher than normal. That was a BAD mistake, on its part. It was last seen by the control tower (Virg), diving into Glen Pedersen's cornfield a mile north of Hetland.

Virg searched that field with a fine-toothed comb to no avail, looking for his plane. Today, maybe the government aviation boys, would have been out here to see what was the cause of the disaster? Virg then conned Ralph Anderson into taking him up in his plane, and they skimmed the top of the corn, back and forth, and sideways in that 160-acre field, and came up empty-handed. What a shame, as our boy was, to say the least, utterly dejected.

The plane met its Waterloo when it went through Glen's cornpicker. Uff Daa as the Norwegian would say, what an ending. Ashes to ashes and dust to dust, and where the plane went, who knows, maybe back to - DUST???

Eva and I used to have Halloween parties here at the house when Myrna and Virgil were small. One time she had a "slug" of kids sitting here in the kitchen with a sheet over a ghost's insides. The young ones couldn't see what was being passed around from one kid to the next. They had a good time, and always had some goodies to eat. The next day, after this episode, I went up to get the mail, and Jessie Hurd, who helped take care of the store and Post Office, wanted to know what went on at our place Halloween night. Doug Kallesen had been into the store and told Jessie about all the insides of the ghost that were passed around under the sheet. He told her "It kept getting worser and worser when the ghost's intestines came around!" Yuk! Lots of good memories for everyone.

Through the years, the Mons Melstad family, our next door neighbors, would celebrate Christmas Eve with a big powwow at their home. They always had enough food to feed a threshing crew, and being a mixture of Norskes and Danes, they were good cooks. They even had lutefisk for some of the old diehards, even though the younger generation turned up their noses at it. Obbie Melstad would change the water on the fish every day for a week or so, to make it taste just right. Eva and I had a standing invitation to go over to their place after most of the tribe had left. We would have oyster stew for supper over at Ma and Pa's place, as all of our families lived close enough to make it home for Christmas Eve. Our folks, and all of us, were thankful that we could share Christmas Eve together.

When Myrna and Virg were small, Eva and I would tuck them into bed, then scoot over to Melstad's to check out what they had left to eat. There was always plenty left, and a big variety, as each family brought something for the supper. When our kids got to be big enough to go with us, they too would head north to sample a smorgasbord at Melstads. Virg was right in his glory when Fern would serve him cold lutefisk. I know

Myrna passed the fish and probably sampled something "less smelly." We enjoyed their hospitality for years, as long as the Melstads carried on this Christmas Eve tradition. This was another example of Hetland's small town sharing with other neighbors – a yearly practice which we all enjoyed. The Melstads enjoyed showing us what they had received for Christmas, as they had their gift opening that night. We enjoyed seeing what Santa had left them before he took off to pass out more Christmas cheer.

Christmas was always a joyous time around our house. Eva would organize carolers to go around town singing carols to shut-ins and older folks. Then they would come back here for treats and a lot of good fellowship. Our kitchen was full of all kinds of candy, cookies, and everything known to man and some women, too! I didn't get into the Christmas spirit until it was time for me deliver boxes of treats all around town and the country, as well as in Arlington and Lake Preston. The kids were right in there pitching with their Mom, and helping me with the deliveries.

One year when Virgil was a little guy, he asked his Mom what she wanted for Christmas. She told him that there was some wax fruit at the hardware store that was pretty nice. He came over to the shop and asked me if he could have a dollar to buy his Mom a present. Up to the store we went, and when we came back he told her he had her Christmas present, and it began with waa. That was a big secret.

Another time this little boy went up to Hazel Rottum's store with a dollar and spent all afternoon buying Christmas presents for all of his aunts, uncles and cousins. It seems to me like he had some Lucky Strike cigarettes for his Uncle Homer and Uncle Skinny, a cigar for his Uncle Dane, and an assortment of candy and other stuff for everyone else. Hazel told us he made her day, as the presents he had came to a dollar and one cent, and she told him a dollar was all right, as that was all the money he had. He had to be a good shopper to get his Christmas shopping done in one day and only spend a buck to do it. He must take after his grandma Andersen. She was that kind of shopper, as she too didn't have much of the world's wealth to buy things with.

The kids bought their Mom a bread machine for Christmas. She baked one loaf of bread in the outfit, and I've been the bread cook ever since. If you doubt my word, I've gone through nine bread machines. As of July 2007, I am now using the tenth one. Now you wonder how one lone man can use that much bread? I don't, but I have a great time giving it away. Some days I even bake three loaves of different kinds of bread, and I enjoy spreading it around to my friends. I might add that I put a lot of different kinds of spices in the bread. Garlic, oregano, cinnamon, nutmeg, turmeric, cumin, thyme and even sage being some of the ingredients. Then some of the

Dale making bread

ladies would call and want to know what all I had in it. Ardis Karban even took out her spices and sniffed of each one to see if she could decipher what I had put in. She finally gave that up and called me, so I filled her in as to what she was eating. I think I did that just to devil these excellent cooks. Anyway I really enjoy giving away fresh bread.

Quite often when a new family moves to town I will bake a loaf of bread and take it to them. The Drewes family came to town, and I took a loaf of bread to them and invited them to come to church and get involved in helping out the town. I found out they needed a picnic table and I offered ours to them, as we didn't need it anymore. They offered to buy it but it wasn't for sale.

One night their cute little red-headed boy, Jesse, came over to see us. He and his sister Tina did that quite often, as we were like grandma and grandpa to them. We thought that was "great," as they are really nice kids, so polite and thankful for what was done for them. This particular night he was sitting on my lap and I told him that Eva and I loved him and he said he knew that. Because we loved him, I told him I was giving him a dollar "if that was okay." He thought that was nice and thanked us for it. Then I told him we were having a yard sale and Eva and I had a nice picnic table for sale and he was the only one invited to the sale. He figured that was a good deal. Then I asked him if he would give me a dollar for the picnic table (which by the way was made out of an old antique Model T Ford frame with inch pipe and 2x6s for seats and tabletop). Jesse said he would, so I told him to give us back the dollar and he had bought the table. Boy, was he excited and wanted to use the phone to call his Mom. He told her, "Mom, I just bought a picnic table from Dale and Eva for a dollar so come over and get it."

The rest of the family came over and Tina had a dollar bill to pay for it, as they knew Jesse had no money. I showed them the dollar he had paid for it so the sale was completed – with a Bill of Sale. The Drewes family got a much needed picnic table and Eva and I had a nice warm feeling in our hearts for doing something special for nice people who were thrilled for the "sneaky" way we used little Jesse to buy the table from us two old folks. This little boy and his family made our day and are very special to us.

I have mowed over to the church for a good many years. How many, I couldn't say. Some of those years if I had charged anything – and I mean anything – for my labor of love, the church would have been operating in the red. However, we wouldn't have been able to print more money, like the US government does, when they are deficit spending.

Out in back of the church there are several trees that have been there for many years. Two in particular were close together, and I had to get the riding mower positioned just right in order to mow between them. That worked fine for many years. However, this one time I was going to go between the two trees, and I didn't get the mower just right (at least, that's what I thought) and couldn't go through to the other side, as the drive wheels spun and the engine quit. I managed to push myself and the mower backward, and then this smart Dane got the brilliant idea of backing up several feet and then taking a run for it at full speed. Do you know what? The trees still stood there, and I had the engine quit, just like that, and I was really stuck between the trees! There was no way to back out, so I proceeded to get off the outfit and finally, literally lifted the mower out backwards. Now, don't tell me why I couldn't get through those trees. How was I to know that each year the trees grew and got bigger around, (just like some of our bellies do) and the mower hadn't shrunk any, so I finally figured out the problem.

Then I made another mistake, adding to this one. I told Howard Karban about it, and he never seemed to forget to remind me of my miscalculation. He told their son, Steve about this hair-raising episode. Now Steve keeps reminding me about it!

When Fern Melstad taught school in some of the rural schools close to Hetland, we always went out to their Thanksgiving and Christmas programs. If we couldn't go, I always gave Fern a buck to buy us some candy at their bake sale. My motto was, any kind of candy, just so it was fudge. Boy, we always got a good amount of candy, as we also did here when we had one of our programs in the school. We were out to the Christmas program at the Karban school one year when the kids were small. It might have been called the Krueger school also, as it was close to their farm. After the program was finished, Orville Roderick asked little Virgil why he didn't sing in the program. Virg told him, "I don't go to school here." Roderick: "I'll give you a nickel if you'll go up and sing." Out went his little hand to get the money first. Up to the front our little minstrel went. The crowd quieted down, and he proceeded to sing a song that had something to do with Christmas, I suppose. He got a good round of applause, and Roderick didn't offer him any more money because anytime Orville parted with cash like that, it was a miracle. He must have decided that one song was enough to pay for at one time. Could be.

Those of you who know where we live in Hetland know that we're just across the street from the school. The teacher told the kids they had to have overshoes. So we had to buy overshoes. The teacher didn't say they had to be worn so many times Myrna and Virgil carried them to school and carried them back at noon and when school was out. They were always considerate of their folks and this way the overshoes didn't wear out so fast, so they were saving us money.

We always thought they were "smart" kids and this was just one good example of it.

Eva and I always thought we had some smart kids. However, at times it made me wonder. Fern Melstad, the elementary teacher and our next-door neighbor, told us that Virg was having trouble with learning his multiplication tables in arithmetic. Every morning he would wake up to, "Virg, what is 8 x 6, 8 x 7," etc. He got straightened out on that, so our testing worked.

Myrna and Virgil with Fern Melstad

One time I went back to the shop after supper and told him to get his problems done. I came home about 9 PM and he was singing at the top of his voice, while hitting the top of the table with his pencil to keep time, happy as a lark. I asked him if he had the problems all done. I supposed he would have them done, as long as he was so pleased with himself. I should have known better, as he said, "Nope, but I've got one done." A few other times I questioned his upbringing. I always told Virg and Myrna and their Mom that the good stuff they got from Mom, and the bad from me.

Myrna had chicken pox one year when the World Series was on, so she had to stay out of school (she was in the grades). That suited her fine, as her Grandpa Andersen had a TV. So they enjoyed each other's company while watching the series.

One year when the Twins and Dodgers were playing in the Series, I went to the Post Office to get the mail. Several ball fans were shooting the breeze and all were for the Twins. I took my mail and was ready to leave, and remarked rather profoundly, I think, "I'm for the Dodgers." Boy, oh boy, you should have heard the chatter, just like the world was coming to an end. They were still lipping off when I told the outfit I had to go to work. Honest – I really was for the Dodgers. The only time I'm for the Twins is when they play the Yankees. Enough of that.

When Fern Melstad got the job to teach school in Hetland, she was worried she might have trouble with Virgil having her for a teacher. She had been our neighbor since he was born, and she told Mom she wondered how it would go. She told us he was a perfect gentleman, as I knew he would be, having a Mom like he has. In Hetland, we never had enough kids in school to have enough pupils so that each class could have a room by itself. When I was in school, we had 1st, 2nd and 3rd grades in the primary room, 4th, 5th and 6th grades in the intermediate room, and 7th and 8th in the upper room. It finally got down to only two rooms with four grades in each, and then to only one room with all eight grades. Our kids received a better than usual education under those circumstances, as the younger ones got to listen in on the older kids. Fern told us more than once that Virg wasn't bashful about raising his hand if none of the upper classmen knew the answer. She said she would call on him, as he knew what the answer was.

One time, this was before any man was on the moon, she asked the upper class if it would ever be possible to put a man on the moon, and how it could be done. Our little boy then raised his hand, even though he wasn't in the higher grade, and Fern wanted to know what he thought about it. He had it figured out, he told her. A man and

Hetland Elementary School, teacher was Fern Melstad, 1955

woman could get married and get on an airplane that could go to the moon, and this couple could have kids and the kids could have kids and they could go on for years until they reached the moon. If he had been in the right class, I wonder what grade she would have given him. We never heard about Myrna ever doing these things, not that she couldn't have.

Virg played the French Horn with three girls from Lake Preston. I took him to practice, and he wasn't doing too well in learning the contest piece. The four would be playing, and pretty soon the girls had to quit playing, as he was lousing up the music, and they had to laugh. At the contest in Milbank, V. W. Madsen, the Superintendent, and I agreed the French Horn quartet didn't have much chance to win anything. Lo and behold, they did a good job, as Virg knew he had to "get in gear" and performed his part to perfection. I ambled over to the scoreboard, and there it was - #1 Superior, Lake Preston French Horn quartet. (They also performed the piece in the grand concert. - ed.) I told Madsen we didn't know much about music.

Eva had kids from other schools who took singing lessons, as they were not getting much help from the music teacher in their own schools. Myrna went out for singing solo when she was in Lake Preston High School. She won both years, as she didn't sing solos until she was a Junior. The music teacher told her he didn't know she could sing, and wanted to know who she had taken lessons from. Myrna said she hadn't taken any lessons. Carroll Saugstad, the teacher, told Eva that she didn't get any credit. Myrna got to perform in the Grand Concert, singing her solo, and also playing her tuba solo.

One time in DeSmet a couple of us wanted to talk to the school board about something. The meeting started at 8 PM and at midnight, we were still waiting for an audience with the board. Finally, the board got through meeting with two ornery Danes from Brookings County and the board told us to come in. It was 1 AM the next day! We were the "caboose" of the meeting. I don't remember who the chairman was, but he wanted to know what we were there for. I scratched my head, and told him we had waited so long that we had forgotten what we had come for. Big deal!

Lloyd Carlson was the board member from the Erwin district, and he was a Swede. When the board had to make a tough decision about closing a school, he was ready to take off for Sweden! Mom used to get a kick out of it, how he would squirm and say they will get mad. I told him one time to get a ticket for Sweden and stay there until it was safe to come back. He agreed, but on the condition that I go along, and when the plane was over Denmark, he would push me out without a parachute. He didn't go to Sweden, and I didn't get to Denmark, either.

Our daughter, Myrna, and Sharon Jibben, a classmate from Lake Preston were the top typists in school. She didn't take after her Dad on typing, although I passed the course. One day, there was to be a typing contest in Arlington for the area schools. What do you suppose? The teacher had the two kids type for 45 minutes as fast as they could go. Boy, talk about a warm-up! Then they took off for the contest. The poor kids typed faster than anyone there, but had warmed up so much they had too many mistakes. Even then, they were among the top ones, but not the winners. I saw the teacher afterwards and wondered what got into her to do such a trick. I knew her and her folks, so knew I could kid her about it. She said she didn't have any idea why she had Myrna and Sharon warm up like that. Probably like the two guys, betting on whether the one could drink ten bottles of beer, one after the other. The other one said, "Wait 'til I go in and try it, and then we'll bet!" He lost. Rather far fetched, but it could be.

Our daughter Myrna was driving in her Uncle Dane's farm field. What for, I don't know. Anyway, Myrna was driving the car for her Mom, looking over the scenery. She didn't see the slough of water that was between where they were and where they wanted to go. Myrna, being sharp, decided the shortest way was to go straight ahead and promptly got stuck in the mud. Uncle Dane got his tractor and pulled them out. He didn't even comment on how his niece was driving. Made a good impression on her.

When Myrna had one of her handbell choirs out here on a concert tour in the 70s, they had a concert in a church in Vermillion. Cliff and Helen Manley lived there, and they had taught school here when Myrna was a baby. Cliff had pictures of her without many clothes on. In the morning before the choir left, he brought pictures of her and showed her choir kids how cute she looked at an early age when she was crawling around on a blanket. The Illinois kids really got a bang out of seeing their choir director when she was a baby. We thought she was cute and sweet then, too, and she still is. Of course, we might be prejudiced. Who knows?

When her choir had their concert in our Congregational Church, the director (Myrna) drafted me to be a part of the program. One of the bell pieces was "The Anvil Chorus." I got a chance to show my versatility by hitting a chunk of iron with a hammer. If I remember right, I had to hit the iron twelve times, and I think I did just that as Myrna knew her Dad could probably count to twelve. I think I was in time when I clobbered the so-called "anvil." At that time it was who you knew and not what you knew, that got me the job. I enjoyed it as much as Myrna and her bell kids did.

When we took Eva to the nursing home in Arlington on November 18, 1999, it was a sad day for all of us. We thought we had lost her the night before, but she rallied and survived. It was lucky for me that Virg and Vi were here that night, and took good care of her. I will be forever thankful.

Our sister-in-law, Shirley Matson, and I were with Eva when one of the social workers came in to ask her some questions. She couldn't answer the questions, so I took care of that. The last thing the nurse asked was "If you could do something right now, what would it be?" Eva's quick response with no thinking was "Help others." Shirley and I looked at each other in total disbelief at how quickly she had answered that question. That was no problem for Eva, because all through her life she had helped others. Both of us would have pondered on a question like that, but not Eva. Her mind was clear as a bell to give that quick answer.

Eva and Dale, 1995

Chapter 5
Family *Matters*

Above: Penny, Clayton, Eva, Homer, Ruby, Elden, Morris, Front: Curtis, Myrna and Virgil, ca 1945

Left: Penny, holding Curtis, Clayton, Cora, Ruby, Dale, Eva, holding Virgil, Myrna, Clyde, Morris and Topsy, November 1944

Family *Matters*

Pa thought he needed a new hat. He and Elden were in Sioux Falls and went into one of the stores to see about a hat. He found one they both liked, so Pa asked how much it was. "Three bucks," the clerk said. "Put it back," Pa told him. He wasn't paying three dollars for any hat, so no hat.

Later, Pa and Elden were in Huron and Pa told Elden he needed some wine. He always said he hardly ever drank any wine, but it disappeared. Anyway, when his kids came to see him, it seems as though those three brothers of mine knew where he kept it, and being part of the family, didn't need to ask if it was all right to partake of a little nourishment to settle an unruly stomach. They went into a liquor store and the good looking girl, as Pa called her afterwards, wanted to know how she could help them. Pa told her that he needed some wine. "What kind?" Well, Pa told her "It was some David." "Oh, you mean Mogen David." "Yeah, that's it." When he came to pay for it, it was six bucks. Elden thought that he would have told her to put it back, at that price, like he did with the hat. No, by golly, he dug up the cash and had his bottle of hooch ready to take home. Elden told his Pa that he thought he would tell her to put it back. "No," Pa said, "She was good looking." We razzed him about paying six bucks for a few shots of wine, and it would be soon gone, when he wouldn't pay three bucks for a hat that would have lasted for years and years. It was his money, so he could spend it like he wanted to.

I took Pa to Sioux Falls several times for cancer treatment - radiation. We had to be there at 8 AM so one time we stopped at a pancake house for breakfast. We ordered the cakes, and then the girl wanted to know if we wanted bacon with them. "Yeah," Pa said. We got our cakes and three pieces of bacon each. Boy, they tasted good, as he liked pancakes, and when Eva sent them over to him for a meal, he really cleaned them up. I paid the bill and on the way out he told me how good everything tasted. Then out of a clear sky, he wanted to know how much the bacon cost. I told him that it was 15 cents a slice. Boy, he hit the roof! Fifteen cents for a slice of bacon! That was too much, and was highway robbery. I told him that he seemed to think everything tasted OK, so why complain? That's all right, if he had known that, he wouldn't have ordered it. The pancakes were 60 cents for three, so he figured it was a "bum steer" or a "bum pig" in this case, instead of beef. He really stormed about that. Fifteen cents a piece; unheard of!

Christmas picture of Clayton, Penny with Barb, Eva, Dale, Elden, Morris, Ruby, Clyde, Virgil, Myrna and Curtis, ca 1947

We had plenty to eat at Grandpa Morris and Grandma Ruby's at suppertime on Christmas Eve. All of the Andersens, though there weren't many of us, would go over to the folks' place and our wives would have oyster stew with all that went with it. There was always plenty to eat. It was a wonderful and enjoyable tradition and one that all of us looked forward to each year.

When Eva's folks, Clyde and Cora Guptill, moved to Hetland from their farm at Springfield, Myrna and Virgil had the best of two worlds. They had grandpas and grandmas from both sides of their Mom's and Dad's families. Our kids had a good chance to really be spoiled, but the grandparents looked out for their welfare, instead. I didn't ever know any of my grandparents, so I know what I missed, and I like to think that my grandparents missed something too.

Clyde had a job of taking the mail from the post office to the depot every day to meet

Clyde, Eva and Cora

the passenger trains. He had a two-wheeled cart to transport the mail when the roads were good, and I made a toboggan for him to use in the wintertime. The kids, when a little older, would help their grandpa push the cart, whether he needed help or not. Our folks enjoyed our kids and the kids enjoyed visiting with their grandparents as well. It was good for all of them and Eva and I enjoyed hearing about our kids' visits. Both grandmas were not in the best of health, so the kids looked out for them, too.

Grandpa Guptill did a lot of nice carpentry work. He made our bathroom cupboards, magazine racks, bookshelves and kitchen counters. We all benefited from his expertise and loving, caring work.

My brother Homer, and Lula Moe were going together, and finally decided they had lived alone long enough and better get "hitched." Eva was a licensed minister, so they wanted her to tie the knot. The date was decided upon and Homer told all of us not to tell anyone when it was to be, as they were to be married at Lu's home. Our kids used to say that their Uncle Homer went to bed late and got up early before he was married, and after the wedding he went to bed early and got up late. Maybe they were on to something, even though they were young.

The big day came. Lyle Waby was in the shop and told me this was the big night for the wedding. I didn't let on one way or the other, as I knew he was "fishing." However, he knew what he was talking about, as he said he had bribed Virgil to tell him when the big event was to happen. He had given Virgil a dime ahead of time to let him (Waby) in on the secret. Homer forgave our little boy as he knew that Virg needed the money.

Homer came to pick me up to go to Lu's home for the ceremony. I got into the car and wasn't in any hurry to get the door shut.

Homer and Lu - wedding

This was after dark, and the overhead light was on as it should be. "Shut the door quick!" He told me. I didn't shut the door, and politely, I think, asked him "Why?" "We don't want anybody to see you all dressed up with me," he said. I still took my time shutting the door. The marriage went off like clockwork, and survived as long as they lived.

Lu and Homer Andersen

Homer was a great one to tell how to raise kids, especially since he didn't have any of his own. He told me he was giving our son Virgil the devil for something. Homer said Virg was taking it all in and knew what the lecture was about. When Homer was finished, Virgil looked at him and said, "Uncle Homer," and then asked him a question about something altogether different than what he had been lecturing him on. "He never heard a damn word I said," was Homer's comment.

Homer and Myrna were arguing about something that happened in a ball game. Neither could convince the other. Virgil was an interested bystander and was really listening to see who was right. Finally, in desperation, Homer told Myrna, "I'll bet you a nickel that I am right." Our girl jumped at the chance to make money off her Uncle Homer, so she took him up on the bet. Homer said that Virgil, out of the clear blue said, "I'll take some of that, too." Our little boy must have figured that his big sis knew what she was talking about. As it turned out, Homer was right and the kids lost the bet. Homer told me that he took Virgil's money, being the eager beaver that he was, but let Myrna "off the hook" without paying up.

I only have one sister-in-law left on this earth, Shirley Matson, who was married to my brother Elden. After Elden died of cancer, she married Maurice Matson.

Elden knew what he was doing when he latched on to Shirley, or was it the other way around? She has always spoiled me as well as Eva and our family, and she still continues to do that to me, and I enjoy every minute of it. When Shirley was born, she must have had her eyes on being a super duper culinary expert, because that is what she has been, and still is today. Yum, if you haven't tasted some of her delicious cooking, then you don't know what you have been missing. Even today, before I began to hunt and peck this out, I enjoyed a delicious dinner of scal-

Donna, Terri, Rhonda, Shirley and Dane at their 25th anniversary

Shirley and Maurice Matson

loped spuds and ham, courtesy of Shirley. And that ain't all. She brought me enough food so that I have NO need to sit down and plan my dinner menu for several days.

Out here in Hetland, we are still old-fashioned. We eat dinner at noon, after having breakfast in the wee hours of the AM. Supper is at night, and if a snack is needed in between meals, we call it Lunch. Norskes and some Danes (not me) call it coffee. I'm not old enough yet to drink that stuff.

Many a time when Elden and Shirley lived out on the farm and I happened to drop in on them, she would be busy making FUDGE or some other sweet tooth bar that was known to tickle the palate. My palate was always ready to oblige, so she didn't need to look any further for a sweet tooth tester. Maybe that is why, at the present time, my mouth is sans many a tooth. Too much sweet stuff? That is a possibility. Well, Shirley always invited me to sample her finished product, and to this day I have never, no never, tasted anything that wasn't good when she had her finger in the pie. Maybe two fingers? When I was ready to head home, I never left without something for the road, in case of a blizzard, and that would tide me over in case of an emergency. After all, I was a mile from home and during that long drive back to Hetland the weather could change in a quick hurry.

Shirley is a sweetheart, and a "smart chick" too, even though she didn't graduate from Hetland High School (it was from Lake Preston High).

Most of the time I lounge around the house in "A" shirt underwear, sometimes even in my shorts. I got a good buy on T-shirts and after our big snowstorm on November 11, 2000, I decided to try out my bargain shirts. It was too hot, and I was telling Shirley about my predicament, and that I didn't know what to do about it. Being of German descent, and sharp as a tack, she asked if I had turned down the heat. I was elated that she solved my problem. After turning down the thermostat, I wasn't too warm any more, and as she told me on the phone it would be a saving on the heat bill, too. Now, why didn't I think of that? She has been a joy to have in our family since Elden picked her out to be his bride. He knew a sweet, nice, loving and caring girl when he saw her. We think the same about her, too.

I took our nieces, Donna and Rhonda Andersen, on their first Halloween escapade. They weren't very big, so I asked their folks if it was OK for them to go with me. Boy, we had fun! We would go to a house and I would <u>beat</u> – and I mean <u>beat</u> – on the door. When the door opened I'd holler,

Donna and Rhonda

"Twicks or tweets!" Those two little girls were speechless as well as spellbound at such antics. They would hold up their sacks and came home with lots of loot. Shirley told Elden that Mory shouldn't be doing that with the kids. His reply, "He's enjoying it more than they are." And right he was. He knew his older brother, having lived with him all his life.

Donna and Rhonda thought that their Uncle Mory was a pretty good shopper. Years ago, Eva and I were supposed to fix the turkey for the Andersen clan's Thanksgiving. There were no birds here in Hetland, so one morning we took off and checked turkeys in Arlington, five miles away. Then on to Brookings, 25 miles away, and then to Sioux Falls, 85 miles distant. We spent the day looking and came back to Brookings, and bought the biggest bird they had. The turkey was "extra special" as Eva did a fantastic job of cooking it, and making dressing too. Shirley and Elden's two little girls let me know after the dinner, "Uncle Mory, you are a good shopper." I think we must have had extra time on our hands, and wanted to look at the scenery. Today, I would buy the first one I saw, and that would be it.

Terri, Shirley and Elden's youngest daughter, was a just little tyke when her Uncle Skinny was in the hospital in DeSmet, The Andersen clan went en masse to see how our loved one was behaving with the nurses. At that time young kids could not go into the hospital room under any circumstances. Period. Little Terri figured out how to circumvent such a dumb ruling and wanted to let her Uncle Skinny know that she was there in person. She got several sheets of paper and wrote a full 3-page letter to her uncle. We took it in to Skinny for him to read. Then we asked little Terri what she had written. "I don't know, I can't read yet," was her honest answer.

Terri with kitten

I am sure that Skinny could read and decipher the Love that radiated from the three pages that Terri had sent to him.

Terri competed in the Miss South Dakota USA pageant. Eva and I sponsored her. She did well, but didn't win, and she had a good time. We were there to see the whole shebang, but unfortunately we were NOT judges, or the outcome may have been different.

Skinny and Penny had two kids, Curtis and Barbara. I used to give them a rough time, probably because I was one of their next of kin, their Uncle Mory. Eva's Dad, Clyde, had a 1937 Ford four door sedan that he wasn't able to drive any more, due to ill health. One day out of a clear sky, Curt said in a loud and commanding voice, "I WANT to buy Grandpa Clyde's car, and I'll give you 25 bucks for it." Wait a minute, hold your horses, we don't want to sell that car. "Why not? I WANT to buy it." "We DON'T want to sell it." "Why Not? I want IT." He was really bombastic about it, as he sometimes was. There was no sale.

Clayton, Penny, Curtis and Barbara

I remember one time when Curt was home on furlough before he was shipped out to lose his life in a no-good war in Viet Nam. We were attending graduation services at his Alma Mater, Lake Preston High School. The preacher ended the invocation prayer, "For we pray in the name of Him who never lost His Cool." Hmm, even to a staid Congregationalist like me, that was what might be termed a different ending for a prayer. Curt must have been thinking along the same lines as his Uncle Mory, when he shouted out loud for all to hear, "My God, a Swinging preacher."

Our niece, Barbara, Skinny and Penny's daughter, was a contestant in one of the Snow Queen contests in Lake Preston and came through with flying colors. She was crowned Snow Queen for Kingsbury county, and went on to Aberdeen to compete for the South Dakota Snow Queen title. She didn't make state queen, but had a good time competing with the other girls. One thing I remember hearing on TV before the actual contest was the announcer asking each girl what their favorite food was, and if they prepared it for themselves, or their mother prepared it for them? Most of the girls did not cook for themselves, so I began to wonder if these beauties could boil water without burning it. I don't remember what our Barb said in answer to the question, but I am sure that she could handle the cooking situation, being related to a line of good cooks.

Come and get it, come and get it, FRESH Sweet Corn on the Cob, FRESH Sweet Corn on the Cob. Anyone reading this get in gear, if you want FRESH Sweet Corn on the Cob. Wow and double Wow. Corn on the cob, right from the field into the boiling water. That's what Skinny and I did. He shucked the corn while I got the water on to boil, and then we dumped eight ears into the water, and we stood by the stove, patiently??, watching, and trying to get the water to boil in nothing flat. This was the first sweet corn of the year, and after a long drought with no corn on the cob we were, to say the least, champing at the bit and drooling at the mouth, all at the same time. After what seemed like ages to two hungry brothers, we finally chomped on to that savory corn on the cob. Skinny tried to convince all who would listen, that Mory had five ears and he only had three. Not so. We shared and shared alike, four each. Brotherly Love?

Now you might ask, "Where does corn like that come from?" Well listen, and I will share a little secret with you. When Elden and Shirley lived on the farm, before he was elected sheriff, they raised sweet corn that was out of this world, and it was second to none. I have never tasted corn like that before or after they quit raising it. These two dear relatives of ours had the right touch, and they knew what was the best corn to plant. We came and got it, and it was raised with loving care.

One time Eva was out in their patch picking corn, and here was a man that she didn't know. He told her he was a cattle buyer from Huron, and Elden always sold him his cattle, and that they were good friends. Needless to say, he could take all of the corn he wanted. He told Eva, "Boy that is GOOD corn." We all agreed. Elden was a GOOD cattleman as well, and always had top steers to sell. Not only that, they would butcher the cream of the crop, and we always got to share deluxe beef. I have heard it said that their kids would sometimes ask, "Do we have to have that OLD steak again?" Maybe they wanted to see what McDonald's had to offer?

One time, I made nightstands for the grandkids. Didn't know which one should go to Melanie, and which one to Elaine. Of course, these were made out of steel so they will last forever, or even longer. They had marbled Formica shelves, one white and the other one black. Melanie came downstairs first on Christmas day, and we asked her which she might prefer. She looked them over and said she would take the one that Elaine didn't want. When Elaine came down, we asked her which she would like. Quick as a flash she said, "That one!" and she picked the black one. That's the one that Mom and I figured would be her choice. Melanie was well satisfied with hers, but she asked Elaine, "How can you decide so fast?"

Eva and Melanie with her table

One year Myrna gave them cameras for Christmas. Elaine had used up her roll of film, and Melanie was going around checking things out without any film in her camera. Must be a difference in kids? Could be that they are related to their folks or their grandparents?

Elaine with her camera

When Grandma Eva was in the hospital in Sioux Falls, no kids were allowed in the patient's room. Virg and Vi and their little daughters, Melanie and Elaine, were standing out in the corridor to see Grandma, but the little ones could only peek in through the door to talk to Grandma. All at once the fire alarm went off and the nurses sprang into action and came running, at the same time yelling, "Get into the room!" Into the room we went, men, women and children, and Bang! The door was closed behind us. Melanie and Elaine were elated, and up on to Grandma's bed they went to get some loving, which before the fire alarm went off, was a No No. The three of them had a howling good time,

Melanie and Elaine

snuggling together like peas in a pod, until the all clear signal came through. Luckily it was only a fire drill, or else we may have all gone up in "smoke." The kids thought it was great, and the timing couldn't have been better for the Andersen clan.

There is a question whether it is better to read "canned" children's stories from a book to young kids, or have the kids listen to stories that will fit any occasion as the need may be? In other words, tall tales from a seasoned tall tales veteran researcher and prefabricator, who (unlike the children's book writer) doesn't charge anything for spinning a tall tale yarn or two. Our kids, Myrna and Virgil, seemed to lean to the former. Every night it was a ritual for them to get a book (one of several) and bring it to Mom or Dad for them to read out loud, of course, to four little listening ears. They would crawl up on to an available lap, snuggle down, curl up and get comfy, eagerly waiting to hear the same old stuff that they had heard umpteen times before.

Eva, being the teacher that she was, could read the pages of the book easier than I could, so she didn't make any mistakes when turning the pages. Now with me, that was a little different story. I couldn't always tell if these two dear young ones were asleep, or if they were just being quiet and listening to the story. Once in awhile, I would turn two pages at once (the story ended quicker that way), and boy did I find out in a quick hurry that these two kids were NOT sleeping. "Daaad," was the loud wail, "You MISSED - a - PAGE." "Oh yeah, I guess I did. Sorry about that." They snuggled down again, and I would go on reading the story, before the interruption. These two little twerps could have told the story to us, without them having to read it. They knew each one by heart. Mom and I wouldn't trade those pleasant memories for anything. Needless to say, our kids' books showed the ravages of time, but they served their purpose. From what I can gather today, reading stories to the little ones is a thing of the past for many families. From past experience they, both kids and adults, don't know what they have missed.

Now let's flip over the coin and see what the other side has to say about telling stories to the "younguns." Our two grandkids, Melanie and Elaine were right in their glory when they could hear Grandpa spin them a tale or two. But on the other hand, I think that Grandma was more inclined to read stories to them. She always told me she was married to an unimaginative Dane. After years of losing arguments around the house, I knowingly let it go at that. There was no use in ruffling any feathers unless the occasion called for it.

Melanie, being the elder of the two kids, took every story in stride, but with Elaine things were different. She knew how to get grandpa cranked up again for another story, as you will soon find out, if you will be so kind as to read on. One time when we were visiting them, I had just finished telling the young "lasses" the story about Brer

Elaine and Melanie on Dale's lap for storytime

Rabbit and Poky the turtle. They always lapped this one up, as I never told the story the same, except for the "ending," which was always the same. You know the old stories which always ended, "and they lived happily," etc.

One time after finishing the above-mentioned story, Elaine told me in a loud and commanding voice, "Grandpa, you sure tell stories, LOTS MORE BETTER than the book." Wow, did that ever puff me up. Out of the mouths of babes.

"Brer Rabbit and Poky the turtle?" Hmm. Now that's something. I don't ever recall hearing that story when I was a youngster. I wonder what that was all about? Well, listen my friends and you shall hear the wild tale of Brer Rabbit and Poky the turtle.

Now Brer Rabbit and Poky the turtle were sitting in the shade of an old apple tree that was located alongside of farmer Brown's garden. They were just relaxing and shooting the breeze, as a rabbit and turtle were known to do. Their talk went along OK until Brer started to get nasty, telling Poky that he was a slowpoke, and couldn't run like a rabbit. Poky finally got teed off with this know-it-all rabbit, and let him have it. "I'll bet you a strawberry malted milk from McDonald's that I can beat you in a race down to that post." Wow, a strawberry malted milk from McDonald's. Brer perked up his ears at that one. "The bet is on," Brer said, "When do you want to start?" "Right now," said Poky. Brer knew that this was a good way to get a malted milk.

Not having a gun to start the race, Brer told Poky that when they were all set to start, he (Brer) would = BURP. Brer dug in his heels to get a quick start, while Poky just waited at the starting line. All set, "BURP," and they were OFF. Brer took a couple of big leaps and he was off like a rabbit. Then out of the corner of his eye, he saw farmer Brown's car going down the road, heading for town. Brer stopped dead in his tracks. Farmer Brown was gone and there was no one guarding the garden. Boy, oh boy was he in luck. Brer had been in the garden before this, but farmer Brown had a shotgun and Brer had some buckshot in his tail to prove it.

The old rabbit checked to see where Poky was and he was hardly moving toward the finish line, so Brer knew he had plenty of time to go over to the garden and help himself, free of charge, with no gun in sight. The carrots were first, and he ate until he was full of carrots. Then some lettuce went down the hatch. Seeing some cucumbers, Brer decided to try one. Uff Daa, he spit it out and it left a bad taste in his mouth, so he decided to get a shot of tomato juice to rinse out his mouth. He found a ripe tomato, pulled up a carrot to punch a hole in it, and proceeded to squirt the juice into his mouth. The bad taste was gone. By now, this rabbit was stuffed, so he decided to take a little snooze. He checked on Poky, who was far from the finish line, so there was plenty of time to snooze and still win the race.

After flicking a grasshopper off his belly, Brer closed his eyelids to rest his eyeballs and went fast asleep and he got to dreaming of McDonald's malted milk. His nose twitched, his ears wiggled and his feet were moving faster and faster as the dream went on, but Brer's fast moving feet were not getting him any closer to the finish line. Finally, when the malted milk was gone, the dream was ended. Brer woke up with a BANG. Where was Poky? Lo and behold, Brer had slept so long that Poky was nearly ready to cross the finish line. No problem. Brer took off like a rabbit and when he neared the finish line, he gave a flying leap to jump over Poky and win the race. But alas, Brer was so full of carrots and stuff from Brown's garden that he didn't jump far enough. Instead he landed on the back end of Poky the slowpoke turtle, and shoved him over the finish line. Poky, slowpoke that he was, became the winner of a McDonald's malted milk.

The moral of the story, if there is one: Run (if you are in a race) before you stuff yourself with carrots, lettuce and tomato juice until you need to take a well earned snooze. When I would tell this story, or one about the four bears or something else, I needed to put my words into action, and that is what I did, so these dear little granddaughters might think and say, "Grandpa, you tell stories, LOTS MORE BETTER THAN THE BOOK." A nice compliment? Grandpa thinks so!

Top: Morris and grandchildren: Donna, Barb, Rhonda, Virg, Curt, Myrna and Terri
Bottom: Tim and Elaine Samolytz, Dale and Eva

Family Matters 65

Top: Dale with granddaughters, Elaine and Melanie
Middle: Ben and Josh Heise with Great Grandpa Dale
Bottom: Ben, Don, Melanie and Josh Heise

Chapter 6
Hetland in War

Top left: Clayton (Skinny) Andersen, U.S. Navy
Top right: Ration book
Center: Homer, Army
Bottom: Elden (Dane), Army

Homer with his U.S. Army Air Corps glider

palachian Mountains, what for I do not know, except that the glider was being moved to some place other than where it was before being moved to where it was supposed to be. Uff Daa. Army rules, I presume. It appeared that Homer came home unscathed, and was just as ornery when he came home as he was when he

Homer and Myrna

went into the service. He was Myrna's hero, as he brought her a pair of little RED boots that he had picked up in South America. Boy, did she strut her stuff when she was all dressed up, wearing those red boots. Needless to say she proudly wore them out.

Skinny was in the Navy, and was injured when a torpedo bomber that he was in crashed into the ocean while on a torpedo run on a Japanese ship in the Aleutians. (He once told Virg that the plane ahead of his was shot down, and his plane was brought down when it flew into the water splashed up when the lead plane hit the water.) The physical and mental effects of those injuries stayed with him for the rest of his life.

While Skinny was serving in the Navy, his wife, Penny, came to live with our folks. Skinny had been bragging what a nice looking girl his new wife was, so we knew what to expect. Pa, however nearly tipped over the apple cart when he met her and said, "Well you don't look like Miss America." I have NO recollection of what Penny said, but she took it in stride. Pa was gruff on the outside, but softhearted on the inside.

Penny and Skinny

Elden was drafted just a few days before the Japs hit Pearl Harbor, and he only received ten weeks of training before being shipped out to the jungles of New Guinea. He was in the Army Infantry, serving with the 32nd Division of the Michigan National Guard. The Japs pounded them unmercifully, as our troops were short on big guns to fight back. They went for several months without eating a decent meal, only canned food.

Elden and Bill Haufschild were drafted at the same time. The local Legion Post is named after Bill, as he was gunned down in Germany.

After returning home, Elden suffered for the rest of his life from the effects of malaria, etc., contracted while serving in the jungles of the south Pacific. After the war, he would curl up in the big chair at home, all crunched up, with

Hetland in War

My only recollection of World War I was when the war was over. I was only four years old but can remember standing at the south window in our downstairs bedroom and seeing the "big" celebration that went on west of the depot. Half of the country seemed to be there, as they had a hay-stuffed dummy representing the Kaiser hanging by his neck from a rope that reached across the street by the railroad tracks. Under the old "coot" was a monstrous pile of hay. After everyone had shot the Kaiser with volley after volley from shotguns and rifles, they proceeded to set fire to the hay. Do you know what? After the blaze got going the Kaiser caught fire and down he came. That was the end of him, ashes to ashes and dust to dust, the Bible says.

Ralph Johnson was Hetland's fighter pilot in World War I. When the war was over, once in awhile he would fly to Hetland and take up passengers for a buck apiece. School would be dismissed so us kids could see what a celebrity looked like, as well as an airplane that could do "loop the loop" and boy, he could loop it. He held the world's record for awhile for the number of loops made one after another. He took his brother in law, Jim Barber, up for a ride. When they landed Jim was really sick. Come to find out, Ralph turned the plane upside down over Lake Preston lake. He flew it like that for a short ways. Jim said, "There I was hanging upside down over the lake." Don't blame him for being sick. Ralph took his sister, Lutie Barber, for a ride too, but that was nothing for her. She didn't get sick.

How well I remember when the Japs bomb[ed] Pearl Harbor. Elden had just been draf[ted] a few days before December 7, and we used [the] truck for a rabbit hunt. We had a really g[ood] hunt and a good time, but it all was spoiled w[hen] we came home and everyone was telling us [the] bad news, that we were at war. That was a bl[ack] day in our memory, as well as in history.

I can see Homer yet when he came home fr[om] the Army. He came from uptown, walk[ing] down the sidewalk south of Starksen's st[ore]. Topsy was lying out in front of the shop whe[n] at once up went her head. Cocking it sidew[ays] she saw her pal, or at least it looked like her [pal], Homer, walking toward us. He was a lot thin[ner] than he was before he went to war. Topsy jum[ped] up and went full speed ahead to meet him [and] boy, did those two have a joyous celebration [and] a welcome home affair. Even though Homer [had] been gone for four years, she hadn't forgo[tten] who he was, even though he had changed in [that] time. Smart dog!!

Topsy was a pal of Homer's. Before he [left] for the service, she would sit on his lap and [put] her head up on his left shoulder and go to sle[ep]. When he came home from the Army after f[our] years, he sat down in the same chair where [he] used to sit. Topsy jumped up in his lap, put [her] head on his left shoulder so that her nose [was] behind his head and snuggled down, just [as] she had done over four years earlier. And s[ome] people say pets are dumb.

My three brothers were in World War [II]. Homer was in the Army Air Force, par[t of] the time flying gliders. Once he flew over the his knees pulled up on his chest and his arms over his head, just like he did when he was lying in the foxholes while the Japs strafed and bombed them.

He never complained, but the war took a terrible toll on him, as it did with the many thousands of soldiers who fought in all wars. He didn't talk about his experiences in New Guinea, but told good stories about liberty in Australia.

Elden

After the war, we heard some fancy tales of what went on while they were in service. Homer would tell Skinny that when he was stationed in Italy our Navy gunners couldn't hit the broad side of a barn while shooting at German planes, but that they were right on the target knocking down our planes when they flew over, going gung-ho after the Germans. Elden would tell Skinny, the Navy man, that the Navy ships with supplies would anchor out in the ocean about two miles offshore and then radio, "Come and get it, Grunts." Either the infantry was supposed to walk on the water or the Navy didn't want to get involved with jungle fighting. There were some lively discussions.

Virg and Myrna

Chapter 7
A-Hunting We Will Go

Top: Successful duck hunters. Standing: Dale, Homer, Obbie Melstad, Gerald Dutcher, Clayton, Sig Peterson; kneeling: Mel Peterson and Elden
Bottom: Virg and Dale with ducks

A-Hunting We Will Go

When Pa bought his automatic shotgun, he and Oscar Stangland went out to pattern their guns to see what size shot worked best. Pa blasted away at the big sheet of paper, and had a really good pattern. Oscar told Pa he had shot two times. Pa said, "Not by a damn sight - I only shot once!" Sure enough, two empty shells were lying on the ground. Pa had never shot an automatic before, and somehow must have pulled the trigger twice without knowing it. They found out that five chill shot looked like the best, and that's what I use in the 12 gauge automatic.

Lewis Crandall had us build him a sawmill, and it was big! He would saw boards out of big trees, which were mostly cottonwood. The saw blade was four or five feet in diameter so he could handle big trees. He wanted to know what I thought about helping him build a duck boat out of 12 inch cottonwood boards, and then we could hunt together. Sounded great! I've dealt with steel all my life, and I didn't know much about cottonwood - but I soon found out! We got the big ship built and finally got it soaked up enough so that the water stayed in the boat. Alas, instead of the water running out of the boat, it soaked into those one inch boards, making the boat so heavy we could hardly lift it.

We managed to get the boat up to Lake Badger a few times, and then decided it would be better to tie the boat to a tree and leave it there, since it was too heavy to move. This worked out OK until one weekend we went to go out in the boat and discovered that some character had swiped it. Those of you who knew Crandall would know that the air was blue! Don't recall if I added anything to the color of the air or not. A few weeks later, the two of us were scouting around the lake looking for ducks, when lo and behold, along the shore at least two miles from where our boat was stolen, we spotted a cottonwood boat that looked familiar. Boy, we were in luck! We were loading our prize on the trailer when here came a kid running down the bank from his farm home. He was all out of breath, and wanted to know what we were doing taking Casey's boat? That let the cat out of the bag, and I told the kid to tell Casey Phelps that Dale and Crandall had taken their boat back to Hetland. I knew who the Casey was, and he lived in Badger. If he had known who that sailing ship belonged to, I'm sure he wouldn't have "snatched" it, as he and I were friends. We never heard any more from Casey, either. I've heard of boats getting waterlogged, but didn't ever think I would own one. We built this boat before the one that Byron Foss and I built.

Pa and Lewis used to hunt ducks together. One time they were out in Lake Preston hunting ducks and it was really cold. Lewis was facing away from Pa when he heard a shot. "Did you get him, Andersen?" Lewis asked. Pa told him to take a look, as his hands were so cold he pulled the trigger and shot a hole in the boat, just above the water line. More explosive talk came from one end of the boat.

Another time, Lewis was hunting ducks in Lake Badger and lost his oars. Rather than stay out in the lake he jumped overboard and pushed the boat back to shore. The water was about four feet deep. Good sound thinking on his part!

I remember the first pheasants that came to this area. They were shipped in, and were in cages at the Barber-Johnson Hardware store. The men took the birds out to Tom Omdalen's place, which is east of where Dennis Ryland now lives, and turned them loose. That was quite a sight.

When I was 15 years old, I was old enough to hunt. Pa told me that he would buy me a single shot gun for my pay for working in the shop that summer. He wouldn't buy a gun with a hammer on it, it had to be hammerless. A hammerless single shot was almost unthinkable, but they were a lot safer to use. The hardware store boys finally found where they could get a single shot hammerless LeFever, but it would cost 25 bucks. Pa didn't care. That was what he wanted, even though it was higher priced than a hammer gun. How well I remember when Pa brought the gun home in a long box, and the sign for advertising said, "Who ever saw a broken LeFever?" in great big letters. Of course we never had seen a broken one, but over the years, we did. I once had to weld something on the firing mechanism. Boy, could that gun shoot! More people commented on how far out that gun could knock down a bird. I agreed with them, but I didn't hear any of them say that the kid pulling the trigger helped bring them down.

In later years, we visited Yankton College where the kids went to school. Don Ward, the president of the college, informed me that he had been out hunting with Virg, and boy could he shoot! I couldn't pass up a chance like that, so I told Don, "Well, what would you expect? Look who he learned from." (Me, of course.) Then Don had some retort for me, as I expected.

Ralph (Gunder) Mauch had a double-barreled Parker shotgun. It was a high priced gun, and really was supposed to "knock'em down." More than once, I think, he would have traded guns, even up, after he had wasted two shells, and I had the bird with only one shot. Virgil has this old standby now, and started out his hunting career with it, too. When he got his pump gun, I told him the only difference between the

Dane, Obbie and Sig.... What a hunt!

two guns was that with the single shot he shot once, and with the pump gun, three times. What a waste of ammunition. We sure had good times hunting together, with me using Pa's Remington automatic, where all I had to do was pull the trigger. Our boy had to pump shells into his, in order to get off another shot. I always felt sorry for him, having to go through all that effort to pump the gun. No labor saved, there.

When we were young, there were lots of pheasants around Hetland. Whenever there was a cornfield planted west of the schoolhouse, we could figure on some good hunting. We would walk the corn from the west, driving the birds ahead of us. When we got to town, especially by the schoolhouse, we had lots of shooting. The pheasants didn't like the looks of the schoolhouse, so they didn't run out ahead of us. Instead, they would wait and fly over town or fly back west over us. It was great sport, as I don't suppose the birds knew what a schoolhouse looked like until we exposed them to it.

I remember one time Jim Barber shot five times at a rooster up by the schoolhouse and the bird never flicked an eyelash at Jim. We always told Jim and Charlie Johnson, the hardware store owners, that they could afford to shoot more shells than we did, because they got them for wholesale.

The first year when our brother Elden hunted, we were worrying about him, as he didn't come home when we thought he should. We were eating supper when in he walked with a lone rooster pheasant in one hand, his gun in the other, and the rest of him smelling like he must have slept in a skunk den! He was proud as a peacock of that bird, which he had by the head, and the rest of the bird was four inches from the head as his neck was stretched out that far. We let out a yell for him to get out, as the smell was permeating our food.

He buried his clothes out in the garden and marked the spot in case he wanted to find them later. He stuck a wooden stake in the ground so he would know where to dig. A couple of days later, he remembered his hunting license was in his shirt pocket. He went out to dig up the license and discovered the stake was gone. Ole Petersen had hauled in a load of coal, and the stake was in the road of the horses, so he pulled it up and gave it a toss. Elden dug up the whole garden and didn't find the license or his clothes. It was unbelievable as to where they disappeared.

Dane's successful hunt, 1945

Pa and I were out hunting in Lake Whitewood during the time of shell shortages. I told him we wouldn't shoot anything but mallard ducks, as they were bigger, and had more meat on them. I would let him have first chance on the ducks. Here came a nice big greenhead, and I waited for him to shoot. Nothing happened. I asked him, "Why didn't you let that greenhead have it?" "That was a teal," he said. Then a teal came buzzing along and bang, Pa let him have it. I wanted to know why he wasted a shot on that little devil. It looked big to him, as he thought it was a mallard, so we decided, what the heck, shells or no shells, we would shoot whether the bird was big or small, and hope for the biggest.

One year several of us hotshot duck hunters decided we would camp out on the south shore of Lake Thisted so we would have the first chance to hunt on an island in the lake. The next day was opening day for duck hunting. We finally got settled down for bed with the campfire going to keep away any wild animals. Nobody seemed to get any sleep as we waited for morning, and the chance to shoot ducks. It was 3 AM when Verle Dutcher loaded up his gun and shot five times into the campfire. That was all the shells the gun would hold. Talk about action! Everyone rolled out of where they were trying to sleep, ready for action in case we were invaded by who knows what. There was no invasion. Dutch just got bored and decided it was time for breakfast. We had the island all to ourselves. The ducks decided to let us keep it, and stayed away from us, as well. A lonely seagull came by and parked himself a short distance from our hiding place. Don't know who it was, but one of our Hetland boys had a double barrel shot gun and decided to pull both triggers and send that gull to wherever they go when they "kick the bucket." The would-be killer of an innocent gull took deadly aim and pulled both triggers. The jolt from the old 10 gauge nearly put him down on his butt. The shots really stirred up the water. The gull flew up, and more or less thumbed his nose at the would-be assassin. That was the end of a fantastic camp out. No sleep and no ducks, only a good breakfast at 3 in the morning. What more could we expect?

Shrimp Cleveland and I were hunting one time, out west of Boyd's slough. Here came a lone duck, coming from Lake Preston, probably heading for a meeting with some of his friends in the slough. He was really moving, like he was late for something. Just to see what might happen, I held up the gun and shot ahead of him, and he flew into the shot. Down he came, stone dead. Shrimp couldn't believe what he had seen, and remarked, "That was a good shot." I told him about two drunks in the same situation, and the one that shot said, "I should have gotten one out of that big flock!" I wasn't drunk either, must have been lucky.

Jim Barber, Sig Peterson, Happy Larson and my brother Homer were hunting ducks way out in Lake Poinsett when it was really dry. They had 50 mallards and the limit was 40. The two with 20 ducks came up on the beach and there was Ed White, the game warden. The other two with 30 birds were further behind with two sacks of ducks. Jim didn't tell him that in his coat pocket was a redhead duck, which was outlawed. Anyway, they got the warden to talk to them with his back to the lake. They other two were just ready to bring those 30 birds onto the beach when they saw the warden. They dropped the ducks and came over to the warden who supposed the four of them had shot 20 ducks. Jim was scared spitless standing there with the redhead duck in his coat, but the warden must have known they were law abiding citizens. After all, they were from Hetland. They followed the warden clear over to the Stone Bridge, a good many miles away, before they went back and picked up the two sacks with the 30 ducks in them. What a relief to think they didn't get their names in the paper as being good duck hunters with too many birds.

Byron Foss, the school superintendent, and I used to do a lot of hunting together. We built a 16-foot boat and used six-inch flooring for the bottom. Did a fancy job on it and caulked everything like my ancestors, the Vikings, used to do, or at least that was the way we thought they did. Lewis Crandall watched us build the ship and told us that it wouldn't leak a drop. He wasn't as smart as old Noah was, who knew more about building the ark than we knew about building the duck boat. We got the boat finished

Dale and Byron Foss

and took it up to our house, had it on a trailer and proceeded to put water in it to be sure it was unsinkable. Lo and behold, we couldn't believe what we were seeing. You talk about something leaking like a sieve, this was worse than that. We couldn't get any water in the boat, as it went out faster than we could put it in. We left the hose running all night and the next morning, when I looked out the boat was full of water and the axle of the trailer was bent down as far as it could go. I don't know how many hundreds of pounds that water weighed, but we had a boat that held water. Later on, we covered this same vessel with tin so we didn't need to soak it up.

One time Foss and I were out in the same boat hunting ducks in Lake Badger. It was cold, and we had been drinking coffee when the ducks started flying. By the time we were done shooting, the coffee was frozen in the cups. We had a crippled duck ahead of us and I was poling the boat while Foss tried to hit the duck with his oar. He missed the bird but hit the barrel of his gun, and into the lake it went. Bubbles came up and when the water cleared we could see the gun lying on the bottom in six feet of water. Now how could we get the gun without me going over the edge and probably drowning in the cold water? Foss, being German and me being Dane proceeded to call a powwow. That gun, a pump gun, looked so peaceful lying in the mud that there was a temptation to leave it in Davey Jones' locker. However, after the powwow broke up, I, being the youngest and with no experience on how to salvage sunken treasures, got a "brainstorm," even though in later years, after I had a CAT scan of my brain, Maurice Matson said they found it but there wasn't anything in it. (I agreed with that profound statement.)

Getting back to this brainstorm, we had a long push pole with an iron handle that I put my hand in so that we wouldn't lose the pole when it stuck in the mud. I told Foss that I would reach down and see if I could snake the gun barrel into the handle. This would have been a good idea except when I hit bottom with the pole we could no longer see the gun. Now what? Would you believe it, we were in luck, as I threaded the barrel through the handle and lifted the gun up so Foss could get his hands on it. Lucky it didn't go off, as our school superintendent was literally looking down a gun barrel. Some good hunter who had passed to his Creator must have been doing the guiding on the bottom of the lake when I couldn't even see the gun through the muddy water. Of course, the hunting stopped for that day.

Another time Foss and I hadn't been hunting for a week or two and we decided to take the boat out on the lake even though there was ice on it. Foss would break the ice and I would use the push pole to break through. When we were finally out in the middle of the lake and I asked Foss how much water he had in his end of the boat. He replied, "About six inches." I had around four inches in my end, as he was heavier than me. I told him, "Let's get to shore or we will go down, and if we survive we will be the laughing stock of the town." I gave him the push pole and told him to get us moving. We didn't have a straight path through the ice and I would use the oar to try and make it easier to zig without a zag. Finally, Byron said he had to quit, as he was all in. Being a school superintendent and sitting on his butt all day, I suppose he wasn't in "A number 1" shape. The boat was nearly full of water and I told him to keep going or we would be done for. He must have gotten his second wind, as we finally hit shore and the boat stayed in the lake. What a relief to see shore again.

I'm reminded of Columbus when he finally found Denmark, or was it the USA? After this harrowing experience, we decided rather than going to the Pearly Gates in a duck boat we had better put tin on it. We never had to worry about water, but the boat seemed like it weighed a ton with all the tin on it. We didn't have a name on the ship but my brother, Skinny, and Sig Peterson had one they called the "May Sink" and had the name on the hull. We couldn't afford the paint for the name after paying for the tin. Jim Barber told me he could have soldered two boats with the amount of solder we had used. He was an expert and I was a novice.

In 1940 Eva went to Springfield, South Dakota to see her folks. I told her that Byron Foss, the school superintendent and I were going hunting ducks on November 10, and if the weather was bad enough, we would go on the 11th, which was Armistice Day. We were out in Lake Badger in the boat, and it was snowing and blowing like winter might be coming. The ducks were flying like they were possessed, and we were shooting the same way, using lots of shells. There was another boatload of fellows from Hetland. They ran out of shells, and headed back to town to get more. The storm kept getting more violent, and all at once there weren't any ducks to shoot at. They were smart and headed south. About that time we too decided we had better see if we could get home. We should have headed south several hours before.

When we finally got to shore, we discovered a foot or more of snow on the ground, and the road home was over a mile away from where we were, out in the middle of nowhere! We finally managed to get to a farmyard where we had to open a gate in order to get out to the nearest road. We couldn't get through the barn yard, as the car would slip toward the barn. I finally put my back against the side of the barn and both feet on the side of the car to keep it from hitting the barn. No luck, we couldn't move. Finally in desperation, we unhooked the boat, and after a seemingly endless struggle, we got the trailer up the hill onto flat ground. With me pushing, and Foss spinning the wheels, we got out of the barnyard and headed for Hetland. We made it, but were lucky, as there were many hunters who froze to death in the big Armistice Day storm. The next day the storm was worse, piling snow banks several feet high. We couldn't see out of our windows. The weather was so bad we didn't try to get out of the house, and the ducks were gone, too. Eva's Dad wanted to know if she thought the weather was bad enough for Mory to go hunting.

Lake Whitewood Lutheran Church always had the lutefisk supper on Armistice Day. They didn't have it, of course, and had 1,400 pounds of fish to get rid of. I don't know if the fish smelled any worse when it aged. They didn't have any more suppers for several years after that calamity.

When Lake Preston and Lake Whitewood were dry, we used to have terrible fires out in the lakebeds, mostly in Lake Preston. Some farmers (that was the rumor) who wanted to get rid of the weeds and grass in the dry lakebed might accidentally throw away a cigarette butt when the wind was from the southwest, and wham! A fire would take off, headed for seven miles to the east, taking care of everything in its path. Every man, fire trucks and whoever was able to fight fires, was out there. One time a fire came down the whole length of the lake and got up on the upland. For a while, we thought it would burn the buildings on the Carpenter farm, just north of the Hetland cemetery. Luckily, one of the fire trucks still had enough water to put it out before that disaster happened. Then the lake could be farmed, free of charge, if you happened to have deeded land beside the lake. I don't know if that would have stood up in court or not.

Some years when the lake didn't get burned, the farmers would cut the hay for their cattle. Sometimes, they would leave strips of grass standing. This was good for pheasants and other game. One farmer west of town had strips left like that, and proceeded to put up "No Hunting" signs. That didn't sit very good with us avid hunters, so what did we do? We went into the lake to hunt pheasants, but before we started hunting, we had target practice at short range on those "No Hunting" signs. After we finished them off they were unreadable, so we started in hunting. To add insult to injury, we went up on this guy's regular land, which by the way was also posted, but we pretended like we couldn't read, so went onto his land and shot pheasants like you couldn't believe. All the time this poor landowner was hollering, "Get out of there, get out of there!" However by that time we were hard of hearing, so we just let the sound of his voice go over our heads, and kept on shooting birds. He didn't come out and chase us off, so we took off on our own accord, looking for more cornfields.

Successful Legion pheasant hunt

One year, we were hunting pheasants out in dry Lake Preston lake. It was below Arne Johnson's farm. There was corn planted in the lake and on the end of the field Arne had put up several "No Hunting" signs and had written on them "please don't hunt in the corn until it is picked." Obbie Melstad wrote on the sign "Why in hell don't you pick your corn?" Arne wasn't home at the time but the next day he was in town looking for that damn Obbie. We wanted to know why he wanted to see him. Arne said there was nobody but Obbie who would write on his hunting signs. He had figured out who the culprit was.

One time we had a big bunch of hunters, Legion men and some of us others, out to Kenneth Hesby's, ready to hunt his fields. We told him to park his corn picker so he wouldn't get shot while we hunted his cornfield. Rather than run the risk of somebody mistaking him for a pheasant, he obediently parked the outfit until we were done. Then he started picking corn again. He knew that the hunt was for a good cause, as the Legion boys were hunting pheasants to take to the Vets Hospital in Sioux Falls for a delicious pheasant dinner. Besides that, one of his kids was in the hunting party, so we had another plus on our side.

We had wonderful pheasant hunting. We would take twenty or more hunters, load them into Barber and Johnson's truck and go out and easily get 70 or 80 birds in an afternoon. That was great sport!

One afternoon, we were out north of Hetland and proceeded to follow an old Model T Ford. We couldn't get by the two old duffers who must have been hard of hearing, as they stayed in the middle of the road without hearing our driver laying on the horn. Anyway, we wanted to hunt. I'm ashamed to say it, but I suggested we load up and all shoot into the air at the command "fire." Do you know what? These two old boys nearly took the ditch, but we sailed right on by and gave them the "thumbs up" sign. Lots of wasted ammunition, but it worked for what it was intended to - we passed them!

When we were hunting pheasants, Donald (Starky) Starksen was never one to shoot a bird if anyone else would. We figured he wanted to conserve his shells and let us shoot up ours. He always managed to get his share of the birds at the end of the hunt when they were divided up. We set him up on one hunt. We propped up a dead rooster pheasant in a plowed field. It wasn't very far out from the road when we came driving by, looking for birds. We had Starky sit in the front seat next to the door. Somebody hollered that there was a pheasant. Starky never even flicked an eyelash, and didn't offer to get out. We told him to move, but he said, "Let someone else shoot it." Nothing doing, we pushed him out of the car and told him to shoot. The dead rooster and Starky were eyeballing each other, and we told him to hurry up and shoot, or the bird would be gone. He finally aimed at the bird and pulled the trigger. That was the best shot we ever saw him make, as that dead bird didn't even try to fly away! We never told him about the ruse, and what he didn't know didn't hurt him. At least we got him to help out the ammunition companies for a change!

In the fall and winter, we would organize rabbit and fox hunts. We would get dozens of men with shotguns, surround a section or two and walk toward the middle point, shooting rabbits as we walked. Some days we would "nail" seven or eight hundred rabbits and a few foxes, and on one occasion we killed a coyote. The rabbits were worth a nickel each, and once in a while we would use the money to put on an oyster feed for the hunters. Lots of fun, but I don't know how we stood up to it, especially when we waded in snow up to our knees or higher. We didn't mind that, even when trying to hang on to a couple of rabbits that we had shot. The moral to that story: "Don't shoot anything until you were closer to the middle where we were to meet." Otherwise, a mile or two of lugging a four-legged creature was what we could call tiresome.

Run, rabbit, RUN! Once, in a hunt out in Lake Preston, we all came together down by the "skunk farm." One lone rabbit started heading south with nearly everyone taking a shot at him. The more we shot, the faster he moved. Oliver Omdalen was the last man on the south end of the two lines. He got down on one knee and pulled one trigger on his double barrel shotgun. The old rabbit flicked his tail, as though thumbing his nose at him, and shifted into another high gear. This old Norwegian wasn't about to take that kind of treatment from a rabbit, so he pulled the other trigger, and that speeding rabbit met his Waterloo. He went end over end for several yards before he stopped dead. Everyone cheered, letting Oliver know that he had stolen the show, and had the bunny to prove it.

We had about the same situation on another hunt. Elden, my brother, was on the end of one of the lines when a rabbit came through the same way. Elden let the rabbit have a blast from his gun, and that old boy just speeded up, free from any more shooting, as there was no one left to shoot him. Something must have gone wrong with the rabbit. Maybe he had been hit, or didn't know up from down, because he made a circle and came speeding back heading through the line of hunters like he dared anyone to knock him off. Elden had the first shot and that was the end of the speeding rabbit. We razzed Elden, telling him that the rabbit came back and dared him to shoot him. The four-legged creature should have kept going so he could have been free to run another day.

On one of our rabbit hunts, we ended up the hunt by an old abandoned farmstead. There was an old barn on the place, and several of our hunters went up into the haymow to see if there were any pigeons inside. There were droves of pigeons and those of us who were out on the road heard a roar from the barn. The roof nearly came off from all of the shooting in the haymow. The dirt from the old wooden shingles looked like smoke. I don't know how many birds died in the blast, but those that survived headed for safer quarters.

Barber and Johnson, besides having the best hardware store in the country, also sold Nash cars as a sideline. I suppose they could drive a car and get it wholesale, without a middle man making any money on them. Besides that, Jim and Charley were good hunters and knew how to get rid of a lot of shells. They would generally have a half case or more of shells with them. We always told them they were shooting up the profits that they made on us hunters. Back then, some shells were 85 cents a box and the better loads were a dollar or so. When World War II was on, shells were hard to come by. They always saw to it that we would get 10 shells each, when a few cases came in. There were 25 shells in a box, and 20 boxes to a case. With only 10 shells, we had to be sure that we saw the whites of the bird's eye before we shot. Del Barber told us that in Omaha there were plenty of shells, but not here.

Charley Johnson's nickname was "Barney." I didn't call him that, as I didn't have many occasions to go riding with him, especially when he was driving a new Nash car. You may wonder about the nickname. He was named after Barney Oldfield, the famous race driver at that time. Charley had one speed when he was on a straight road, that being "wide open" with the throttle to the floor.

Charley, my brother, Skinny, and I went to Badger one time when they had a coyote hunt. No rabbits. The lakes were dry, and there were coyotes yelling at the top of their voices at night, no doubt trying to get the moon to talk back to them. Charley was driving his faithful Nash car. There were no coyotes in dry Lake Badger, so we all headed for Lake Albert. This lake had been farmed, and good crops had been taken out of it. The three of us went around to the east side of the lake, as the brain trust in charge of the drive told us to. More Badger people and farmers were to come along after us. No one showed up, and we sat and waited for more reinforcements for the drive out in the lake.

All at once, we saw something standing out in the middle of the lake, big as you please, just like he owned the lake. A horse, perhaps? Nope. Skinny hollered, "It's a coyote!" That's what it was, and boy, was he big! "Barney" put the throttle to the floor, and we took off in a cloud of dust, heading out into the lake to head off this monster of destruction to the farmers' livestock. There was a strip of plowing between us and the coyote, but that didn't stop our old race driver, Barney. We hit that strip of plowed ground going 60 miles an hour! Boy oh boy, I thought that the Nash was done for! Skinny and I held on to whatever we could grab, but Charley had hold of the steering wheel, and never let up on the gas. Whew! We made it, and kept after the four-legged beast, who by now knew that he had better be moving it as it looked like danger was approaching. There was - us. To this day, I marvel that we didn't hit a rock and break our necks.

This old coyote knew where the rock pile was, and he was really picking them up and laying them down, heading for the shore! However, he underestimated our race driver. A rabbit got up and Charley passed him like he was standing still! We got close enough to this monster so Skinny, in the back seat, emptied his gun shooting at this guy, who by now was going in full speed. But that old Nash had more speed than a mere 60 miles an hour, so Barney pushed harder on the throttle, and we showed that wild animal what speed was! Charley caught up to this streaking beast so I could get a shot at him, too. I emptied the gun and never touched him. Just as we were about to shoot, the car would hit something and bounce, and I mean <u>bounce</u>! I would only get one shell in the gun, and time was running out or this varmint would be in the rock pile. Finally, I hit him up by the left shoulder, and he began to run out of steam, or whatever kept him going. Then we finished him off, and there he lay, a monster of a brute. Charley sat there and shook, and so did we. What an undertaking, to think that the three Hetland boys nailed the only coyote of the day.

The rest of the hunters had watched the fracas from the top of the "hogsback," as we called the peninsula that jutted out into the lake. There was no more hunting after all of that excitement, and we all went home. I suppose the "wheels" of the hunt left the creature where he gave up the ghost, as they weren't worth anything except for fertilizer. Jim Barber's comment, when we told him about it was, "Damn fools, you all could have been killed, going across the lake at that speed!" He probably was right, but I don't think any of us thought about that, when our goal was to commit mayhem on that ferocious, wild beast. We survived to hunt another day. I might add that Charley and Jim were brothers-in-law, Jim being married to Charley's sister, Lutie. She was one of the sweetest ladies you could ever expect to know.

Charley Johnson went out north of town one morning, and came back shortly with five nice rooster pheasants, which was the limit. Boy, he was strutting his stuff in the store, showing off his kill. Finally his dad, Herb, let him know that he understood the season didn't open until noon. Boy, oh boy, Charley grabbed those birds and high-tailed it for the back room, and the birds were out of sight. No wonder he had the limit, shooting from the road, and back in town in less than an hour. The poor birds didn't think any law-abiding citizen would take advantage of them and shoot at them out of season. If they had realized that after they were dead it was too late, as they would soon be in the frying pan and cooked to perfection. Boy, pheasants are <u>good eating</u>! I can just see the headlines in the paper, if a game warden had been around. "Hetland businessman arrested for shooting pheasants out of season." He had the limit, too. Charley would never have lived that down.

After we were married, my girlfriend and I would go road hunting, as there were lots of pheasants just daring anyone to shoot at them. I suppose I felt sorry for her, with me having all the fun shooting. We talked over the situation and decided she could get a license to hunt, too. The single shot was too long for her, so I very dutifully proceeded to saw off the butt of the gun so she could shoot straighter. I gave her all of the fine points on how to handle and shoot this old trusty gun which had helped furnish a good many meals for the Andersen tribe. She wasn't a novice at shooting, because before we were married we would go hunting gophers with my rifle. She had gotten so that she could shoot pretty good, as the gun had a scope on it. So one day in hunting season we took off on our first married hunting experience. I don't recall that we wore any special attire for this noble adventure, but at least we were on our way, exploring new fields of married life. Wow! This was better than hunting by myself! I never realized how much better hunting could be than to have my sweetheart with me and armed to the teeth, waiting expectantly for something to "blast" at.

We didn't have long to wait. Lo and behold, there, right along the fence line, on her side of the road, stood a gorgeous rooster pheasant. Boy, he was standing straight up like he was the cock of the walk. He didn't flick an eyelash when I stopped the car. Even then, he didn't move, but acted like he was the king of the hill, or proud of something. I didn't know which. So, I told my sweetie, like Annie Oakley of pioneer days, to get the gun out the window and let that smart-alec have it. He acted like he was daring her to shoot. Finally, after careful and deliberate aiming, KA-BOOM! Off went the gun, and away flew the rooster, scared by now, of course.

The kick of the gun knocked my girlfriend backwards, so her head was on my lap. Of course I didn't mind that at all. This was really cozy, as

Eva with a .22 cal target rifle

she had laid her head on my lap before. I used to tell her that I couldn't understand women (I still don't!). Before marriage the girl crowds up close to the man driving the car and after marriage, there is lots of room on the seat between them. What happened to that snuggling up to each other, just because they both said "I do?" By the way, this bird had been standing, and I hasten to inform you that I never shot at a bird unless it was on the fly. This way they had a chance, and I had a challenge to nail the bird. Virg was just a little guy and was out hunting with me when we saw a rooster in the ditch. I got out with the gun, and he wouldn't get up, but just ran away from me. When I got back to the car our little boy was really disgusted. "Dad, here we don't have a single pheasant, and you let them run away from you." It rubbed off on him, because he gives the birds a chance, just like his dad.

Let's see where were we? Oh yes, I remember. Eva had shot at a pheasant, the bird took off for parts unknown, and us two married folks had experienced a cozy relationship, but no bird. Hot dog, how exciting. Now let's get back to this fancy shooting. All at once there was a flopping of wings in the grass, and the grass was moving. What was going on out there? I got out of the car with my trusty automatic at the ready, and stalked across the road, gingerly looking to see what the fracas was all about. It was unbelievable – there lay two dead hen pheasants, and it was against the law to shoot hens. My female marksman, or markswoman, I should say, had gotten two birds with one shot. No wonder that proud rooster was not going to move when he had a harem at his feet! But on the other hand, he was a lousy provider, letting the females take the shot intended for him. What a cowardly way to act - disgusting to say the least. By the way, my pretty Annie Oakley gunslinger decided once was enough, no more shooting. She just rode along and kept me company, which was nice. She always looked after my welfare, and that of our kids, too.

Our first Topsy was with me in the old Model T, driving out in the dry Lake Preston lakebed. I had the gun pointing out the window. She always sat beside me in the front seat. All at once, up went a pheasant. I didn't get the car stopped before I shot, and down came the bird. Just that fast (and how she did it I'll never know) that dog went across between the steering wheel and me, through the open window. She rolled on the ground jumped up in a flash and nailed that old boy, just like that. All I had to do was open the back door so she could jump in with the dead bird. Then she was back in the front seat, panting with excitement, ready for more action. With hunting dogs like our two Topsys, we got spoiled when we had to look for a bird, especially if it was just wounded. More than once, we would drop a rooster and Topsy would take off pell-mell. She would go right by the place where the bird hit the ground, often 50 feet or more, and come back with the bird in her mouth, looking as proud as she could with another prize for her master. What joy!

Dale & Topsy with a pheasant

Skinny was a rural mail carrier out of Lake Preston before he became postmaster, so in the fall he could see where the geese were prone to feed. One Armistice Day Skinny, our Norske neighbor, Orris Sylvester (Obbie) Melstad and I embarked on a goose hunting expedition to a cornfield south of Lake Preston. According to Skinny, the geese were as numerous there as the sands of the sea at LOW water mark. Three Nimrods were ready for action, just bring on the

Obbie and Dane with geese

geese. We had newspapers with us which we crumpled up to look like?? geese, and put them out on the ground in the cornfield. These were what were known as poor man's decoys, and we were in the poor man class. So the three of us deployed around the newspaper decoys and we were ready for action. Bring on the hungry geese, we were ready for the slaughter.

Well, we waited and we waited, and after a couple of hours of twiddling our thumbs, Obbie and I were ready to throw in the towel. We let Skinny know what we thought about his goose hunting cornfield, and started back toward the car. That was a mistake. While we were walking north, Skinny kept looking south for the geese, and all at once he hollered, "HERE THEY COME." We tore back to our designated shooting spots and watched and waited. Boy this was something to behold. When those smart birds saw our newspapers they started to drop anchor and floated in, right over Skinny. BOOM went his gun, and down came a goose. But alas, NO second or third shot as his gun had JAMMED. By now Obbie and I had sprung into action, and even though we were on the far side of the geese, we managed to down three more birds.

Then it was time to give Skinny a good going over. "Why didn't you wait five seconds longer so that we would have had all of the geese in the middle of us?" He fended off all of our questions, and being a Dane, he gave us plausible excuses, even though we rolled our eyeballs at some of his answers. Finally Obbie, in exasperation, pulled up his loaded gun, put the end of the barrel into Skinny's belly, and turning to me said, "Shall I shoot the S.O.B. now, or let him live a little longer?" As I loved my brother, I calmed down Obbie's ruffled feathers and Skinny lived to shoot another day.

By the way, Skinny was an excellent shot, although in this case he was "trigger happy."

We were hunting in Lake Whitewood where the farmers left strips of grass when they cut hay. Topsy suddenly stopped dead in her tracks and pointed at what I thought must be a pheasant. After all, she knew that was what we had been hunting. I came closer to her, as she was pointing with her tail out and front foot off the ground, even though she wasn't a pointer. I told her "Go get 'em, Topsy!" This smart dog never even twitched an eyelash, and never moved. I got closer, ready to finish off the bird in the bush when he flew up. Then I saw the reason why she didn't move in when I told her to. Here was a beady-eyed, white-striped skunk looking her in the eyes. I let out a yell, "Get out of there, Topsy!" This time she nearly fell over backward to do as I told her, and we took off, away from that source of immediate danger. The way it was, this varmint lived to spray another day.

Fern Melstad, our neighbor, taught school in several of the rural schools around Hetland before finishing up here in the town school. Obbie, her brother, would take her to school in the morning and go to get her when school was out. On occasion, he would be busy and couldn't take time off to get her after school, so he would ask me to go and get her. That worked out OK, as they were always good to help us out, too. Once when she was teaching in the Max Neilson school, Obbie asked me to pick her up. It was hunting season, so I took the gun along, as well as Myrna and Virgil, and we drove to the schoolhouse north of town. After school was out, Fern was in no hurry to get home, so we took the long way around, an extra two miles. Lo and behold, just a short way north of the school were a slug of pheasants, sitting in George Nelson's pasture. I jumped out and shot once, and down came three pheasants, and all of them had been flying! Think of that, three birds on the fly, and with only one shot expended. Wow, that was something!

Now I know that some of you Doubting Thomases (and some with other names, too) are wondering how this big event could happen – one shot and three birds knocked down, and they were on the fly, too. I'll admit that sounds unbelievable, and if I hadn't been there and witnessed the whole affair, I think I might have joined you doubters, too. Now, those of you who are hunters probably have found out the hard way, as I have, that you are better off not to just shoot into a cloud of birds, but rather to pick out one and let him have it. That's what I did, the one rooster got into my sights, and two more came down with him. So in putting my blacksmith mind to work and after careful and exhaustive research, I have come to the startling conclusion that those other two birds must have gotten in the way of the shot pellets, and therefore they met their Waterloo. Any better explanation from some of you doubters?

By now, you shouldn't have any reason to doubt my veracity. Let me assure you that I had three witnesses, although I think the kids were too small to remember it, and now Fern has gone home to her Maker. I can take you out and show you the exact spot that all of this happened. However, the pheasants are not there, they ended up on the Andersen's table in Hetland. Three in one shot! Our prime pheasant paradise is no more. Hardly any birds are left around here.

When Virg was a little boy, I thought he was too young to go duck hunting on the opening day. His Grandpa Guptill took him hunting. We have a picture of the two of them with their ducks. He did better going hunting with his grandpa than with me, as they had ducks (the

Virg and Clyde with ducks, 1949

limit, no less - ed.) and I didn't get any. He and his grandpa had a great time and the picture radiates love for each other, with them holding hands and beaming as if to say "We showed you!" I'm glad they did.

I haven't been too smart throughout my life, and some of my episodes will prove it! Eva's dad, Clyde, and I took Virg out into Boyd's slough in our boat to hunt ducks. The season started at noon. The pond was alive with ducks, and there wasn't anyone else hunting there - just us. We poled out into the water at about 11:30 to be ready for 12 o'clock shooting. Birds were flying all around us, and we got into the weeds to be out of sight. Well, you can guess what happened. We had scared the ducks off the water, and when the season started, there were hardly any ducks left to shoot at. Why we didn't wait until noon to go out on the water, I'll never know. That was the year before Virgil started hunting, carrying his own gun. It wasn't a very smart way to teach him how to hunt! He is smarter than me, and is more scientific about hunting as well as other things - he takes after his Mom.

I used to take Myrna and Virgil with me when I went duck hunting. Generally, we went out on the dike in the east end of Lake Preston. I would holler at the kids that it was time to get up so we could get going. This went on for a few years. One year I told them it was time to get up and get ready. Myrna must have decided that she was needing the sleep more than freezing out in the lake, so she let us know that she was staying in bed. I don't blame her, as it was warmer and drier in bed than standing out in the weeds hoping for a duck to show up. It was great to have them along, and Virg never did decide that sleeping was better than hunting. I'm glad that he still has that same philosophy.

Virg and his cousin Curt borrowed their Grandpa Morris' field glasses to locate ducks and geese. They were lying in a ditch somewhere in Kingsbury County watching some birds. It being hunting season, they got back in their car and took off. Don't think they got any birds, but that wasn't the worst of it. They left Grandpa's field glasses in the ditch. They must have figured the ditch had moved, as they couldn't locate the ditch or the glasses. Grandpa didn't say anything derogatory as he probably figured they might have inherited some of his characteristics, since some of his blood was flowing through their veins.

Our son Virg wanted to go hunting ducks, but he had to take Myrna to Lake Preston, as she had to play for the Snow Queen contest and had to be there early. I told Virg that it wouldn't work out if he went hunting, and he had better stay home. He gave me that "all knowing look" and assured me that there wasn't any problem, as he would be home in time. To accomplish this marvelous feat, he would take the alarm clock with him. I was gullible, and figured that was a brilliant idea coming from one of our offspring. He took off in good spirits, knowing that he had "soft soaped" me, his dad, into letting him go out and settle down in a corn field to gaze into the evening sky looking for a foolish duck to get into gun range. I knew the anticipation he was experiencing, as I also liked to hunt - probably inherited it from my dad.

We had an early supper and waited for Virg to come to take Myrna to Preston, but alas, he didn't show up. I was afraid something might have happened to him because he was a boy of his word, having taken after his mother. Then I got the hair-brained idea that maybe he had so many ducks that he was having trouble carrying them. Either idea was "far fetched," so I ended up taking Myrna to her appointment. When we got home, I was glad to see that Virg had gotten home OK, and was all right. I asked him how it happened that he didn't get home on time, since he took the alarm clock with him. He said he had left the alarm clock in the car while he went out in the cornfield after ducks. He probably had good eyesight, but his being far out in the field away from the car wasn't the best way to see when he had to head for home. In spite of all of that, he managed to grow up to be a good kid, even if he has me for a dad. I probably would have forgotten to take the alarm clock as well. That's just one of the things that makes life interesting. (Maybe it would have been a good idea to give Virg a watch, as well as a gun? - ed.)

Whenever it rained really hard, the streets around here were full of night crawlers. To me these were just overgrown angleworms that were great fishing bait. After one big rain, Obbie and I picked up several coffee cans full of night crawlers. What were we going to do with them, as they wouldn't live long out of the ground? I told Obbie that he could take them, as I had no use for them. Earlier, I had nearly a three-pound coffee can full of crawlers, and we had a big rain that drowned them all.

Obbie got a brainstorm as to how to have night crawlers any time we needed bait. He had a two-foot piece of chimney pipe that was open at both ends. He dug a big hole, and put the pipe down in it, so he had a good place to keep the night crawlers until eternity. He dumped the wigglers down the pipe and put some dirt on top to cover them, I suppose, to keep them warm. When we were to go fishing, our smart Norske went out to his lair to get the worms. They were all gone. Instead of staying where they were supposed to, they just dug themselves down through the open pipe and took off underground to wherever they wanted to go. Boy, he took a lot of static for that! All that work of digging a hole to let the night crawlers get away!

We used to put steel rods in the ground and then charge the rods with electricity in order to get the night crawlers out of the ground when we didn't have a lot of rain. Sometimes it worked, and then again, it didn't. I suppose it depends on how much of a shock they could take before sticking their heads out above ground.

Obbie and I made a bunch of fish flies out in the back room of the shop. I had a sports magazine with pictures of all kinds of flies, so we tried to duplicate them. Ours were not very fancy, but after we tried them out, they were a "howling success." The two of us went up on the north side of Lake Poinsett, by the inlet from Dry Lake, to try our luck at catching bass with our new lures. The shore was lined with fishermen, and nobody had caught a fish. That scenario changed in a hurry. We two old pro fishermen, with homemade lures, were about to show the experts something that even they had never expected to see. We cast our lures out into the fast flowing water, and BOOM! we each had a nice bass on. With the first cast, at that. That's when all of the languishing fishermen sat up and took notice. Boy, everybody knew that the fish were biting at last. There must be a big school of them out there now, waiting to get into a frying pan.

Everyone started to cast like it was the last day of their fisherman lives, but to no avail. There were no fish to be caught. But when Obbie and I tossed out our lures, we either had a fish on, or the fish was traveling so fast that he bounced off our homemade flies, ready to tackle that strange object again. Whatever was the case, we caught fish – the limit, no less, the limit being eight apiece. Before we had to quit, this fellow beside me wanted to know if he could throw his line out where I was casting while I was reeling the fish in. "No problem," I told him, "go ahead." Sometimes I had to wait for him before I cast out into the deep. Still he got no fish. Then he asked to see my lure, and wanted to know what kind it was. I told him homemade. This poor guy looked the lure all over, then dumped his tackle box out on the ground. Boy, talk about lures! That guy had them. He wanted to look at my bait again, as he had found something he thought looked something like mine. It was some kind of Coachman, whatever that was. He put all of his stuff back in the fishing box and gave that new outfit a whirl. Nothing happened, no fish.

Obbie and I packed up with 16 nice fish and started for the car. By this time, word had spread far and wide that two guys were catching fish, and nobody else had a nibble. Obbie carried the fish out in front of him so everybody couldn't help but see them. When someone commented on the nice fish we had, our friend, whose nickname was "Baron," didn't let us down. His reply was, "We threw the little ones away and just kept the big ones." I didn't let on that he was stretching the truth. We kept them all, big and small.

Another time the Baron (Obbie) and I were fishing on the south side of the Lake Poinsett inlet. Right above us was a single strand of telephone wire, not very high off the ground. It was really decorated with all kinds of fishing lines and lures wrapped round and round the wire. Obbie looked at the lineup, and commented, "Anybody dumb enough to wrap their line around that should not be fishing!" It wasn't long before I heard my fishing partner let loose some strange words that wouldn't be heard in church. He was looking up in the air, and sure enough, there was his line going round and round the telephone wire. "What was it you said about anyone dumb enough to wrap a fishing line up there?" He had a good reason, he forgot about that damn telephone line. That was a good enough answer for me.

Fisherman Skinny with The Big One

Chapter 8
All Creatures Great and Small

Top left: Dale's feline friends
Top right: Morris and Mugs
Bottom left: Morris and Sport
Bottom right: Dale and Sport

All Creatures Great and Small

Morris' dogs —

Our Pa was a great lover of animals, especially dogs, and he had several of them. The first one was an Irish Setter that came along on the passenger train with a bunch of hunters from Chicago. They let the pack of dogs out here when the train stopped. Somehow the engine started up before all of the dogs were on board, when the train was ready to leave. Sport, as Pa later named him, got bumped and broke some of the bones in his back. The drayman, Ole Peterson, had some stuff for Pa and backed up to the shop to unload. There, on the floor of the wagon, lay this nice looking red Irish setter squirming in pain, looking at our Pa as if saying, "Please help me." Pa wanted to know what that was all about? Ole told him the details about the dog getting hit by the train, and that the owner of the dog gave him a dollar to dispose of him. Pa said, "I'll give you a dollar to drop him off here." The deal was made, and poor Sport, unable to move, lay on a blanket for a week or two, and then started to show signs of movement in his legs. Before long he was standing up and moving around.

From all reports, Sport was a Super Duper hunting dog, and all of the townfolk wanted to go hunting with Pa as long as Sport was with them. Needless to say, Sport knew who was entitled to the birds. One time Pa and Simbl, the hardware store owner, were out hunting ducks in Lake Preston. Sport was bringing all the ducks to his master. The hardware man held up his gun and pointed it at Sport and yelled, "You Red Irish S.O.B, you do that again and I'll shoot you!" Pa let him know that if he shot Sport there would be a dead man too. Sport survived.

The folks used to tell about me chasing Sport around the house in my little walker. He would take it only so long, and then he would crawl in behind the kitchen range, to get rested up and take a snooze. Now I wonder what ever got into me to do a thing like that, to chase Sport until he put a stop to my shenanigans. Pa said that Sport always had a rough spot on the top of his backbone, where the back had been broken and grew together again.

Pa had another dog he named Sport, an English pointer called Spot, and a black Boxer cross pug-nosed dog that he called Blackie, that everyone else called Mugs.

When Andy Sorensons moved to town they had a white bulldog - a fierce fighter, according to their kid "Cap." We believed that, of course, and always kept our dog Sport (who, by the way, was not afraid of picking a fight) from getting close to the bulldog. One day Sport saw the bulldog across the street from the BS shop, under the clothes line, where my line is now. We didn't have time to grab Sport before he took off across the street to do battle. The other dog saw Sport coming and was ready to commit mayhem. He headed toward our dog, and that was a <u>bad</u> mistake! I don't know how it happened, but Sport had hold of him someway and threw this other critter up in the air. The would-be killer dog landed on his back, got up on his feet and high-tailed it up the alley, with Sport breathing down his tail. After that skirmish, we had no qualms about walking down the street with old Sport, as that other four-legged fighter was long gone when he saw our medal winner.

Jim Barber had a police dog named Fritz that could be vicious around dogs and cats. As a matter of fact, one of his favorite pastimes was running down a cat and killing it by snapping its back. Old Sport jumped him once, but Fritz was too big for him. The Barbers went over to Herb Johnson's one time when Herb had a cat with kittens. The cats and Fritz were all in the house. All at once, here came the ferocious dog with the mother cat on top of him, with her claws dug in. Fritz didn't wait for the screen door to be opened. He went right through it, with the cat letting him know who owned the little kittens. He never killed another cat, as far as I know. I saw him chasing one out south of the schoolhouse, and he could have killed it, but about eight feet was as close as he dared to come. He must have remembered what cat claws could do, when said cat was mad.

When we were kids, an old tomcat came and found sanctuary at our home. He was skin and bones, and must have been a homeless cat. His ears were nearly frozen off and his face was pitted like he had been in a few free-for-all fights. We babied him, fed him, gave him milk, and he became one of the family. We had him before Elden started school, and he was with us after he graduated from high school. I don't know how many lives he had before he came to live with us, but he must have had more than nine altogether, the way he survived with us. Of course he started to get fat after he had all the food he wanted and he got to be a good looking Tom, even though his ears were only about half as long as they should be. Fight? Boy, he knew how to show other cats who was king around the Andersen place! I remember him chasing a cat up the tallest tree and the chased cat got to the end of the last branch when Tom nailed him. Both hit the ground, with Tom on top. The fall shook them loose, and the strange cat left, never to come back.

We had a minister, Arthur Green, a wonderful outstanding man of God. He had a dog named Hans. One day, Skinny was riding Dale Boyd's horse. As they rounded the corner of Nelson's garage, the horse shied and threw him off. Skinny was cut up, and when he got home Ma had to clean up the cuts. She wanted to know what happened. Skinny told her about riding the horse, and when "Hans Green" ran out it scared the horse and he fell off. Anyone would know that Hans Green was the preacher's dog, of course.

Eva did a good job of training our first Topsy. Topsy would walk along with her when Eva was pregnant. She would throw sticks, etc., and Topsy would bring them back to her. If anyone had tried to touch her mistress, that dog would have sprung into action, quick as a flash. She was her dog and protector. Eva brought this little pup home to me from Sioux Falls for my birthday. Madge Dietz, one of the teachers here, was with her. They put this cute little girl down on

Dale and Topsy I, 1938

the floor, and do you know what? She felt right at home, and showed us she meant it. Why do I know that? She squatted, and soaked the floor with Vitamin P, as the hospital nurses call it. We all had a good laugh over that. It wasn't the last time that the floor needed some water on it, but what the heck, she was an important member of our family, and a loving pet.

This pup was born in November or December, and Eva gave her to me on January 16 of the next year. That fall, when Pa and I went hunting, she went along with us. She, of course, had no idea what this new adventure was all about. We were hunting in a patch of grass out at George Wolfe's, looking for birds. Topsy was out ahead of us, as she used to do for Eva, when all at once, KA-BOOM! Up went a rooster. We shot it down and it landed on the other side of a little hill. Topsy took off at full speed over the hill. Pa and I just stood there and wondered what next? We couldn't see either the dog or the pheasant, so we didn't know what to expect. We didn't wait long until, wonder of wonders, here came our little pup with a nice big rooster in her mouth. That was a joy to behold! She came over to me with her tail wagging, and I talked sweet talk to her, for her to give me the bird. No way! She sidled over to Pa and let him get a good look at what she had found. Boy oh boy, she strutted around like a proud peacock, showing off her prize. She finally condescended to let me take the bird. Eva had trained her well, even though at that time her little friend didn't know what the training was all about. She soon found out.

Our first black Labrador dog, Topsy, would always go along when I got the mail. If I didn't get it, my Ma would take care of it. Topsy always had to carry some of the mail home with us, being a good bird dog. I suppose a letter in her mouth reminded her of a pheasant without the feathers. The dog always came into the store when the door was open in the summer time. On one occasion, Ma didn't give Topsy anything to carry. Topsy didn't think much of that, so she went over and picked up a loaf of bread from the rack, and went out the door. Another time the same thing happened, only then she picked out a head of cabbage and carried that home. That was a good way for Harry Starksen to make a quick sale, as Ma always paid for the groceries rather than have the Sheriff come to collect for them.

Topsy had an aversion to Harrison Ballou. He kicked at her one time, and she never forgot it. One morning I was going to work and she was along with me, as always. We were west of the house where we live now, walking on the sidewalk. All at once, Topsy stopped dead in her tracks. The hair stood straight up on her back, and she started to growl, at the same time looking at the shop. I couldn't see anything different over there until we were in front of the shop. There stood an old kitchen chair in need of repair, and that poor dog just stood out in the street, acting like she was going to eat somebody up. Later on in the day, Harrison Ballou came to the shop, and it was his chair. How that dog could smell his scent on that chair clear over on the other street, I'll never know. No wonder she was a good pheasant dog, as well as being a loving friend. And some people say that animals are dumb? Phooey!

Most every dog in town had no time for Inga Gaasedelen. The feeling was mutual. Many a time in the winter, when the doors and windows were all closed, our Topsy would be lying on the floor, all stretched out, and sound asleep. All at once she would jump up, the hair would stand up on her back, and she would start to growl. What do you suppose was wrong with her? Inga was going by on the sidewalk, getting in her walk. We never could figure out how Topsy could tell there was someone outside of the house.

Topsy had good ears, as well as a good nose. Many a time she would come and lay her head on our bed at night, and would be panting and scared. All at once we could hear thunder in the distance. She was deathly scared of storms.

I took Myrna and Virg out to a farm where the farmer had several Cocker Spaniel pups he wanted to give away. I wondered how we would decide which one to take, as I was going to let them decide. They both picked the same little black dog, cuddled him all the way home and called him Tags.

Tags was always Eva's dog. When she was making doughnuts she would tell him to roll over and he would flip and flop to get a fresh donut, something he didn't do easily the rest of the time. If she happened to drop a sizzling donut while transferring it from the grease to the cooling rack, it never would hit the floor. She could never figure out why it didn't burn his mouth.

Virgil and Tags

If Tags heard another dog bark at him he would hightail it for home, put his butt against the front door, and when he felt safe he would bark back.

Spot was another stray dog Pa picked up. He was a black and white dog, and looked like a pointer. Pa figured he was a good hunter, so we took him out west and proceeded to shoot the shotgun. When we looked around, the so-called "bird dog" was high tailing it for home! We found him in the porch, behind the washing machine. Spot would lie in the big armchair in the living room to pass his leisure hours, since he had nothing else to keep him occupied. When Pa's mantle clock struck 11, the dog never moved, but when it struck 12, he was out of the chair and out to the door with his tail wagging as though he was waiting for something. Indeed he was, he was waiting for dinner to come through that door. Eva or I would bring over dinner for Pa, and that dog evidently could tell time or had some built-in timer so that he knew what was coming when the clock struck 12. And then, we call some dogs dumb!

Virgil had rabbits in Grandpa Guptill's garage. What ever happened to them, I don't know. He fed and watered them real well. Consequently there were lots (and I mean LOTS) of rabbit pellets, or whatever you call those little round things that those four-legged pets deposit on the ground. We had a big garden south of the town hall at that time, and he carted over a good many pails of this delicate fertilizer and put it on the garden. Boy, did that stuff work! We had tomato vines that were out of this world. Talk about big, and besides that, lots of tomatoes to eat. They tasted extra good, so evidently the rich rabbit fertilizer didn't permeate and spoil the fruit. If anything, there was good added flavor, instead of anything "off taste."

We were in Huron one day, and the kids thought they would like to have a parakeet, which was the rage at that time. Haven't heard of anyone having one of those birds anymore. We went into Newberry's 5- and 10-cent store to see about a bird. There were several choices, and the kids picked out one they wanted. Cost a buck. The clerk got the bird out of the cage, and all at once the bird took off! Around and around the store it flew. I have no idea what became of that flying bird, but it was scared. So, the clerk had to get another bird to leave Huron and make its home at the Andersen home in Hetland. The kids called it "Twinkle," maybe because they saw a twinkle in his eye. I call the bird "he," as we didn't check out the gender, and there weren't going to be any young ones, either. Their bird had the run of the house. He flew around and sat up on the window casing, and ate the wallpaper and plaster, too, and even sat on the kids' glasses. He raised havoc with the wall, but what the heck, he probably needed something different than birdseed to clear out his digestive system.

Mirm Demske had a parakeet, too. As always, everything they had was the best. Some of us were up for coffee (milk for me) at the café one day, and got to talking about, of all things, parakeets. I said that the kids had a new bird, so Mirm said she had one that would have cost $50, but a good friend of theirs gave it to them for nothing. Then she let me know that her bird could talk. I wasn't dumb enough to ask her what the so-called talking bird could say. Then she got real nosey, and wanted to know if our bird could talk. "Nope, he can't." "Where did you get him, and how much did he cost?" Well, this old girl didn't need to know, but one of those city "know it alls" wasn't going to back me into a corner, even though it was none of her business. "We got him at a dime store, and he cost a buck." That took care of the question. When I came home and told Mom and the kids about this episode, Myrna and Virgil were really upset. "Dad, why did you have to tell her that we got Twinkle in the dime store? Why didn't you tell her that we got him in Newberry's," which was also called the 5- and 10-cent store. I hope that I haven't been known for beating around the bush, and I just called it like it was, a no-frill store, a dime store. Regardless of where this little bird came from, he was a nice bird, even though he wrecked the walls of our home.

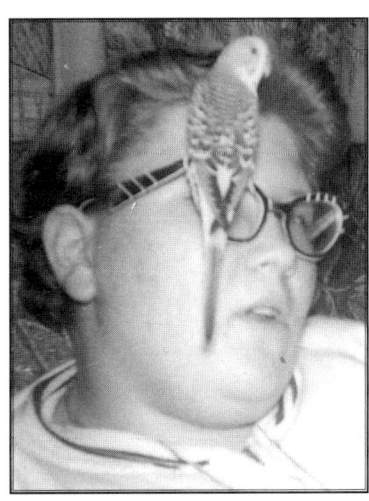

Myrna and Twinkle

One Easter, Virgil got two baby chicks for an Easter present. We had them in a box in the sitting room of our home. With lots of TLC, and plenty of good stuff to eat, these two little chickens started to grow and get pretty frisky. The box we had them in was a foot or more high on the sides. Those two would try to jump up onto the edge of the box in order to see what the rest of the house looked like. Finally they made it. They didn't dare to jump down on the floor, and when Mom would see those two up on the edge, she would go in and give them a good scolding and put them back inside the box. One day, she heard the darndest commotion in the front room. Twinkle was really talking like he was possessed. She went in to see what all of the ruckus was about. Boy, talk about a standoff! Here were those two chicks out of the box, standing on the rug, looking at Twinkle. He was about two feet in front of them, on the floor, and they were all looking at each other, eyeball to eyeball. The bird was just screeching, imitating her mistress, probably telling the two chicks to get back into their box. Maybe he was alerting Eva that those two characters were not where they belonged. Either way, she put the chicks back in the box, and picked up Twinkle and gave him some good loving, which he liked. Even though he came from the dime store, he knew how to talk when it was necessary.

These two chicks grew up to be great big whoppers. They would see some kids out in the alley and take after them. When they gave up the chase, and had the kids on the run, they would stop in the middle of the road, shake their wings and crow, just like they would say, "Boy, we sure made those kids run!" We finally took the two roosters out to Elden and Shirley's where they could have the run of the farm. By now they were really big, and would chase the Andersen kids around the farm. Finally, Shirley got tired of that and got them into the frying pan. She invited us out for dinner, too. Before we sat down to eat, something was said about the chickens. Virg perked up his ears and wanted to know if those were his chickens. They were, and he wouldn't eat any chicken when they were his two pets. I didn't blame him one bit, as we, too, had chickens when we were kids.

We had two good Labrador mix hunting dogs named Topsy. The last dog was one of the reasons Virg got all of the birds. She was his pal, and when a bird was shot she would retrieve it. Who do you suppose she took it to? Of course it was Virgil's bird, whether he shot it or not. Topsy seemed to know her master was an excellent shot and I don't think it entered her mind that any-

Virg with Topsy, ca 1958

one could shoot like he could. I shot a pheasant one time on the far end of a slough while Virg and Topsy were clear over on the other side. She saw the bird come down and came across the slough to get it for me. At least, that was what went through my thick skull. She picked up the bird and didn't have the least intention of giving it to me. Virg let out a little whistle, and she carried that bird a quarter of a mile or more so that he could carry the bird without overloading his dad.

Virgil's Topsy would always ride alongside of us in the front seat. I don't know how that girl knew when Sunday came along, but somehow, she was onto it. She knew that I needed to go over to the church early every Sunday. She would be out by the car, dancing and prancing until I opened the car door for her to get in. Mugs, Pa's dog (that he called Blackie) knew the way she was acting that we were going to the church. As soon as we started the car, Mugs would go full speed uptown, and go between Ralph's garage and the Legion hall. He was at the church about the same time as we were. How they knew what was going on, I'll never know. We hardly ever missed a church service, but if we did, the parishioners would tell us that Topsy was lying in front of the door, waiting for the service to be over. She would look each one over until all were gone, and the door was shut. Then she would come home. We weren't there! Steve Karban told his folks one Sunday morning that we should name our dog Saint Bernard, as she attended church when we weren't there. Never thought about this before, but maybe, just maybe, she was representing us so we couldn't be counted absent. Could be.

When I was growing up, when we threw a ball or practiced hitting it into the wild blue yonder, we had to go and get it. With Myr-

All Creatures Great and Small 101

Dale and Topsy II... Throw the rock!!

na and Virg that all changed. Topsy didn't care what she retrieved, whether it was a pheasant, ball, rock or a flying model airplane. She would be on cloud nine when she clomped on to it and brought the object back to the sender.

When the kids were going to bat the ball out into space, Topsy would be out in front of them, eyeing the ball, like a pointer would when pointing a pheasant. As soon as the ball was airborne, she was after it. Many times it was a ground ball or a line drive right at her. She would catch it, and still have her teeth intact, as some of those balls were really moving when she caught them. If it had been in a regular ball game, the batter (according to the umpire) would have been out.

Virg, being the mechanical genius that he is, inherited from both Grandpas from the family tree, decided to make model airplanes that he could fly by control lines. Boy did we hear lots of buzzing when those planes got airborne. His dog Topsy thought flying planes was great. He would be over west of our house, on the school lawn, zipping the planes up and down. Topsy was right in her glory (being the bird dog that she was), trying to catch the plane. Virg would zoom it down at her and she would jump up into the air trying to catch it. Virg would zoom it up, just as she was about to "nail it."

We had Topsy spayed and had brought her home from the vet's clinic after the surgery. She was all pooped out, lying on a rug by the door in the kitchen. All at once, KA-BOOM, Virg fired up one of his planes over on the schoolyard. Topsy jumped up from the rug, ran to the west window and put her front feet on the window sill, and began to yowl like she was sent for and couldn't come. We had to run out and have Virg shut the outfit off, or Topsy would have gone nuts. She wasn't out there to oversee what her master was up to. It was a marvel that she didn't tear the stitches loose, but she didn't, and lived to tell the story.

Topsy would bring a rock into the shop and drop it at my feet, wanting me to throw it so she could go get it. We always had the window over the workbench open in the summer, so I would throw the rock out through it. There were six 8x10 panes in the window, and one of them was broken out. After it got colder, I shut the window, and would throw the rock through the hole, missing the glass. When it got even colder, I put in a new pane of glass. Then what do you suppose? The next morning Topsy brought in a rock and stood there dancing around, waiting for me to toss it through the window. That's just what I did! The new glass was so clean that I just threw the rock into the glass. There was a crash of broken glass, so I found out about my "memory lapse." When I put in the next pane of glass, I left the tag on it so I wouldn't do the same dumb thing again.

Virg and Topsy were out in front of the hardware store one day – wherever he was, his dog was always with him. He had a ball that he would throw, and Topsy would go get it. Nothing pleased her more than retrieving something. He would throw the ball, and Topsy would bring it back, then drop it for him to throw again. Martin Wonsbeck took this all in, and then told Virg that he bet he could throw the ball, and she couldn't find it. Virg had faith in his dog, and the two bet a nickel as a wager. Martin had the ball, and pretended to throw it east, between the bank and the store. Topsy took off at full speed to get the ball. Martin still had the ball in his hand, and threw it west, across the street, where it rolled nearly to the alley by the BS shop. The poor dog went back and forth, back and forth, smelling for the scent of the ball, but she couldn't come up with it. Martin wanted his nickel, but Virg told him to wait awhile, as his dog would find the ball. Martin still wanted his money. Finally, Topsy kept smelling along the ground, and started west across the street with her nose to the ground. When she got to where the ball had hit, and then rolled, she didn't have to wonder where the ball was. Her nose was "sharp as a tack" and she promptly brought the ball back to her master, prancing around like a kid with its first toy. She dropped the ball at his feet, and was ready to hunt some more. Virg had his hand out for the nickel, and his pal hadn't let him down.

Our kids came in laughing one day, telling how smart their dog Topsy was. Leo and Miriam Demske owned the hunting lodge uptown, and had a café and bar in conjunction with the hotel. Everything that they had was the best, having lived in South Bend, Indiana, and then moving to South Dakota. "Mirm" always said that the women out here didn't know how to cook, because they didn't use garlic in their menus. For her to make that snide remark about our excellent cooks was a low blow, as our ladies in Hetland didn't take a back seat for anyone, as far a cooking, or anything else was concerned.

Leo had two big black Labrador dogs which, like their master, figured they were kings of the hill. We had strung 2" mesh chicken wire up high between trees out in the yard to make a backstop where the kids could play ball. One day, one of Demske's dogs took after Topsy, chasing her in a circle. Topsy headed toward the wire fence, but when she got there, she went on the north side of the tree. The fence was on the south side. The kids laughed when Demske's dog went on the other side of the tree, at full speed, and head first into the fence. You know what happened. End over end, backwards, went this big bully, flat on his back. He was smart enough to pick himself up and hightail it for home. If dogs laugh like we do, Topsy had a good laugh and patted herself on the back for pulling off such a fine feat. No wonder Myrna and Virg thought their dog was smarter than Demske's. She was. (By the way, Topsy learned to do this the hard way. One day when she was uptown, Virg called her from the front steps. In her hurry to come home, she ran headlong into the backstop, experiencing the same effect felt by Leo's Lab. The memory of her experience served her well.)

Our last Topsy and Mugs would always go along to get the mail. Topsy would be ahead of me, and Mugs would bring up the rear. Ed Crow had a talking dog; anyway he thought that the dog could talk. I never heard what the dog had to say. One day Crow's dog was outside between the bank and hardware store. Topsy saw him and took off full speed, heading for the talking dog. Mugs saw her take off, so he "spun his wheels" and took off too, not knowing what the excitement was all about. Topsy hit the other dog at full speed and knocked him down, and then Mugs jumped on him too. I rescued the dog, so he could continue to talk. I told Skipper Peterson about this, and his comment was a profound, "Why didn't he holler for help?" He, being from Norwegian stock, couldn't understand dog talk either.

Our dogs, especially the two Topsys, were always cleaning themselves up, in other words taking a bath. When we wanted to give them a bath in a tub, that was a different story. Something like Dennis the Menace in the funny papers. When done bathing those dogs would really shake and throw water all over. With Mugs, cleaning up was an altogether different story. He could be dirty as a pig and never clean the mud off.

These two dogs would meet the two bread trucks every day to get a "handout." They were never disappointed. Mugs never missed a chance to get something to eat. One day the Swanders Baking Company truck driver opened a box of powered sugar doughnuts, and the Old Home Bakery driver brought out plain doughnuts. Mugs ate all 12 of the sugared donuts and spit the plain ones out on the ground. When the dozen sugared ones were gone, and no more were coming, he ate the plain ones too, one at a time, in a single gulp.

Getting something to eat, or in other words, a handout from anyone was right down his "alley." The Old Home bread truck came to town from the north and would stop at Demske's Hotel and take in bread. They always drove Ford trucks. When Mugs heard the truck stop at the hotel he would get up and amble up to Starksen's store, as that was the next stop for Les and the bread truck. Les always gave Mugs something to eat.

The Fenn's Ice Cream truck driver would give them ice cream bars if they were both there.

Dale, Topsy and Mugs

One day the guy told me to come on out, as he had found something that Mugs couldn't eat in one gulp. He opened up a flat box of ice cream, and Mugs couldn't get all of it into his big mouth at one time, so he ate it in two gulps. His face was square across, and about two or three times bigger than a regular dog. We always figured that he was a cross of Boxer, Labrador, and Bum!

I returned to the shop after dinner one day and saw Topsy over by the iron pile. She started to nose around in the grass. Mugs was a few feet away from her. I looked to see what she was interested in. It was a nest of baby rabbits. When I got her away, Mugs jumped in and cleaned out the nest. He got them out one at a time, squealing like heck, and swallowed them whole. It wasn't a very pretty sight, with legs and head hanging out of his mouth before they went "down the hatch."

One day, Pa and I were out on the south side of his house and Mugs was there also. I heard the truck stop at the hotel and Mugs did too. He cocked his head and listened but didn't get up and go uptown. The truck stopped at the store and Mugs was all ears but didn't move. Shortly after that the Old Home truck left town and when it got to the railroad tracks Mugs really took notice. A few days later I saw Les uptown at the store and I told him what had happened. He said he missed Mugs and then said "You know what? I drove a different truck that day." Smart dog, Mugs was!

Pa would turn the air conditioner on in the house so Blackie could lie under the unit to keep cool. Pa would sit outside in the shade, and let his dog enjoy "cool comfort."

One time Dr. Askey came to the shop to give the two dogs a shot. I held Topsy's head, and Askey stuck in the needle. Topsy jumped and gave a little "yip!" When he stuck Mugs, he didn't flinch, but looked back at Doc like he thought a fly had sat on him. One time, Askey and I were shooting the breeze out in front of the shop when a bird sitting on the wire above him pooped on his head. He got some water and a rag from the truck and proceeded to clean up the mess. After all, being a vet, he wouldn't want to go out to a farmer with bird droppings sliding down his face. He wasn't like the preacher who had the same experience. The preacher felt the deposit on his bald head and said, "Thank God." A parishioner who saw this asked, "How could you thank God when the bird let you have it?" The preacher replied, "I thanked God that elephants don't fly!"

When the kids came home from school in Lake Preston, Topsy would hear the car whenever it crossed the railroad tracks. She would get up and stretch, so as to be in good shape when the kids stopped the car in front of the house. She would be howling and jumping, and of course wanted to be petted. They could drive across town, and the same thing happened. Myrna used to say that with all the fuss Topsy made, she must have thought they had been gone for a long time. Maybe the dog was lonesome, as we all are sometimes.

I used to go over to the folks' every night about 9:30, before they went to bed. Our second Topsy would lie by our big chair sleeping and wouldn't move any time when I got up to walk into the kitchen. When I got up to go over and check on the folks, that dog would get up and stretch, and go to the door, ready to go with me to see them too. She never missed knowing when I was ready to go. Maybe it was some way that I got up from the chair, or else she could tell time without a watch. She was smart. When she got too old to hunt, we would ask Pa if he wanted to go hunting. Topsy would go crazy, and wanted to go too. We finally spelled h-u-n-t-i-n-g to Pa, and Topsy would stand in front of us and cock her head from side to side and wag her tail ready to go along. We couldn't take her, even though she was a "super" pal to have along.

Virg and Vi called us one time that they were coming home, and would be here before bedtime. I told Topsy that the kids were coming. She cocked her head, and gave me the "knowing look." When we were over to check Pa out, I thought I heard a car door shut. I looked out the window, and saw that the kids were home across the street. I told Topsy that the kids were here, and was she excited! She stood with her feet on the ledge of the big window and yowled like she was possessed. Pa wanted to know what she was so wild for. I told him the kids were here, and he wanted to know how Topsy knew that. I informed him that I had told her the kids were coming. His response was, "You told her? Now I've heard everything." When I let the dog out, she beat the kids to the door of the house. She was tickled pink, and let them know it.

Another time I was over there in the evening and the dog was all stretched out, enjoying the loving she was getting. I told Pa that Myrna had called. Wow! That dog sat up and cocked her head from side to side, listening and listening. Pa wanted to know what was the matter with her. "I just told you that Myrna had called, and that she knew who I was talking about." Of course, he didn't think she was "that" smart. We knew better.

After Ma passed away, the second Topsy and I would visit Pa every evening. I would sit in a chair beside his, and Topsy would stand and then lie by his chair. He didn't just pat her gently, he would really whack her - and she would enjoy it, too.

One night I noticed something lying under his bed. I crawled under the bed and found his little tape measure, which he always carried even after he couldn't work in the shop. I wanted to know how that tape measure happened to be under the bed. He felt in his pockets, and it was his ruler. What and how did it get under the bed? He told me that Blackie (we called him Mugs) had gotten mad at him and crawled under the bed, I suppose to pout. Pa always gave his dog a lemon drop before he went to bed. He got the lemon drop and called Blackie to come and get it. The dog must have still had his nose "out of joint," and wouldn't move. Pa said he crawled under the bed and dragged Blackie out to give him the lemon drop. Now this dog weighed 80 or 90 pounds - or more - and Pa was 93 years old, so it must have been a struggle for him to drag that pooch out from under the bed! I asked Pa what the big idea was? He told me he didn't want Blackie to go to sleep and be mad at him. Then to top it off, he said Blackie wouldn't open his mouth to eat the candy, so Pa pried open the dog's mouth and pushed the candy far enough down so it could be swallowed! I still can't see how Pa, at his age, could manipulate such a deal.

Delbert and Gladys Zeller came to see us once when Topsy and I were over to see Pa. I saw their car was here, and told Topsy that Delbert and Gladys were here. She was wild to get into the house. When she saw Delbert sitting in the chair by the bay window, she tore across the room and put her feet on his lap. Then she realized she wasn't supposed to be that far into the living room. She went back to the doorway, and proceeded to give him a serenade. We had a rug by the big chair near the doorway to the living room. She knew that was as far as she was supposed to go. Anyway, our two good friends received a royal welcome, even though Topsy seemed to neglect Gladys. I'm sure that our dog wasn't playing favorites by not snuggling up to her. They both were her friends.

After about 13 years we had to have Dr. Askey mercifully put our second Topsy to sleep. He told me to get out while he took care of our dear friend, and I wasn't about to stay anyway. Doc told me that most people didn't treat their dogs like we did. Our good friend, Doc, said to come back in 15 minutes or so, and he would have Topsy in the coffin we had made for her. I didn't come back in 15 minutes, but stayed away as long as I could before my emotions would let me take her home. She is buried out north of our house, and has a steel marker with her name and dates on it. What a special friend, and member of our family. She was definitely Virgil's pal, and she had an uncanny sense of loyalty, and was sharp as a tack in mentality.

After Virg and Vi were married, they had a brown Lab they called Coco. One time they were visiting and some friends of theirs from Aberdeen were here, too. They had a pup from the same litter as Coco. Boy, those two little twerps tore around the house worse than wild men. They were really having fun. Finally, our Topsy was fed up with all of their bedlam. These two came tearing along, and all at once, Topsy let out a bark - WOOF! Do you know what? Those two pups stopped dead in their tracks, and that was the end of their fun. They wouldn't listen to us, but they knew that Topsy meant business when she said stop.

When Eva went to the Care Center, I had 11 cats that depended on me to keep them fed. I went to the Care Center during the week to eat dinner with her. After the meal was over, the help checked each resident's plate to mark down how much was eaten. At our table, and sometimes at other tables, I cleaned up what was left and brought it home for our cats. When I turned the corner uptown, those smart cats "got in gear" to give me a royal welcome home. I generally had a half-gallon or more of food for them, and boy, were they wild to get it! Standing on their hind legs to give me a chorus of yells, they let me know that they were hungry. They cleaned up everything in the dishes – beans, beets, spinach, carrots, meat, potatoes – you name it, and they ate it.

Although I don't have as many cats now, they give me something to do, and I enjoy their company, even though at times they frustrate me by how they seem to take advantage of me. I think that perhaps they look at me as a "soft touch." Maybe they are right. Who knows?

Eva with Snookie, 1999

Dale and friends, 1999

Chapter 9
Just for Fun

Friends on sleds, one mile south of
Hetland. Skinny and Dane are standing

Just for Fun

Games we played —

As I look back there were games that don't sound very exciting, but they were a lot of fun, and didn't cost anything to play.

Snowball Fights: When we were growing up we would make forts out of snow blocks – and they were some forts! They were across the street from each other and the walls were about a foot thick. We had portholes to throw snowballs at the other side, just like the medieval forts had them as places to shoot out of. We made up a supply of snowballs, and made a pile like a pyramid, like cannonballs used to be stored. We had the back entrance made in a zigzag so that the enemy couldn't charge and breach the fort from the rear, without a pitched battle ensuing.

Mumbley Peg: When we were growing up and going to school, we must have had a different set of values than kids do today. Now if a kid has a knife, he will be in big trouble with schoolteachers and the law. Evidently we didn't know that a pocketknife could be used to hack people to pieces. We all had a favorite knife and used it to play "mumbley peg." In case you don't know what mumbley peg was or is, I can fill you in on what the game was. We would sit on the ground and take turns on trying to get the open blade to stick in the ground when you flipped it over from several different angles from your hand. The first one was to hold the knife flat in your hand and then throw it up in the air to make the blade stick in the ground. There were several different ways to try to accomplish this daring feat, and the one who completed all of the maneuvers first was the winner.

Marbles: We used to play marbles several ways. Sometimes we would make a circle on the ground and put marbles in it. We would try to knock them out of the circle. If you succeeded, you kept the marbles. Other times, we would draw a line in the ground or use the lines in a sidewalk to see who could get closest to the line. The one who did got all the marbles. Maybe this was a forerunner of the South Dakota Lottery.

We used to play kid games in the back of the hardware store, rain or shine. One game was where we would go and hide and whoever was "it" tried to find everyone. When some couldn't be found the game was over when the kid hollered "Run sheep, run." We had one kid who would say "sheep run, sheep." It still brought out the sheep.

We had many good times in the back room in the hardware store, and Jim Barber and Charley Johnson never complained. There was a dirt floor in the storage room and we could play marbles, tossing marbles at a line in the dirt, to see who could get the closest. We would draw a circle and shoot the marbles out of the circle. Any way it could be done. We got to keep any marbles that we could knock out of the ring and likewise, whoever got closest to the line in the dirt or sometimes the line in the sidewalk, got all of the other marbles that were further away.

We used to go down to the stockyards which at that time were operated by Lyman Ballou. It was quite a thriving operation too, as several carloads of cattle and hogs were shipped to market each year. Anyway, we would choose up sides and have "corncob fights." Can you imagine what an old, soggy, manure-coated cob feels like when it hits you in the face? Imagine how our clothes smelled after getting plastered with all that nice juicy pig manure that had a way of sticking to a cob. We thought it was great sport and it didn't cost us any money, as we didn't have any anyway. It was a cheap pastime, even though smelly.

One time Debs Starksen and Snort Buhn, the barber, were playing checkers in Skipper's restaurant. The boys had drilled a hole in the wall behind Debs place so they could put a water gun through from the other room. The game was going along okay and Debs was studying his next move. Snort looked up and saw the water gun was in place and loaded for action and ready for the next act. Snort told Debs "It's your move, Charlie" which was the cue to let him have it with the water gun. The gun worked. Debs, with water dripping off his head, picked up the checkerboard and smashed it over Snort's head and at the same time exclaimed "You're damn right it is." A few days later Debs made a new checkerboard out of an aluminum sheet that wouldn't break under the same circumstances.

At the Stangland farm on the south side of town, Gub was showing us how he could ride the big bay horse bareback with no saddle. He crawled up on the horse and sat there so smug, as though he was a real cowboy. The devil must have gotten the best of me because I couldn't resist what I was thinking. I picked up a hard old corncob and hit the horse with it in the belly. That was a big mistake, as the horse's hind feet left the ground and Gub left the horse, all in the same jump. That wasn't the worst of it, as the old nag turned around and was kicking with both feet trying to plaster Gub. Gub was over the fence in a hurry and gave me heck for inciting the beast. I don't blame him, as it wasn't a very good way to treat a friend. I should have had my head examined!

We used to go down to the sliding hill that was south of Jerry Bunday's elevator. We would slide on our sleds or ski by the hour, day after day. We would go out into Lake Ole, which was at the bottom of the hill, and see who could go the farthest, especially on the sled. We also

Skinny and Homer with their sleds

had a homemade toboggan and would use this too, as well as a ski jump. More than one kid or adult got cut up running into the fence near Lake Ole. When we got cold we would go up to the elevator and roast plain ear corn on top of the potbellied stove until it got good and black and then we'd eat it because we couldn't afford regular popcorn.

I used to like to argue when I was younger. Maybe I still do? When we would come into Bunday's elevator to get warm after being out in the cold at the sledding hill we would get into some odd arguments. One in particular was "Who made God?" We never got it solved and still don't know and Jerry Bunday, a staunch Congregationalist, couldn't tell us either. Another was "How many angels could sit on the head of a pin?" Never got that solved either.

We had an ice skating rink south of the town hall. We didn't have any outdoor toilet or even a place to get warm. After skating up and down that rink, we would have to get rid of that good Hetland water after it had passed through our kidneys. The best place to squirt the hot fluid stuff was behind Skipper's tin-covered restaurant. For some unknown reason, the tin was charged with electricity. Now don't get me wrong, I had nothing, absolutely nothing to do with this, as I didn't like to get a shot of electricity anywhere, especially in the middle of my anatomy. This being the best out-of-the-way place to feel better, it was natural to aim at the building and "shoot." Boy, what a wallop! More than one novice got initiated, but let me assure you he didn't try that shooting maneuver a second time! Never heard if any of the girls experienced the jolt we got. At least they never told us gents about it.

Later on we had another skating rink on the north edge of town. Had a warming shack, too. One night, John Cleveland was going to show us how good they skated in Norway. He was going up and down the rink swinging his arms and butt in a leisurely fashion when BOOM! Down he went. We all laughed, but not for long. John had a broken leg and it never did heal right, as he always limped after that.

We used to skate on Boyd's pond on the east end and Boyd's slough on the west end of town. Had an old shack west of town at the slough that was made out of a couple of crates that were used to ship pianos. We would burn wood in the stove to keep partly warm. One night the shack burned down. Never heard if the fire marshal checked it out but there were rumors of "foul play." The rumor was that it was being used for "immoral purposes." No insurance to collect, either.

Back in the dirty '30s, Two or three of us hauled in dozens and dozens of loads of clay to build a tennis court east of the blacksmith shop. We used the hardware's old International truck and hauled the clay from John Kvinge's gravel pit. We used hand shovels and worked day after day for weeks to get enough clay to build a court. This was in the dust storm days and we wouldn't dare to cross highway 14 until the dust storm let up enough so we could see a few feet to see if there were cars coming. We had to have the old truck in super low to even get started moving. When we finally, after several months, had the court ready to play on, it was surprising how many tennis players there were in town who didn't volunteer to "lift a shovel" to make the court a reality. We even planted trees and had benches so the spectators could sit and watch the game. We dug the trees from a grove out east of town. Lots of fun, and we enjoyed doing something for the good of the town and the people who lived here.

Jim Barber had an outside electrical outlet on his garage. We used to initiate some of the farm kids when they came to town. We would get the novice to fill a steel pail with water and then throw the water at the outlet and hang on the pail to the last second before the water hit the hot current. Boy, did you ever hear some hollering after the "shock" when they didn't let go of the pail early enough. I'm ashamed of being a part of this as we could have killed someone from the "jolt."

We used to build kites, and they were big kites too - four or five feet high. It took a lot of tail to keep them from making nosedives, but when we got them up it was a sight to behold. Several kites in the air at once, going clear across town. At the time we would have a half-mile or more of string, so that kite would be a long way out. If the string broke, and sometimes it did, we had a hard time to find it if it went down in some farmer's cornfield. I don't know what kind of heavy string we used, but we would put it on a wooden winch bolted to a post, and use a crank to pull the kite in as we couldn't do it by hand. Lots of fun, and it didn't cost us any money, as the storekeepers gave us the paper to make the outfit. The tail was made from scraps of cloth that Ma gave us.

We caught crawdads down in the "Dago Pond." We built a raft out of railroad ties, and used it to go out in the pond. We tied a red piece of beefsteak on a string and dropped it to the bottom, where we hoped a crab would grab it. When one did, we would pull him up, grab the crab and deposit him in a pail. We got on to a way to save money by using a red cloth instead of trying to get money to buy steak. Other times we would see a mound in the mud and dig down to pull out a crab. We would take the crabs up to Spot Laymon's drug store were we would heat water to a boil and drop the crabs in. When cooked, we ate the tails. Spot let us use his heater as long as he could get some crab to eat. As of now I doubt if I would eat them after scalding them to death in that boiling water.

One year we played touch football on the schoolyard in our shirt sleeves on New Years Day. Don't know what year it was, but most any other year it would have been cold and wintry.

Some of the farmers were even out plowing their fields, as there was no frost in the ground. That was what was called an "open winter." Later on in the new year it proceeded to get colder, so we didn't have to get out our summer clothes.

A letter from Mabel Anderson about baseball stories that was in a recent issue of South Dakota Magazine brought back memories to this old blacksmith. I was one of the two pitchers on the Hetland baseball team that played the Danes, from the Badger area, out in the middle of (nearly dry) Lake Poinsett during the dirty thirties. We drove out a mile or two from the Stone Bridge Resort, located on the north side of the lake, and which was just south of (dry) Dry Lake. "What's that?" you might say, "Play ball out in the middle of a lake? Was that a place to play baseball?" You bet it was. Sand as hard as a rock, as far as the eye could see, and NO fences to hit the ball over for a sure home run.

Chris Cornelius was the speed ball pitcher for the Danes, and his brother Martin was the catcher. When one of our players, Scrub Russett, (a Norwegian) would come to bat, he would taunt Chris by yelling at him, "Go ahead and hit me, you S.O.B." Chris would, and send Scrub to first base every time that he came to bat. The grapevine had it that there was BAD blood between them over some "chick." Oh, lest I forget, we won the game.

Years latter, after Poinsett was again a lake, Martin and his two daughters drove to Hetland from Bryant, to test my ? memory. The first thing Martin wanted to know was, "Mory, did you EVER play ball out in the middle of Lake Poinsett?" Yup, I had. Martin turned to his girls and said, "Now will you believe ME?" How about that? One Dane vouching for another Dane. I may have played against, or known some of Mabel's next of kin, but I don't know what her name was when she resided in the Badger and Lake Norden area.

When we had card parties, the teachers were always invited. We had a redheaded Irish teacher by the name of Murphy. I don't know what kind of hairdo she had, but I doubt if she could have put her head into a bushel basket – it was that frizzy. One night, or I should say morning, at about 2 AM we were playing whist, and we stacked the deck of cards on her. She had aces, kings and queens in two suits, and my partner and I had the other two suits, solid. She granded, naturally, with all those sure tricks. I sat behind her, and was the first one to lead out. Before I put out my first ace I said, "Here comes Otto Larsen," which to us old card sharks meant, "Here comes a run of cards, big ones too."

Murphy turned around and looked at the door to see who Otto Larsen was. Nobody came in through the door, so I played my first ace and kept on taking tricks and then let my partner in, and he took the rest of the tricks. Murphy didn't get one trick, so she found out who Otto was. Everybody started to laugh except the redhead, and then it dawned on her that she had been "had." She turned to me and accused me of stacking the cards. We finally admitted it, but there was no harm done, as we didn't play for money – just for fun.

One time we had a carnival in town. The chief sponsor of it was Satchel Butt (I'm being polite in calling him Butt, as we used another word that had only 3 letters. Use your imagination what that was.) A Norwegian Streel friend of mine and I decided (don't ask me how we decided) to spend a dime apiece to go into the "Hoochie Coochie" show. Today, to dress it up, it would be called burlesque or a strip show. We got into the tent, and being young, we hobnobbed with the rest of the clientele who were all older than we were. They were evidently not members of the Christian Coalition, but could have been, hoping that none of the "coalition for right" crew would notice that they had spent a dime to see some girl display what she had to show the men. The money probably would have been welcome in the next collection plate. I might add that there was a four-foot barrier between us and the females. I suppose that was to designate which side of the fence we were on.

Finally after the tent was full, we heard soft music and two well built girls started to wiggle their behinds and associated other places, and then off their robes came to show us more of what girls looked like, and were proud of. They still had on more clothes than what we see everyday on TV, but looked pretty naked to us boys. The youngest and best-looking girl kept dancing and wiggling over to where we were ogling the festive event. Finally she stood in front of my Norske friend and really began to wiggle. I thought "Now what?" She looked him in the eye and asked, "Where are your hands?" He got red as a beet and brought his hands up in the air and everybody laughed but me. I was embarrassed for him. Lucky for me I had my elbows up on the fence like all the old timers did. I pretended to be an old pro at ogling half-clad women, but my friend had been out in the sun longer than I had. You notice I didn't mention his name, as he must have seen the error of his ways. He got to be a Lutheran preacher.

I didn't get carried away that far, and just kept on being a blacksmith. I must not have seen the light! You need to trust me, but this was the first and only time I ever set foot in one of these strip joints. By the way – I wasn't married then either. I think it is only fair to add that I heard by the grapevine that later on the ticket price went up to a quarter, and then the girls shucked everything off. Guess nothing was covered up for that price. We didn't have the quarter and had already risked a dime of our hard earned money. That was nearly a half day's work at hard labor. Enough about that sleazy side of life. I'm too old to spend money on such foolishness.

Several years later, another carnival came to town, and set up in the hall. They had a BIG mail sack and wanted two volunteers to tie a guy in the sack. They looked for two big suckers to do that. Bill Mogler and I were given the honors to tie big knots in a half inch rope. We had knots for ten feet and we pulled like "jackasses" to make them tight, and were they tight! We got to our seats, the curtain was pulled and the guy was out of the sack. I don't know how he did get out but it wasn't because we didn't tie the knots tight enough. The hawkers sold boxes of candy for a nickel. Some of them had a trinket in them. Bill and I were the only ones in the hall who got anything but candy.

We would put on plays in the town hall. We had one where the only actors were men—no women allowed in that play. Fern Melstad was the prompter, and we would get off on a tangent and not follow the script. She would talk louder and louder, and finally we would get back in the script. She said she would never be prompter again. I wore one of Eva's long dresses so I could cross my legs, as I don't think panty hose were in vogue those days. Kenwood Cleveland was playing with a ball of yarn and by accident (planned) dropped the ball off the stage. One of the school teachers was sitting in the front row, and reached down to pick it up. Kenwood yanked on the string so she didn't get the ball. It would only roll so far. The poor lady was red as a beet and the crowd loved it.

Sig Peterson stopped in the middle of the stage and stared toward the back of the room. He kept walking back and forth across the stage and shielding his eyes, looking toward the back. Finally, most of the crowd couldn't stand the anxiety any more so they were turning around and looking too. Finally, Sig stopped and really gawked. We finally asked him what he was looking at. He replied, "There is a fly on the back wall." That brought a roar, and everyone turned toward the stage to watch the show. Sig stole that show.

When we were kids, it was the custom to make May baskets on the first of May to give to our friends. Of course, we had to give our teacher a basket, as maybe, just maybe, she would feel so good after eating all the good candy that she would "up" our grades. Don't know if that philosophy ever worked, but it was a thought. When I was in the second grade, I hung a basket to my teacher, Ruth Heinz. She was a cute "chick," in good shape and quite a runner. After the basket was hung, the recipient of the goodies was entitled to kiss the giver, if said giver could be caught. Anyway, I wasn't about to let any girl – especially my teacher – kiss me, so I took off running as fast as my little feet could go. She took after me, and boy, could she run! I could feel her hot breath breathing down my neck, so I decided I'd climb a tree and be safe. Alas, I was doomed! She came up that tree like a squirrel and gave me a great big smack on the lips. Boy, was I embarrassed. To this day I don't recall which it was – a dry kiss or a wet one, but it was a good smooch. I had botched a try at escaping a girl who was determined to catch me, even to climbing a tree. Mission accomplished.

We used to have some really good times on May 17th, the Norwegian Independence Day. Charlie Starksen was King until he died and Mrs. Sam Vidvei was Queen. We had big parades, with a Viking ship with the King and Queen riding in it. I think they copied the trim on the boat from some of the ships the Danes used when they conquered Norway.

One year, the day of the celebration I went up to the post office to mail a letter. Charlie had the Norske flag lying on his desk. I took the flag off the desk. Somehow it nestled under my arm and I took it with me back to the shop. Now, let's get this straight; I didn't pretend to steal that flag. It just came along with me. It didn't take Debs long to notice his desk was short one flag. Here he came, shook his finger at me and wanted to know what I had done with the Norwegian flag. I didn't tell him that I didn't take it, but asked him how it was that he would accuse me of taking it. He said it was gone and nobody but me would take it. I never could understand how he got such a crazy idea, even if true. Debs informed me that there would be no parade until the flag got back to him.

Six o'clock came and still no flag. The Norskes were desperate, so they caught my brother Homer, and tied him to a post in the basement of Starksen's store. He was tied hand and foot, and then the clowns had Zib Melstad and Joe Boyd for guards, each with big 2 x 4 clubs. The rest of the Norskes blocked the stairs so us "law-abiding citizens" couldn't get down to rescue Homer without a pitched battle. Rather than "rock the boat" I got the flag and the parade started. Lots of fun with no lives lost. Looked like a good compromise.

King Debs Starksen and Queen Andrina Vedvei

Halloween in Hetland —

One time some of the big boys moved George Pettis' small barn and parked it in front of the city opera house door, on main street. This was Halloween, of course. The crew dismantled a wagon running gear and put it together on top of the barn, with the wagon pole hanging over the edge of the building. Lucky the wheels didn't have any place to go or they would have rolled over the edge.

Somehow, George got the barn back on the spot east of main street where it had previously resided, so that the Pettis kids had a place to shelter their horses when they (the kids) came to school.

Another time a hard-working crew hauled cans (toilets) out to the north corner and put them in nice straight rows. I wasn't in on this, and my brothers weren't either, as our Pa always told us not to get involved in such "antics."

Debs Starksen was quite a guy to get out on Halloween and was the ringleader for the kids in town to tip over outdoor privies. He always managed to see that his own "can" stayed upright.

One Halloween, some of the boys (not me) loaded a toilet onto a flat car when a freight train was parked here in town. The "can" had been bolted to a six-cornered building used as a flour bin behind the Hartley and Nordmeyer General Store. This building would hold a carload of flour, made up in 50-pound sacks. Every fall the building would be filled, generally with Daniel Webster and Gold Coin flour. The train took it someplace, never to return. The culprits had cut the bolts that held the toilet to the building before sending it off by the Northwestern Railroad, who by the way, didn't get any payment for transporting said can to wherever it was unloaded.

Ole Peterson had come to the shop and wanted to know if he could borrow Pa's bolt clippers, as he needed to cut a couple of bolts. Pa told him not to break them. Of course Ole knew how to use them, and that was no problem. The day after Halloween, Ole brought them back, with a chunk broken out of the cutting jaws. Some of the "wheels" that owned the building figured that maybe, just maybe, Pa was in on the moving exodus, as he was the only one in town with a bolt cutter. Pa knew that Ole was in on it, but kept quiet.

Pa and Henry Mauch were on the town board. One Halloween they asked if I wanted to be a cop to see that nothing was done in town. They would pay two bucks for patrolling the streets. I told them I would, if I could have Tommy Thompson to be a cop, too. Henry said, "Dale, he's the worst of the bunch." I told him to trust my judgment, and Henry finally said OK, if I knew what I was doing. I asked Tommy if he wanted to make two bucks being a cop. He sure would, as two dollars was a lot of money in those days. We made billy clubs, and were ready for action. I didn't tell you that Tommy was the leader of the kids we were to watch. They didn't have a leader, as Tommy served notice on them that we would beat them over the head with our billy clubs. Without a leader, the crew didn't know what to do. We kept watch on them while they contemplated what to do, in their headquarters in the haymow of Dutcher's barn. At 3 AM, one of the would-be gang members decided they didn't dare buck the law – us – and speaking to the others, said "The Hell with it – let's go home." Mission accomplished, and no damage done!

Chapter 10
Characters of All Kinds

Top: Obbie with Terri Andersen
Bottom left: Enough snow for you yet?
Bottom right: Dale loves Hetland!

Characters of All Kinds

One morning Lewis Crandall (L. A.) came into the Post Office and got his mail. A woman came in to the Post Office, and Lewis tipped his hat to her and said "Good morning." Rose Crandall, his wife, retorted: "You old fool, I slept with you last night." He hadn't noticed who she was. After all, it was only 10 am.

Crandalls had a wood burning stove in their kitchen, and the stovepipe went along the ceiling going to the chimney. One day, Rose really fired up the stove, and the stovepipe got red hot. This being about ten in the morning, Lewis was still getting his beauty sleep in the bed upstairs. Rose said "I hollered at the old fool to get up as the house was about to burn down." Lewis didn't get excited and by the time he had gotten dressed and come downstairs the hot pipes were back to normal and the home was still intact.

Lewis always called Pa "Andersen." He came into the shop one morning all excited and told Pa, "Andersen, do you know what Rose called me this morning?" Pa asked him what. He replied, "A diddle ass." Need I say more? Lewis was a college graduate, having gotten a diploma from Eastern Normal, now known as Dakota State, in Madison, SD.

My brother Homer (Hobo) and Lewis were on the road south of Lake Preston. Lewis was pulling his corn sheller behind his old Chevrolet car as he always did, because he didn't have a tractor. Homer looked back and told Lewis he had better pull over to the side of the road, as someone wanted to pass. Lewis pulled over, and the corn sheller passed them and went into the ditch. It had come loose from the car hitch. No big deal, "just one of those things."

The same two were returning home after dark, and every other car would put their lights on bright. Those of you who knew Crandall would realize the language he used then! Homer told him it would help if he dimmed his lights. Lewis couldn't understand that, as he thought the lights should come back to bright mode by themselves. "Not so," Homer told him, so the problem was fixed.

Another time, Lewis rolled his corn sheller over on the corner south of Hetland. I asked him what happened. He told me he was coming from the west and when he made the turn into town the sheller rolled over. Then he said, "I was only going thirty-five miles an hour." Can you imagine taking the corner going thirty five miles an hour, even with a car and no sheller? We put dual wheels on to stop that nonsense. Even that didn't stop the rollovers, as Lewis parked the sheller too high up on a cob pile, and the wheels settled into the cobs and it rolled over on its side. Lewis was just far enough away from the sheller or he would have been a "goner."

Pa and I built a big sawmill for Crandall, and did he have a field day sawing up trees of all sizes. He had a blade that was 4 or 5 feet across, so he could handle most any tree. One time the long drive belt came off the tractor pulley and knocked Lewis flat on his back. Those of us who saw it laughed, but it was no laughing matter as he could have been killed, just like that.

Frank Cleveland was an old settler from "old Vermont" as he always called it. He evidently had been around tobacco fields so knew how the stuff grew. One day he came from the Post Office with a big package under his arm. We wanted to know what that was. He opened it, and it was rolls of leaf tobacco, so he offered everyone a chew. I figured my age was against me, so I'd better not risk a chew. Lewis Crandall was there, and I doubt very much if he had ever indulged in anything like this. "Let me try a little of it," he told Frank. I might add that by now I was inclined to sit down in the chair by the stove and enjoy myself, one way or another. The first thing I knew, before I really had gotten settled down for my siesta, Lewis came on a fast walk over to the chair, pale as a sheet, and said, "My God, boy, get up and let me sit down!" The way he looked, I scrambled out of the chair as fast as I could, because he looked really peaked around the gills. Then we wanted to know if we should carry him home to Rose, his wife, so she could see what a little pinch of tobacco did to her pride and joy. He survived, but I'll bet he never tried anything like that again. I don't think the state knew about Frank getting this "weed" in the mail, so there wasn't any tax to be collected, either. What a loss.

Frank Cleveland and Pa went to some so-called quack doctor, or bone cracker, as they were called. They went to Marion, SD which was the headquarters of the bone cracker. Frank walked into the doctor's office, leaning on a cane. After a couple of leg pulls, he walked out of the building carrying the cane under his arm. Boy, all the waiting patients were dumbfounded that he walked in with a cane, and walked out not using it. The next morning, Frank came into the shop, and we wanted to know how it happened that now he was using the cane. "I just wanted to show you that I could walk without it," was his reply

Spit. That reminds me of an old farmer who lived south of town, who always had tobacco running down his chin. Don't know if he was level headed or not, as we didn't check to see if both sides of the flow were even or not. This guy drove a Model T coupe, and in those days there wasn't a door on the driver's side to get in and out of. You had to slide across the seat in order to drive. This Norske came into Ole Anderson's garage one day and wanted his brake, clutch and reverse bands tightened up. If those bands, as they were called, got worn too much, then the car didn't want to move or stop, as the case might be. Ole told the proud owner of the Model T Ford that he would tighten the bands if the floorboards were taken out so he could get at the source of trouble. The reasoning behind this was that this old boy had to spit so often that when he was driving the car he couldn't get the window down soon enough in order to spit out of the window. To save all that trouble, (in those days you had to crank the window up and down, no automation like today) this old boy had a better solution. He would spit the tobacco down beside his left leg and deposit the works on the floorboard. It being winter, all of this "junk" froze, so that there was a pile of tobacco spit about four inches high on the floorboards. That's why Ole wouldn't start the job until the old boy lifted out the three wooden boards.

Later on, this guy went broke farming, and moved to Sioux Falls and got a job in a café, and of all things, he was a dishwasher. His neighbors decided that they were not going to eat in any café with their friend as a dishwasher. I might add that this character was what was called a "wet milker." In other words, the milker would sit down beside the cow, on his little one-legged stool with the milk pail between his legs. When he was ready to start extracting the milk from old Bossy, he would spit on his hands, supposedly to get a better grip on the cow's projecting nipples. Of course at times, some of the spit would accidentally go into the milk pail. But what the heck, the pail would get full of that white stuff that much faster.

Chris Brixen was an old Dane who lived up north of town, and he was quite a character. Pa knew him in Denmark, as they lived in the same community. Chris had a hard time talking English, and I don't know if his Danish dialect was any better. When he went to buy oil for his car, he would tell the garage man that he wanted some "slip easy for enyine yoints." He had the right idea, because the oil made the engine joints slip easier. Back in those days, some of the farmers and others smoked pipes. Some were corncob pipes, as they were the cheapest, and others were ritzier and cost more. Brixen chewed tobacco, as well as smoked a cob pipe. When the pipes got too clogged up, the smoker would take his jack knife and cut out all of the old burned out crust from the inside of the pipe and dump it out. I have seen Chris do just that, but instead of dumping the junk out, he would cup it in his hand and throw it into his mouth and chew it. If someone else would be sitting beside him and cleaned his pipe, our old Dane would hold out his hand and get all of the droppings from the other man's pipe, and into his mouth it would go. I can't imagine how powerful that stuff was, but it didn't bother Chris at all. He enjoyed it.

Brixen used to play cards with Charlie and Annie Starksen. One time Starky and Elden were over to the Starksen's and were playing whist, which was the popular card game at that time. During one game Annie held up her hand with a card in it and shouted, "Ha, ha, I'll just put my big AH-SS on it." Brixen couldn't say ACE in English, and Annie said that was what Chris called it. Elden and Starky just about had a fit. If the old boy had won playing cards with Debs and Annie, the next day he would be sure to be in the store to see if he could start a "claahs" to show the rest how to play.

It took Cecil Crandall to imitate Brixen to a T. We always got along with Chris, in spite of his sometimes-eccentric language. He was telling me one day that he and Pa were going over to the old country. I let him know that I had better go with them. "And what for should you go along?" was his retort. "To keep you sober," was my reply. "No, by goss, you aren't going along." Neither of them went.

Bill Buhn, the owner of the hotel, had a way of playing tricks on people. He could imitate a train whistle and would do so when a group of people were waiting for a train. They would grab their stuff and head for the depot, but there was no train.

Sometimes this proprietor would put a lantern in his hard coal heater, and put red cellophane over the glass and make it look like a fire was in the stove. Somebody would give him heck when where wasn't any heat coming out. Then they would open the door of the stove and find the lantern.

He used to sit on the sidewalk uptown, all dressed up, with a fancy flat top straw hat on his head. He had a long cane fishing pole, which he would hold with both hands like he was ready to catch a fish. The line would be way out in the street, with a bobber on it. People would come walking along, stop and look at Bill sitting there in rapt anticipation of catching a fish. They would look out at the bobber and ask Bill what he was fishing for. "Suckers" was his everyday answer. Guess he caught a few that way, but never heard that he broke his line landing a "big sucker."

Floyd Grems was a beekeeper in town we called Buzz Buzz. You could say hello to him and say, "It's a nice day." Nearly always his reply was, "What's good about it?" He always needed two more weeks to get his bee work done, but when that time was up, he needed two more weeks.

He wasn't married, and told me he went with a girl a few times and then she began to talk marriage. Buzz Buzz said that was time to leave her alone!

He could be an obnoxious pest but was well read, and kept up on what was going on in the world. One time in the pool hall he told us something, and as usual no one believed him. We gave him such a bad time that he went home, which was just up the street, and get the paper with the article in it. He took off like a rabbit to prove he was right. He had been reading the papers on one of the tables, and we had seen the article in the paper, too. We knew he was right. After he had left, we took the paper with the article in it and put it in the back room. Finally he came back, fuming and without a paper. He proceeded to go through all of the papers on the table, and still couldn't prove he was right. Boy, he was really upset, and we still kept on bedevilling him that he didn't know what he was talking about. He never did prove that he was right, because he couldn't find the lost paper. Doubt if he slept well that night, thinking about showing us the article. It must have been that we were sneaky or heartless with old Buzz Buzz.

Art Calvet, the depot agent, had a bottle gas stove, and Byron Foss, the school superintendent, had an electric stove. They would argue over which stove operated the cheapest. Cal finally turned out the pilot light on his stove and made his wife, Blanche, use a match to light the burners. He would even go over and read Foss' meter to see that Byron wasn't lying. Never knew who won out.

Cal bought a new Plymouth car, and as was the case with those models of Plymouths, it wouldn't start in cold weather. Cal would brag about all of the virtues of his new car, but we gave him both barrels when we saw him getting towed down the alley to get it started. He had given the tower orders not to go up on Main Street, but to stay in the back alley so no one would see what was going on. We knew, and didn't let Cal forget that we had seen what was going on, even though the car was being pulled in the back alley.

One time, in the spring, Calvet dug out his old bathing suit and went to Lake Preston to go swimming in the city pool. Every time he got up on the diving board to dive he would get catcalls and whistles and clapping of hands. The more the crowd cheered the more puffed up Cal became. After it was all over, he realized his bathing suit was full of holes. The moths had eaten it up. The cheering didn't have anything to do with his diving. He couldn't understand why somebody didn't tell him about the holes. Why should they?

It was a good show! I don't think he ever went back into the pool again, if my memory serves me right.

Pete Gaasedelen and his brother Nels each had a saloon on Main Street, side by side, where the Legion Hall now stands. They made scads of money, as the other towns were dry, so those two made cash keeping the Arlington and Lake Preston drinkers supplied. The local paper, the *Hetland New Era*, would even print that, "so and so from Arlington or Preston had been visiting in town." Most everyone knew what the visit was for – they were out for firewater. Pete and his wife Inga lived upstairs over their saloon. They had a big bay window, which extended way out over the sidewalk, so they had a good view in three directions when they sat in this big window space. Boy, that is what we would call being uptown.

Joe Burcham, who lived on Main Street south of the tracks, had a similar idea, only not such a fancy setup. Joe had a big mirror outside his west windows, and had it adjusted so that he could sit in his big chair in the northwest corner of his living room and look in the mirror and see everything going on uptown on Main Street. Boy, Joe should have gotten a patent on that feat of ingenuity. He didn't have to turn his head sideways to keep up with the goings-on in town. He got many hours of enjoyment out of this setup when he was older, and no longer able to get outside like he used to.

Now, getting back to Pete and Inga. These two people were what we would call "loners." Pete would come downstairs and sit on the bum bench and visit with whoever was there to visit with. I think Pa was as close to being a friend of Pete as anyone else in town. These two just didn't want to be friendly with anyone. They didn't have to worry about finances, as they came out of the saloon business "well fixed." Pa and Pete, both being Danes, would get into some real arguments, as you might expect. Pete was a great big guy and always – and I mean always – wore a black outfit, not a suit, but anyway it was black. We never knew if it was the same outfit he wore every day, or whether he had a change of clothes. One day in the shop, there was a salesman who had finished up on Pa's order and he was ready to leave. Pete and Pa got into a heck of an argument, as they quite often did. They were giving each other a working over until they ran out of steam, and Pete finally left for home. This poor salesman told Pa, "Well, I guess I can leave now." Pa wanted to know what he meant, "leave now?" "Well," he said, "I couldn't leave when you two were going at it. I knew there would be a fight, and I thought I could stop it!" Boy, he didn't know Hetland people.

Once Pete came into the shop and told Pa, "Ever since I came to town, they (the townspeople) have tried to hang me, and now, by God, they want me to buy the rope!" He left this earth without a rope around his neck.

Inga Gaasedelen was something else, too. I never could figure out how she and Pete got together unless they figured that there was no one else out there like them, so they might as well give up looking and tie the knot. In this way, they would save somebody else from having to put up with such characters. Inga was ahead of her time, as we never knew from week to week what color her hair would be. It was never, ever one color. It would be two- or three-toned, and varied in color. She would be in style today.

I don't know if Inga ever visited with any other women in town. However, she would come across the street to Tom Anderson's store, when and if they needed anything to eat. But she would come into the store on other occasions. Tom had a bath scale on the floor in front of one of the shelves in front of the outside door. That was convenient for anyone who forgot to check his or her weight at home. Besides that, I have never seen any other store with a scale inside the door that you could step on, free of charge, to see how you were doing, weight wise. That was just one of the many quirks that our upright businessmen did for their valued customers.

Inga would go over to the store several times a day, not to buy anything, but to test out that scale. I'll fill you in on why she would do this. In the first place, it didn't cost her anything; secondly, she had the walking exercise to and from; and thirdly, she wanted to be sure to check the scale for accuracy. It varied on her from time to time. Sometimes the walk across the street caused her to gain weight from the last reading. At other times, she would lose weight from her sojourn. I've seen her step up on that scale, look at her weight, step off from it and then climb back up again to see if she had the same reading. Then she would head for home, but in a few hours, back she would come. What the poor woman didn't know, and it was driving her nuts, was that on the side of the scale was a little adjustment wheel, and you probably guessed what went on. When somebody in the store saw her coming, they would reach down and turn the scale so that the scale either showed more or less than the actual weight. The poor woman never caught on to why her weight varied from hour to hour. I wasn't in on this sort of a game.

Pete Gaasedelen and Pa were having a discussion about something. Pa asked Pete if it wouldn't be a good idea to pool their money and then divide it two ways. "No," Pete said, "I think it's better the way it is now. Only one of us has to work." It wasn't Pete who had to work, as he had made his retirement money running a saloon. Pa kept on working, and Pete was still not working. No justice at all, as there are some that work, and some that don't. I'd rather work if I could, as I don't think the Lord put me on this earth to sit on my butt, but I don't have much choice now. Time marches on, and waits for no man, or woman, either.

Pete Gaasedelen lost his life one evening on the railroad tracks east of the depot. He liked to get his exercise walking the tracks, and this night it was really dark when he was hit by the section mens' engine-powered handcar. Finished him off with one bang. He wore a hearing aid, but always turned it off to save the battery as well as money.

Henry Mauch, the banker, was a kind old soul, and he had several tin cans with all kinds of old coins and money from foreign countries. He would let us kids go out in the back room of the bank and we would ooh and ahhh for a long time, looking over the coins and checking them out in a coin book, to see how much they were worth. We would never get tired of going back and checking out the coins to see if any new ones had been added. I never knew of any kid taking a coin and I know that Henry trusted all of us, otherwise we wouldn't have had the chance to look over such a large collection of coins.

The Bank

When Arlington had a golf course over by Volga, only the elite played, or that's what the consensus was. Ralph Mauch, our banker's son, who we called "Gunder" - why, I don't know - went over and played a few times. However, he made the mistake one day of coming uptown with his golf knickers on. None of these professionals from Arlington would be caught dead without being properly clothed before they went out to chase that little ball around the golf course. We called it "cow pasture pool." I don't know if those were derogatory words or not. Anyway, here Gunder was, among his cronies, or his friends, when Obbie Melstad came along. Obbie took one look at his friend's fancy attire and quietly told him in no uncertain terms, "If you come uptown again with that outfit on, we'll take them off of you, right here on Main Street." How's that for an ultimatum? Gunder never came uptown again with that outfit on! He told me afterwards that "By G–, they would have done it, too!" He would have looked cute, running for home without any pants on. At least he got the message and didn't dare to chance losing his attire.

Obbie Melstad used to smoke carp in an old refrigerator. He would generally use corncobs, and sometimes some fruitwood - plum or apple. One time he came down to the shop with a couple of samples for Howard Karban and me to taste. He had enough left over, so he gave the two samples to Howard to take home to his wife, Ardis. I asked Obbie which fish was cooked with white corncobs, and which was cooked with the red cobs. We told Howard to keep the fish separate, and ask Ardis which tasted the best - the one cooked with white cobs, or the one cooked with the red cobs. He told us he might forget which one was which, but we told him not to forget, as we wanted to know what she thought. She is a good Norwegian, and an excellent cook. We never had a report back, and to this day I am still in a quandary as to which was best. Oh well, Obbie is gone, and I don't think it matters that much after all these years. Carp never were very good, anyway.

One time Ole Peterson came up town holding a skunk by the tail. Carried him up and down the sidewalk. If you ever saw people move, we moved. Ole said the skunk couldn't spray as long as his feet came off the ground. We didn't tell him to put the critter down to find out if that was the correct diagnosis. Never heard how the skunk made out when he was "let down."

Sig Peterson used to have a bunch of skunks in a pen by their house. It was fun to watch them when they would try to squirt on us, as they had been fixed so they wouldn't smell. They surely acted frustrated when they couldn't defend themselves when they saw danger coming. Don't know if the mother skunk told them when she saw danger approaching, "Let us spray!" A preacher under the same circumstances prayed, "God save me and mine."

One time Sig Peterson was driving for some hunters and the farmer caught Sig for trespassing. He was hauled into court to supposedly plead guilty. Instead, Sig packed a suitcase and went to court in DeSmet. We told him we would come and look at him through the bars in the county jail. When the judge and lawyers saw him come down the courtroom aisle with his suitcase they huddled and threw out the case. Not guilty! They didn't want to go to the expense of giving him room and board.

Chris Rasmussen - we called him Chris Rass - was an old bachelor who would come to the BS shop. He drove a team of mules, and Pa would "work him over" about not getting married when he had those mules. Chris would give me a nickel and tell me to go uptown and buy something, as he didn't want me to hear all of "this stuff" as he called it. You guessed it. When Chris came, I came too, and always got a nickel to get something to eat.

Pewee Scherkenback brought a sack of assorted knives to the shop to get sharpened. He ran the hotel, and the knives were dull. We sharpened them and Pewee went uptown with them, but stopped at the drug store to see Spot Layman and left the sack on the "bum bench" in front of Starksen's store. Debs came out of the store and saw the sack sitting there. Being an inquisitive Norwegian, he looked to see what was in the sack. Seeing the knives, he took them to the back of the store, opened a gallon of red paint and proceeded to "dip" all of the knives in the paint and then put them back in the sack. Pewee eventually came out of the drugstore and took his prized knives over to the hotel. He came back in a hurry to cuss Debs out when he discovered the painted cutlery. He was lucky that he discovered the ruse before the paint had time to dry.

When Gub Stangland was Minnehaha County Sheriff in Sioux Falls, he would stop in to see me any time he was in our country. We of course had to go uptown for coffee (I drank milk). One spring, he was here and we went up to the café for lunch. Several federal game wardens were there when we walked in. There were some more Hetlandites there, as well. Anyway, we started to work Gub over about all the lawbreakers in Sioux Falls, and he wasn't doing anything about it. Those game wardens, many of them who knew Gub, were looking cross eyed at the way we were pouring it on to that poor sheriff. Finally he turned to the wardens and told them, "Don't pay any attention to these guys, this is where I grew up." Then I popped up and told the rest of the gang, "Let's go out and shoot some geese, as long as all of the wardens are drinking coffee." They didn't think much of Gub's friends.

When Gub was dying of cancer in Sioux Falls, I would quite often go down to see him. He had his bed set up in the front room of their home, and had nurses to help out with his care. The last time I was to see him, the poor guy couldn't talk. I told the nurse that I went to school with Gub for 11 years, and then I decided that was long enough, so I graduated and left the other class to shift for themselves. Gub couldn't comment, but he really grunted and showed that he enjoyed company, even though he was speechless.

He always told us that he had red hair because his Ma had accidentally spilled peroxide on it when he was a baby. Could be, but there were also some other redheads in the family, so it must have been a coincidence if all had the same experience. In Sioux Falls, they naturally called Wilbur (Gub) Big Red, and his brother Eider, Little Red. Incidentally, if you have ever read the *Ole and Lena* books with jokes about Norwegians, the author is this same Eider – "Red" Stangland, one of our Hetland boys. We always told him that he laughed all the way to the bank after selling a million or more of these books. If you haven't read them, I would suggest you look them up. He always gave Eva and me autographed books. He was a Hetland booster and never let anyone forget that he was from Hetland. He was also in the clown unit of the El Riad Shrine, and he has now gone home to his Maker.

When Delbert Zeller and I were initiated into the Shrine in Sioux Falls, I was talking to a boy on the street, when here came a clown and looked at my name tag. "Ah, you are from Hetland." "Ya," I told him, "you little red-headed Norwegian." It was our Brother Eider in his clown get up. He was a joyous Norske.

One time the fellows were in a big argument in front of Starksen's store. Debs Starksen finally got frustrated with the way it was going. He was probably getting the worst of the argument. He went to the back of the store and grabbed a 5-gallon fire extinguisher, and as Happy Larson got into his car, Debs sprayed the inside of the car and Happy with the dope. Happy grabbed the fire extinguisher and stepped inside the door of the store and proceeded to spray the inside of the store, even though there was no fire. Some mess it was, too!

Another time Debs tried to sell one of his customers a new pair of overalls, but the prospect wouldn't part with the money. Debs wanted to get rid of a pair of overalls, so he poured acid in one of the back pockets of the customer's no-good overalls. Alas, needless to say, Debs sold a new pair of overalls. Quick sale!

Here is an example to show you what kind of people we had in town. Hans Tande owned one of the elevators here in town, and also bought fur-bearing animals. Idor Hesby sold him some creature that he had caught, and Hans paid him for it. Idor was satisfied with the money he had received for the animal. A few days later, here came Hans looking for Idor. Hans gave Idor $1.25 more for the animal, because he had sold it for that much more. He was as honest as the day was long, and he wanted Idor to have the extra money, even though the deal was final.

Chapter 11
Have You Heard About...
(Town stories)

Top: Sign near US Highway 14 at the Hetland Corner
Bottom: Centennial Mens' Sextet: Eva, Evald Gaard, Gordon Mydland, Lloyd Gaard, Mayo Nielson, Erling Tenneboe and Dale

Have You Heard About...

Celebrating the Bicentennial –

Back in 1976, when the United States celebrated 200 years of freedom, we had a wonderful celebration in town commemorating the big occasion. The Hetland Legion and Auxiliary, the Hetland Congregational Church, North Preston and Lake Whitewood Lutheran Churches and the town of Hetland decided to sponsor a celebration. When these people sponsor something they go "all out." For two or three weeks, farmers and townspeople cut trees, hauled junk, mowed everything that needed mowing, and in general made the town shine like it has never shined before. An ad was put in the Preston and Arlington papers that there would be a celebration in Hetland on July 4th, with fireworks, lunches, ball game and good fellowship. We took up donations to raise $1500 for fireworks.

The 4th of July came, bright and clear, just as we had hoped and prayed it would. This was on a Sunday and benches and chairs were put out on the school lawn, along with a piano, and we had a sellout crowd for church service that morning. I'm sure that the old-timers who used to live here and had gone to their reward were overwhelmed with pride as they watched from the "other side" how everything went so smoothly. Main Street and the street west toward the schoolhouse were roped off, and people could feel free to let their kids roam at will with no danger of being cut down by a speeder. The North Preston lunch stand was set up in the trees where the old drugstore used to be. It was given a coat of red, white and blue paint in honor of the special occasion. Hamburgers sold for a dime, pop for a nickel and pie for a dime. Whole families came for picnics, and one band of Norskes had 75 relatives who brought their noon meal to celebrate a family get-together. I don't know if they were proud to be Norwegian or if they were celebrating Leif Erickson finding South Dakota.

Picnic tables were all over town, and everything was perfect for the big event. There were cars everywhere. Elden, my brother, was Sheriff at the time and he was here but not in uniform. He told me if he had known there would be a crowd like this he would have brought the patrol car from DeSmet. I told him we didn't need it, as we didn't even have one cop and didn't need one. No one got out of line, and as far as we knew, there was nothing stronger than good old Hetland water to quench the thirst of the multitude.

There were no drunks that we knew of, and everyone parked where our parking crew told them to, except one wise guy who thought he knew better than the director. He backed over a small culvert south of the school, but luckily there was no casualty.

To climax the day, the $1500 worth of fireworks were set off by a crew of demolition experts who had the big explosives dug down into the ground near the "Dago Pond" south of the schoolhouse. At that time, $1,500 bought a lot of fireworks, so there was lots of noise and excitement when they were shot off. There were cars parked all around town from Lake Ole to Boyd's slough, the Hetland Cemetery, and along Highway 14 south of town, as there was "no more room in the inn." It was a gigantic undertaking and a marvelous success as about 5,000 people, <u>yes - 5,000</u>, were here to celebrate with us. There was practically no advertising, except by word of mouth.

The lunch stand made about $200, which was divided up among the sponsoring organizations, and all we had hoped for was to break even and not go into the red.

The next day everything was "all quiet on the western front," and it all seemed like a wonderful dream. It showed what could happen in a small town when friends from the surrounding country were willing to pitch in and cooperate to make an event a "howling" success. There was no trash to clean up, and the garden planted in the lot south of the town hall wasn't even trampled. Everyone respected someone else's property. It was a wonderful experience, and showed what the people of this small rural community of Hetland could do when everyone "put their shoulder to the wheel."

Hetland on National Television –

Back in 1986, if you had come to the Hetland Congregational Church on a Sunday morning, and I told you that NBC television was going to be in church that day, what would have been your reaction? Ha-ha, what else is new? You're pulling our leg! Big deal! Hot air, etc. Those of you who know me know that I wouldn't pull your leg – unless that was necessary. In this case, it wasn't. Three men from NBC came to church, and Hetland was on its way to stardom via NBC-TV's 1986 show!

This crew came directly from Disneyland in California to Hetland, SD. Do you suppose that was quite a change for that TV crew? Ray Farkas, the head honcho, had called Eva on Saturday and told her what was going on. She filled me in on the deal when I came from work. Ray asked her if I would talk and she told him she thought so – another time when my "pride and joy" volunteered for me! That was OK, as they

Dale on the Centennial float during the parade

were easy to get along with. Anyway, the three headquartered at our place, so we got to know them very well after they had been in town for several weeks.

NBC wanted to get a picture of what the depression had done to the small towns in rural America. They had checked Minnesota, Iowa, Nebraska and South Dakota. Someone in Mitchell at the TV station suggested they come to Hetland. They took pictures and had interviews day after day, and then flew in a Norwegian, Lucky Severson, from New York City to double-check how things were going. I told him that it was a heck of a note to bring a Norwegian out here to talk to some Danes and other oddballs. Then my curiosity got the best of me, so I wanted to know how he was named Lucky. He said his dad was playing poker the night he was born, and had been lucky. That was how that came about. Didn't know whether to believe him or not, but I didn't question his answer.

He interviewed Eider (Red) Stangland and me to get the lowdown on the community. We sat on the bank steps, so everybody could get in on the big deal. Eider thought maybe we could get a McDonald's in town with only one arch. They were interested in any bad deals in town, and I told Ray Farkas that we didn't have any feuds like the Hatfields and McCoys.

One day, Ray asked Eva if she could get a few Hetland High School kids together for pictures and to sing the school song. She said she thought she could, and he told her three or four would be enough. When we got together there were more than 50 people! Ray hollered at the cameraman to get the big lens, as there was a mob here! Eva played the piano in the east upstairs assembly, and we sang the school song with plenty of "vim and vigor." It made the old school proud of its graduates. Then we went outside and gave the school yells, led by former cheerleaders who know how to get the best results to spur the old Red and Black Broncos to "clean up" the opposition. The Hetland teams didn't take the back seat for anyone else, and we had the trophies as evidence to show that we were telling the truth. Tales of what we had done weren't just a bunch of hot air!

After the show aired, Eva and I had calls from all over the US and Canada from people that said they had seen Hetland and the two of us on TV. Ray Farkas called us later to say that NBC had more comments about the Hetland episode than anything they had done before.

The crew was here for several weeks in order to make a 15-minute show. It was a wonderful experience, and we enjoyed it. Eva and I were in Sioux Falls a week or so after the show. I was getting gas and a fellow came up to me and said, "I saw you on TV the other night." The girls in the Medical Clinic were giving me a bad time with the comment, "Here comes that TV star," when I walked in.

Myrna heard the camera and soundmen talking on our front step. One of them commented, "Wouldn't it be nice to live here?" Ray Farkas told us they were missing something, living in the city, compared to our way of life. I told him I wouldn't trade my growing up in Hetland for any place in the world. He said he believed that.

Sometime later, Ray's daughter was in South Dakota campaigning for a vice presidential candidate whose grandparents had lived in White. The girl was staying in Brookings at the Holiday Inn. Ray lived in Washington, DC, and called the motel to talk to his daughter. The desk girl said she had just left for White for a campaign meeting. Ray wanted to know where White was, and the girl told him so many miles from Sioux Falls and Brookings. Then the big city guy nearly floored her when he wanted to know where White was from Hetland. Can you imagine a fellow from DC asking such a question? Then he wanted to know if that girl knew Dale and Eva Andersen in Hetland. She said she did! It was LuAnn Jensen, who was living with her husband, Joe, in Homer and Lu Andersen's farm place. She couldn't get over it – how far from Hetland?!

132 *BS Stands for Blacksmith*

Top: East side of south Main Street, ca 1908
Bottom: Morris Andersen residence, 1990

Have You Heard About... 133

Top: Telephone office, pumphouse, restaurant and hotel and Ralph's Garage, ca 1990
Middle: Legion Hall, 1990
Bottom: Post Office, ca 1990

Back in the "good old days" the streets would be lined with cars, and before that with horse rigs, especially on Wednesday and Saturday nights. Albert Dahms had a special spot in front of the store that was most recently the Post Office. He would be parked there at 6 PM as regular as a clock. Woe be it to anyone who accidentally parked in that spot before Albert got there. I suppose it was like having a reserved church pew. Back in those days, we had a popcorn vendor making fresh popcorn. You could get your shoes shined, AND I MEAN SHINED, for a nickel. Haircuts were a quarter and when one of our barbers cut your hair the style of those days, you didn't need to furnish the bowl to go around your head to see if the cut was even, as he had the straight line method down to a "T"! It looked just like a "bowl line." We looked sharp too!

On Sunday mornings, in case your shoes needed touching up or you didn't get them shined the night before, you could still get a shine for a nickel. Chuck Starksen would also sell one of the Minneapolis papers for a nickel. It was twice as big as an ordinary paper. I remember one time Harrison Ballou, one of our upright citizens, told Chuck he would buy one if he had change for a $20 dollar bill. Chuck told him he didn't have the change but would give him a check for $19.95. That was fast thinking on Chuck's part and he had the money in the bank, too. But, alas, you guessed it, the prospective customer didn't have the twenty dollars. No sale!

In earlier days, Bill Buhn used to run the hotel here in town. They had a big cast iron cooker like they used to scald hogs in. They would fill that up with meat, potatoes and vegetables every day to feed their clientele. They fed about 150 people each meal when Hetland was a thriving town.

Salesmen would come into town on the morning passenger train at about 6:30, stay in town or rent a livery rig and go out into the country to peddle their wares. We had four passenger trains a day, so if a salesman came into town in the morning, either on the 6 o'clock from the east, or the 10 o'clock from the west, he had a chance to leave at night to go either way.

Snort Buhn was one of our early barbers. One day, Debs Starksen went over to the shop and asked Snort if he would shave one side of his face for half price. Snort said, "You bet - which side?" "The outside," Debs replied. "OK, get up in the chair," Snort said, and lathered him up. Then he reached down in the bottom of the drawer to get a razor, and proceeded to shave the old boy with the dullest, most worn-out straight-edge razor he had. One big howl, "I'll pay full price," so Debs paid a dime for the shave instead of a nickel.

We had the best hardware store in the county in Hetland - the Barber and Johnson store. They had the International Harvester dealership, and more than once us kids would go up to the store and help put a grain binder together. It came with each piece separate, and the parts were in wooden boxes. Jim Barber was more apt to be the foreman than Charlie Johnson. There were binder parts all over the floor, and I think that Jim could almost put the machine together in his sleep. We got so we would tighten bolts and whatever else needed to be done. We didn't think about getting any pay for doing this.

You could go into the store and ask for most anything, and Jim and Charlie would have it. At one time, if you wanted a casket to put a "stiff" in they had several upstairs you could choose from. Or, if you wanted a shotgun, rifle, BB gun or chamberpot to carry out to the backhouse, they were there to oblige. When hunting season came, they would have a duck boat in the big front window with duck decoys, rushes, guns and shells, so you could buy what you needed. A license cost a buck, and you could hunt and fish with it. They got a dime for making it out. The First State Bank got the first hunting licenses, and I would start checking the bank after the 4th of July so I'd be sure I got a license in time.

There were shelves on the north wall of the hardware store with dozens of varnished pull-out drawers, or boxes, with a picture on each to show its contents. They were loaded with different things to sell. These shelves reached from about two feet from the floor all the way to the ceiling. A varnished wooden ladder hung down from a track above. It was on rollers, and could be moved along the shelves to the right box or boxes. The next step was to climb the ladder and get what the customer wanted.

If you only needed one or two of something, that's what you could buy. You didn't have to buy a whole package, like you do today. It was service with a smile.

Some smart guy invented self-starters to put on tractors and cars, instead of having to lean on the crank to get them started. Our engineer, Charley, who with his partner Jim, were selling IHC tractors, etc. would try to talk the would-be tractor purchaser out of buying a tractor with a self starter. That was just a waste of money. Imagine today, given a choice between a crank and a self-starter – who would want a crank?

They also sold oil heaters – real good ones too – two-burner stoves called Superflame. Some people would take the "guts" out of their old coal burning furnaces and these two boys would install a Superflame without a case on it inside the shell of the furnace. Then they would put the old tin back like it was originally, and that made a good furnace, and it was still in the basement. Then, wonder of wonders, for 25 bucks they could put a thermostat in the outfit, and the heat could be controlled from upstairs. No need to go down in the basement to change for more or less heat. What do you suppose? Charley fixed up his old furnace like that, but he wasn't about to spend any money to make it convenient to change the stove setting. He told us he would rather go downstairs and adjust the heat, rather than spend $25. I told him I'd never heard of such a crazy idea, as he got those outfits for cost, so he wasn't out that much money. No go, he wouldn't change his mind and break down and get modern. After all, oil heat in itself was a far cry from having to go downstairs and shovel in coal. Maybe Charley figured he could get his daily exercise, going up and down the stairs.

One time, a bunch of us were standing around the store and the weather wasn't too good. Charley looked out and said aloud that anybody must be a fool to stay in this country. Jim had a profound reply, "Never mind, wait awhile and you will be gone." All of us got a laugh out of that, and Jim wasn't stretching the truth, either.

Charley Johnson was the unofficial weatherman. In other words, he didn't collect any money for doing this. His gauge always showed less rain than what the ordinary gauges showed, his being more scientific. Charley, being a graduate engineer (with a slip of paper from the "cow college" in Brookings to prove it) had concocted an elaborate system to find out how much rain had fallen. In other words, you didn't stick a yardstick into a coffee can full of water to know that you had less than a foot of rain falling on the parched land.

I'll try to explain what I'm getting at. Up on top of the elevator shaft, the highest part of the roof on the hardware store, he had about a four-inch funnel hooked onto a pipe going through the roof of the store. The pipe was connected to a big container down below in the store. After a rain, our weatherman had to climb the stairs to the second floor to retrieve the water that was stored up, for him to deduce how much rain had fallen. From here on out, I can't explain how he came up with the magic figure, whether it was a trace of rain or several inches. He, being the engineer, had a series of procedures to go by, and then he would announce the verdict. Of course, we always doubted the accuracy of this so-called "wonder of the world" rain gauge.

One night we had rain, not much, and the more daring climbers in town (not me!) climbed up to the rain spout and poured extra rain water down the tube. The next morning, our whiz kid went up the stairs to check and write down his findings to report to posterity. Lo and behold, the gauge had run over! Now – what was he to do? In no way could he account for the overflow water. He began to wonder if he had dumped the gauge from the last rain. By now, he was in a hurry to check his "rain diary." Nope, he had emptied out the previous rain. Out the door he went, and down home in a quick hurry to check out, of all things, a coffee can in his back yard. We didn't know that he would ever stoop to check the water with a measuring stick in a coffee can, of all things! Guess he had this can out in case some disaster befell his prized water gauge. Of course there wasn't any amount of water in the can, so finally, for fear that our stalwart businessman would have a stroke, we told him what had transpired. He sat down in the chair to rest and relax after all the extra excitement that morning.

Lewis Crandall used to have the agency to sell Huber tractors. They are no longer in business, and I don't know who took them over. Later on, Crandall had a threshing machine and threshed for the farmers. He had a great big Huber tractor to pull the threshing machine. This tractor had huge steel wheels with lots of lugs in the drivers. They were eight or ten feet high. The machine operator had to climb up several steps to get up onto a platform where all the controls were. There was a steel ceiling over the whole tractor to keep out the sun's rays. To start the outfit, there was a big wrench several feet long that went down and some way latched on to something to start the tractor. The tractor operator sat up there to shut the outfit down, if necessary. Incidentally, this is how his son Howard Crandall got his nickname of Huber.

Lewis would put his hat into the separator to see if any of the grain was going over the sieves into the straw pile. My brother, Elden, was the flunky one year to help Crandall keep the machine going. This youngest brother of mine must have been related to me. One day, when Crandall wasn't looking, he took a scoop shovel, filled it with grain, and put the grain-loaded shovel inside the machine. Lewis came around to see how everything was going and to use his hat to see if any grain was being lost. Elden pulled the shovel out, cleared off the straw, and lo and behold, somehow the shovel was full of grain. Crandall held up his hands and hollered to Pete Nelson to shut everything down. Something was definitely wrong, if that much grain was going to waste.

When everything stopped, Lewis told Elden to crawl inside the machine to see what was the matter. My brother didn't relish crawling into all that straw, especially when he knew that nothing was wrong. Rather than mess up his clothes, he had to confess to Lewis how he had pulled the wool over the boss' eyes. Pete threw the lever and the threshing started, but at least the bundle pitchers had gotten a rest.

Tractors in those days had babbit bearings, not like the bearings today. Crandall had torn down a worn out tractor or two. (By the way, out west of the BS shop, we still have two channel irons that came off from one of those tractors. They were the main frame of the tractor.) One day a couple of "scalpers" came to town, looking for stuff to buy. Lewis told them he had lots of babbit he would sell them. That sounded great, so they told him they would take the babbit and see about selling it and come back and give him

the money. Lewis was gullible, just like me, and took them at their word. They came down to the BS shop to see if we could use some of the metal. They wanted two cents a pound for it, so we bought it after weighing it up at 200 pounds. We paid four dollars to these two honest crooks and they left town, leaving Crandall empty handed, with no money. Pa chewed snuff, so we melted the babbit and poured it into snuffboxes, as the hot metal wouldn't burn through them. After the meltdown, we only had 150 pounds of metal, which we sold for a nickel a pound. Lewis would really complain when we sold him his own product for a nickel a pound.

I remember when the first combine came to town at the hardware store, which had the International Harvester Agency. I think it was a five- or six-footer bought by Soren Larson, who lived out on the bank of Lake Preston. The lake was dry at the time and it looked like half of the country was there to see what happened. The machine got moving and straw came out the back and grain went into the hopper. This was better than pitching bundles into a separator. Of course there were some farmers who said it wouldn't work on hilly ground, as the threshing machine had to be level. Needless to say, the combines still work on any kind of hills.

When a crew finished threshing in a field there was always some grain left on the ground where the separator stood. The grain would go to waste, so us "kids" would take a sack and put the grain into it, and go down to the Jerry Bunday elevator and maybe get 25 or 30 cents for our industrious endeavor. We didn't call this stealing, as we just went and helped ourselves before the birds filled up on oats, wheat or barley.

Threshing... note the steam engine, separator, hayrack and car

We used to have two cream stations in town buying cream from the farmers. One day, the cream station owner opened a five-gallon can of cream, and there, floating on top of the cream, was a nice big mouse, stone dead. He put the cover on the can of cream and told the farmer he couldn't buy the cream with that dead mouse in it. "You can take it out and nobody will know the difference," the farmer said, and he also said that if he had known the mouse was there he would have taken it out at home. He was mad, and grabbed the can and headed for the other cream station. The same thing happened there, but this time a state inspector walked in and sealed the can, so the mouse didn't get sold with the cream. What a loss!

My brother, Homer, helped in one of the cream stations. One day a new farmer in the area brought in a can of cream. After Homer had tested it to see how much it was worth, he made out the sales slip and asked the new customer what his name was. "Adolph Bjelke," was the reply. Homer wrote down Balke. "No, no, B A, B A," was the response from Adolph. He couldn't make Homer understand anything different than BA. Finally, in desperation, Homer gave the guy the pen to write out his name. He wrote Bjelke. How would anyone know that, as Adolph couldn't pronounce his own name and it always sounded like an A. He was a nice guy. He came into the shop one day with their aluminum kettle, full of holes. It was wartime, with no new kettles to be bought. "If you can fix it, my wife will really love you." I fixed the kettle and never heard if she loved me or not. She was a well-rounded woman.

I remember when the First State Bank here in Hetland got the first radio in town. It came in a long black box about four or five feet long, and probably ten inches square. It was an Atwater Kent, which was one of the earlier and best radios. The bank had it in the southeast room, on a long table. The first recollection I had of it being used by the general public was when the World Series was on. The New York Yankees were one team, and I'm not sure who the other one was. I was against the Yankees then, even though I was a kid, and I've never changed, and never will – I like to see them get beat!

I don't know how many earphones were connected to the set, probably not over two or three at the most. People were lined up through the bank and out into the street in order to get a chance to hear, "strike one" or "ball one" or whatever was happening. That was all, as the one next in line got to listen to something that was unheard of. More than one fellow went to the end of the line so he could get back into the bank and be lucky enough to hear the announcer from New York telling about a ball game in that city. The old-timers had a lot to talk about, hearing someone talking over the air, and coming out of a box. Today they are still talking, only about what is going on here at the present time. No more standing in line to grab an earphone.

Joe (Slug) Johnson, besides being one of our cops, was also the one who kept the pressure up in the town water system. We had a big 15 horsepower gas engine that was used to pump up the pressure in the big supply tank. The big flywheels on that old Fairbanks-Morse engine were four or five feet in diameter. You had to pump in just the right amount of gas in order to start the big brute. Then the idea was to grab one of those big wheels and try to pull it over in order to start the engine. It was a big pull, and many a time the dumb old engine didn't want to start. It would have been nice to put one foot inside the wheel on one of the spokes to help get more leverage, but that wasn't safe to do. I would have liked to try that, but didn't. In the summertime, we had to check the pressure several times a day, and when it was low, it was time to start the engine, sometimes three or four or more times a day. All this for 15 bucks a month!

Starvation wages. When Slug was out with the Mons Melstad carpenter crew, he had me take over the job.

One Sunday, Skinny went with me up to the pump house to pump up the pressure. Lo and behold, the lights went off before I could see how much gas to pump into the critter. What do you suppose this dumb boy did? I lit a match and held it above the open gas, so that I could see when the gas level was just right. When my dear brother saw me light the match, he went through the outside door like he was sent for and started late! He didn't even use the step, but ended up out in the street. We both should have been blown to kingdom come, but someone was watching over us. The engine started, too.

Well, as long as I was taking over Joe's job, my Pa, being on the town board, told me to go to one ornery businessman and collect the six-month water bill, which our friend wouldn't pay. It amounted to six bucks, as our town charged a dollar a month, and you could use all the water you wanted. How much could we expect for a dollar? That was cheap, even at half the price. I wasn't hip on carrying out this collection business, as I didn't like to do it then, and all my life I dreaded collecting a bill. Pa was the same way. He didn't want to go after someone to collect an old bill, and consequently it never got paid. So I went - gingerly, I might add - to try my skill at collecting the bill that Joe hadn't had any luck with. I told the potential payee that I needed six bucks for the water bill. Nope, he wouldn't pay it. That's what I had figured out, too. Then I volunteered that the town could shut off his water. Then what would he do? Boy, that made him mad, and he must have forgotten what he was saying.

I might enlarge on this subject a little, as this ornery old boy wouldn't go to the hardware store and pay Charley Johnson, who was the overseer of the town finances, what he owed. "All right," he stormed at me, "Go down to Charley and get a receipt for the money, and I'll pay you." Well, I thought this was a backward deal, but I told Charley what the deal was. He just looked and wrote out the receipt that the bill was paid. I took it back, and gave the guy the receipt. He didn't part with the money until he looked over that paid-in-full receipt. I collected, and he was square with the town again.

In its heyday, the Hetland Fire Department wasn't too bad. After all of the business places on the north and east side of Main Street except the livery barn burned to the ground, the powers that be decided something had to be done to try to stave off such disastrous fires in the future. The town put in a water system and piped water to every home and business place that wanted it. We were one of the few that didn't get in on this luxury, as our folks didn't have the money to do it. Our old cistern and cistern pump had to suffice. The town pressure tank held 10,000 gallons of water and a reservoir held 30,000 gallons. We even had fire hydrants to hook fire hoses on to. The volunteer fire department consisted of anyone who wanted to take part in fire fighting. We had two hose carts with several hundred feet of 2 1/2 inch hose. The carts had handles on the front pole so two men could pull and guide the cart and we would run like rabbits to get to the fire. The two wheels were about five feet high, and had steel tires on the wooden wheels. When one man pooped out pulling or pushing the cart, some one fresh would take over the job. Besides these two outfits we had two more carts that had chemical tanks mounted on them. I don't ever remember these being used. Later on, we bought a couple of fire extinguishers that we could carry so that was the extent of our fire fighting equipment. We finally even got rubber coats and hats, but they disappeared, as someone must have needed them for something besides fighting fires. They were probably taken by some "crooks" from nearby towns.

John Cleveland's elevator caught fire one day. The Hetland fire department got in gear and started to put water on the hot spots. Hetland water was good for more than just drinking! The flames were coming out the roof, and Obbie Melstad was manning the fire hose. The elevator was too far from the fire hydrant, or else the hydrant was too far from the elevator, so consequently we could only use one hose. But on the other hand, we only had one fire, too. Obbie quit shooting water on the flames, and told John to go and get a case of beer, otherwise we would let the building go up in smoke. John was all excited; "Please get it out, and I'll get the beer." So Obbie started dousing the flames, and saved the elevator. After it was all over, we didn't see any beer. Maybe it was hijacked before the thirsty firemen could get it.

We had other fires in town that didn't turn out very good. Fires all through the years have been the downfall of small towns, and still continue to be that. Zib Melstad had a Ford with a leaking gas tank. On that model Ford, the gas tank was right under the windshield, and over the motor. The gas was dripping out of a hole in the tank. Zib went over to Barber - Johnson Hardware and bought some kind of solder that had to be lit with a match, and then applied to the hole to be plugged. Zib lit the match and proceeded to ignite the solder, put the lighted dope under the tank, and tried to seal up the hole. Boy, that was a big mistake. Every drop of gas was on fire, dropping down on the engine. The car was soon ready to blow up, we thought. The two fire extinguishers were emptied, and the fire kept getting hotter. The firemen then pushed the car down to the hydrant by the telephone office, hooked up the hose and got the fire out, but by then the car was just a shell. Another experiment that didn't pan out as it was supposed to. I never heard if there was enough left of the car so it could be sold for junk.

Telephone office, 1990

One day the fire whistle blew and Bubs Neilson drove his car to the telephone office to ask John Olson where the fire was. John said "Your house." Bubs ran out the door for home, which was south of the railroad tracks. He didn't get back up town for several hours after the fire was out. The car was still standing in front of the telephone office. Someone asked Bubs what the car was doing there. He went across the street and drove the car to the store.

One time Gunder Mauch was in Skipper's Café visiting with his friends. Nine o'clock came, and he decided he had better go home and think about hitting the hay, as he needed the rest. He just got into the house when bang, the fire whistle took off. Off he went for the pump house to help get the hoses out to put out the fire. What fire? He got uptown, and there was no one around at the pump house. So he went over to the café and the boys were just sitting there visiting as they were when he had left them. So - back home he went. Come to find out, his dad, Henry had the radio on listening to Ed Wynn and the Texaco Gas Company ad. They would blow the fire whistle to let people know that Ed Wynn and Texaco were on the air. That's what he heard. He told me about it afterwards, but nobody else heard about it. When a bunch of us would get together with these older guys, one of Gunder's famous quotes was, "Well, shall we talk about women right away, or lead up to it gradually?" He was a real nice guy, and a good asset to the community.

Henry Mauch owned 15 acres west of town where the dump ground was located. The town paid Henry $15 a year rental for a spot to haul garbage, and that seemed like a high price to my dad. He and Henry were on the town board, and Pa told Henry that $15 was too much rent. OK, Henry said, he would cut it to $10. That was a good deal, and as time went on and Henry died, the town boards seemed to forget that there was any rent due to anyone. Finally I told Gunder as long as he wasn't getting any rent from all of those acres, why not deed it to the town and write it off as a donation? He thought that was a good idea, and being a lawyer, got the land transferred to the town. Now Hetland owns land from the Dago Pond to the mile line west of town, and even owns the south part of Boyd's slough. How much cheaper could we, as townspeople, get land and a deeded slough with water in it? Nobody could post "No Hunting" on this without permission from the powers that be who have the say-so on this donated land. At least we don't have to worry about being several years behind on the yearly rent. Then to put the screws on the dump ground, the government said the dump ground was done for dumping. After 100 years of dumping some smart aleck politicians looked up in the air and decided the dump might pollute the Gulf of Mexico, so that was the end of our use of the old dump ground. It still sits out there west of town, nice, quiet and peaceful. Long live the bureaucrats! Phooey!!!

When the Telephone Company decided to make the Hetland telephone exchange modern, we had all kinds of problems. From what I could gather by the grapevine, it wasn't the best job of installation of the new equipment. As time went on and a lot of bitching occurred, it got better.

One Sunday PM our phone rang and I answered it. Lo and behold, there were three other fellows all saying hello, too. The poor operator was frantic. "What's going on up there? How come there are four of you on the line. I only dialed one number," she said. I told her that's the way the system worked – no good! "I have a long distance call for such and such a number," she said. I knew who the number belonged to, and he was one of the four on the line with the rest of us. I said, "Orville (Ryland), are you still there?" He was. So I volunteered for the operator and suggested the rest of us hang up and Orville could talk without us listening. That was just one of the oddball quirks of the new system.

When anyone on the Hetland line tried to call the operator, it was a big struggle. Sometimes it didn't work worth a hoot. Someone told me that if I dialed "0" and the "5" that the call would go through the Arlington exchange, and the operator would be on in no time. One Sunday morning before church, I decided to try out this new-fangled idea. So – I dialed "0" and then "5" and then the episode began. Ding-a-ling, ding-a-ling, then a pause. "What number are you calling?" asked a voice from somewhere, wherever the call went to (as if she didn't know). The dialogue continued. The operator; "What number did you call?" "0 and then 5." "What did you do that for?" My reply "Because it takes forever to get the operator from here, and I was in a hurry and was told to dial 0 and 5 and it would go through quicker." Her comment; "You shouldn't do that, but how can I help you?" "I would like the time, please." Loud laughter from the other end and then she quit laughing and gave me the time. Eva asked me why I did all that. Just for fun, I guess, but I think that poor girl was wondering what kind of kook we had up here.

Incidentally, by now I presume you are wondering why I was in a hurry to get the time. After all, we had over a block to drive to church, and we didn't want to be late. Besides that, if the preacher preached overtime, he couldn't pull a fast one on me and tell me my watch wasn't right.

Right there I would have had him over a barrel, when I told him that mine was official time from the Telephone Company, and I was sure they had Greenwich time, which was the last word in time. I used to tell John Johnston, one of our preachers who had been a missionary in China, that if he didn't want to eat burned chicken he had better get his preaching done on time (John ate dinner with us every Sunday).

In 1936, Jim Neilson died and there was snow coming out of our ears. In other words, there was lots of snow everywhere. The road out to the Hetland cemetery hadn't been opened all winter and farmers had used sleds with horses to get around. The day of the funeral, Max Neilson brought his dad to the Hetland church in a bobsled. Elza Rice was highway superintendent and sent his brother, Carl, with a F.W.D. (front wheel drive) snowplow to open the road to the cemetery. We had a big crew of men to shovel out the plow when Carl went into the ditch or got stuck. It took all forenoon and until 1 PM to get to the cemetery, a mile away. Carl stayed in town to reopen the road if necessary, as the wind was blowing a gale and really drifting snow. It was a real South Dakota blizzard. We finished the funeral and Carl started back to DeSmet. He got two miles west of town and turned around, as he couldn't see the road. He stayed in town until the next day. At that time the county had to also keep the federal roads open and highway 14 was one of those. Sometimes they would put a V plow on the front of a bus and then hook two busses together and try to plow out the roads.

Charley Bryan had a patent on a rotary snowplow that at least would throw snow. He didn't have any money, but worked us to build it for him, and then share in the profits. We couldn't see working on the plow for a year or two, so we turned him down. He got the county to start building it and they gave it up, so the snowplow went to the railroad roundhouse in Huron. They quit working on it, so we finally took over the job and finished it. Ford Motor Company and other big outfits came to Hetland to look it over. There was an engine mounted on the outfit to run the blower and fan. It would really throw snow. The only trouble was that there wasn't any truck big enough to push the plow into the snow banks. Tractors were small, so that didn't help either. All the work went down the drain, as well as the iron used to build it. The plow sat down by one of the elevators and was finally cut up for junk. If it were around today, there would be outfits powerful enough to push the rotary plow into the snow banks. Charley was ahead of his time with his patent. Incidentally – if you wonder how we knew that this outfit would throw snow, not having the power to push it into a snow bank, we would throw shovels full of snow into the fans and watch it take off for parts unknown. We had fun doing our share of the work, and furnishing steel for the plow, but didn't collect a dime for it. Other investors died poor, too. Such is life.

At one of the school carnivals when Foss was here, there was a lot of activity, and the gross proceeds were $1,100. Before we closed up the schoolhouse, somebody came and told those of us who were left that there was a strange car with two guys in it cruising around town. Maybe they were looking for the proceeds of the carnival. What should be done? Foss, Cliff Manley, Joe "Slug" Johnson, and I huddled together as to how to get all of that money to someplace for safe keeping. We had two cops at the time, "Slug" Johnson and Fred "Knock-'em-stiff" Buckley. John Dillinger wouldn't even have dared to come to town with those two tough cops keeping an eye on things. Finally, Slug said he would go home and get his shotgun in case of a holdup. When Slug came back, we turned out all of the lights and Manley tore out of the door and around the west side of the schoolhouse, headed for home with the eleven hundred bucks, and he was scared stiff! He made it OK, so the money was saved for future use. The three of us marched down the street, with Foss on the inside, Slug in the middle with his shotgun at the ready, and me on the outside, I suppose as a buffer for the other two, and also to give Slug time to empty his gun on any would-be robbers. Boy, what a harrowing experience, but it worked, as no one tried to deter three or maybe I should say, two of Hetland's citizens, when they were protected by such a ferocious cop. This is probably like what the GAR was like in the earlier days, only in this case it would be the GAH (Grand Army of Hetland) instead of the Grand Army of the Republic.

With "Slug" and "Knock-'em-stiff," the people of Hetland should have felt secure. With one cop to start the action by slugging a would-be bandit and another to knock them stiff on the way down, it was no wonder that Hetland was one of the wonders of the world. Besides being the only Hetland in the world, we had it made. By the way, I don't recall if these two eager beavers ever got paid for the honor bestowed upon them, or if they performed their duties for nothing. After all, they were the absolute law in town.

One night some crooks broke into the bank and blew the safe. Don't know how much they made off with, so I have no idea if they got good pay for their efforts. A Federal man was in town checking for the government to see who might have done such a dastardly deed. I might add the same night these outlaws got into the blacksmith shop through a window and stole some of our tools to help out in the burglary. Some of the tools had Pa's initials stamped on them. Ah-ha, the eager beaver government man thought, he had the mystery solved. This guy came down to the shop and started asking all kinds of leading questions about the robbery. Pa caught on real soon that this Sherlock Holmes was trying to implicate him in the robbery.

That's when all Hell broke loose. Pa let him know that he wasn't a thief, and had nothing to do with it. Besides that, if he had been in on it he wouldn't have been so dumb as to leave his tools, especially with his name on them. The federal guy backed off and said, "Oh, no, I wasn't trying to get you involved in it," but Pa let him know differently. The guy left and Pa was still out of federal prison. The crooks are still at large, too, enjoying their loot.

Henry Mauch came down to the shop one day and told Pa that he could sleep nights now, as he had bought a big safe that was built like an egg and a cutting torch wouldn't be able to cut on the round surface. At least that was the salesman's selling point. Pa told Henry that the torch could cut through the round steel, and proceeded to show the banker that he could cut through that kind of steel. Henry felt dejected and said now he couldn't sleep any better than before. He had been hoodwinked by a slick salesman. The bank was never robbed again, so we were in luck, although the bank went "belly up" in the depression years.

Once when I was up in the bank, Henry Mauch was looking all around for something. Finally I asked him what he was looking for. He told me he was looking for his glasses. They were perched on top of his head and I told him so. I was the Sherlock Holmes who solved the mystery of the lost "specs."

The old brick First State Bank building is now getting a complete facelift, due to the efforts of a few members of the Hetland Historical Society. The bank will be like it was when it was an active bank, aiding the community. Lack of funds hinders progress on restoring images of our little town's past glory. We need some well-to-do donors to help keep the projects going. The old schoolhouse, a great white building and symbol of learning, would be next if the money were available. It is still a thing of beauty, although some knuckle headed vandals have raised havoc with the inside of the school.

We had some young guys living in the south part of town who were more or less "daredevils." I think they were trying to outdo Evil Knievel when they tried out an experiment that didn't pan out too hot. One night when the boys were sure everyone in town was curled up in the sack for the night, they decided to see what would happen in their driving adventure. Don't know how far north of town they had the starting line, but anyway, they took off for the south, really winding it up to see what would happen when they came to the railroad crossing. In a few seconds, these eager beavers found out! They must have hit the tracks at a terrific speed, as they were airborne just like that. A couple of hundred feet south of the tracks, on the west side of the street stood the old Youmans Lumber Yard office. These boys hit the north side of the building and kept heading south, but not before they had totaled out the whole building, tearing off the whole front of it. Wow! That must have made some noise, and probably woke up the neighbors. Anyway, these boys found out what being airborne was like, and they walked away from the whole mess unscathed, and lived to drive another day. I never heard how far south they went before getting the car under control. They were lucky, as all of them could have ended up buried six feet in the terra firma.

Since I have been living here, I have seen Highway 14 in three different locations. First it went on the south side of Lake Preston lake, and came into the town of Lake Preston from the north. Then it was moved one mile further south, so that the road went by the north side of Lake Whitewood, coming into Lake Preston from the south, before turning west and heading toward Rapid City.

This last time, the road was moved a half mile further south of Hetland, and made a straight shot through Lake Preston town. There was a big battle on this, as the road was planned to bypass the city of Arlington. Boy, that was a low blow, and after a long and heated exchange, the road went back through Arlington. Some of the businessmen there wanted me to sign their petition to keep the road through town. I wouldn't sign it, and had a lot of static because I wouldn't sign. I told them when I wanted to go east, I didn't want to slow down through their town, as I wanted to get to where I was going and get there in a hurry.

Now these same people are complaining that the traffic through their town needs to slow down to 30 miles per hour or else! They have been giving out tickets to show that the law means business. If the road had gone around town, there wouldn't have been any flap about the low speed limit. The mayor even got up (I was there) and told the state guys that it would be too bad for the liquor store if the road didn't go by it, as theirs was the only liquor establishment on Highway 14 between the State Line and Huron.

Obbie Melstad called Arlington "Ghost Town" which wasn't very complimentary. They have a lake there that they call Lake Arlington, but we in the older generation call it Lake Spittoon. It's so small you might miss it if you had to spit. As of now, the lake has been dredged and an island has been added. The lake looks pretty neat and is a thing of beauty. Our early assessment isn't valid any more.

Before the first electricity was turned on in town the big day came when the switch in the mill in Lake Preston was to be turned on. Pa told Merle Melstad that it would never work. Merle was in the blacksmith shop when the lights came on. Bang-they went off and Pa said "I told you so." Just then the lights came back on and that was the way Hetland got its first electric lights.

When we were kids, the opera house had movies every Saturday night. Tickets cost a nickel, and quite often there was music to complement the show. The musicians (pianist, drummer, etc.) were down in the front in what today in high class performances would be called the "pit." The little Andersen boys never got to get in on the high class stuff, as our folks couldn't afford to give us the nickel. Gub Stangland would go up and down the street with a big megaphone, hollering at the top of his voice that the show was about to start. He got a ticket for his "broadcasting," so he got to see all of the shows – free!

Town Hall, 1990, (Former Opera House)

Later on, we had free movies that the business places paid for, only they were shown outside, sometimes on the front of Herb Johnson's barn or on the side of a store. The businesses gave away tickets when a customer bought something. After the free show the tickets were put into a big drum and shaken up before drawing to see who the several winners were. One old rich Norske who lived south of town would stop the can shaking by coming up to put in his tickets. You guessed it, he had his name drawn nearly every time. Everyone but this character was disgusted at the way he worked it to get his tickets in at the last second. Didn't hear if he took any of his assets with him when he left this earth. He was well off.

After the NBC "1986" program on Hetland was aired on TV, we had a call from a brother Mason who used to live in Arlington, and at this time called Arkansas home. He told us his wife used to come to Hetland to play the piano for the pit musicians, and always had a great time while she was here.

We watched Charlie Weidenkopf drive into his garage, which he had concocted from part of his barn. He had a new car with a shift on it, which was different from the old Model T. He was dubious about driving it in for the first time. He finally got up enough nerve to give it a try. I don't know how many of us were standing outside, watching him in this big undertaking. He got through the door without scraping off any paint, and then he hollered, "Whoa!" and CRASH! He plowed into the south side of the barn. He pushed the pedal like he did on the Model T and the car didn't stop. He got the car shut off, with no damage to either the barn or the car. He was pretty pale around the gills when he finally came out of the car. I don't think he had any trouble after that. Our modern day cars would have had to be in the body shop for a major repair job. If I remember right, his son-in-law, Harry Starksen, did the same thing when he put his new Model A in the garage for the first time. No damage to either the vehicle or the garage.

At a school meeting, the Lake Preston superintendent proclaimed that they had the best school in the country. I couldn't pass up the temptation, even though I didn't know the guy, to tell the crowd that they might get by with that boast, as long as the Hetland School wasn't in operation. Of course, they would have to take the back seat for us. Some agreed with me, but of course they were loyal Hetland fans. We didn't mind being first. The Preston kids used to tell the Hetland kids after our school was closed, that they were smart because they were from Hetland. Our local kids didn't take the back seat just because they were from a smaller school and the school records won't make a liar out of me, either.

One time Ole Stangland left his car parked and idling in front of the telephone office. Eider Stangland was a little guy and was left alone in the car. He proceeded to check out the gadgets in the car and shifted the car into gear. The car shot across the street and stopped when it hit a light pole. The Hetland News reported that Master Eider Stangland had tried to learn how to drive at an early age.

There used to be a monstrous flagpole in the middle of Main Street. It was in line with North Street, the street going west toward the schoolhouse. It seemed to us smaller tykes like it must be a hundred feet high, but it wasn't. The base of the pole was 4-inch pipe and as it went up higher, the pipe was smaller. There was a huge flag that really flapped in the wind, and those of you who know South Dakota know that the wind can blow! The base that held the pole was solid concrete, about five feet square and four feet high. We used to sit on this big slab, dangle our feet over the edge and watch the traffic go by. This big slab of cement had another purpose, too. If you wanted to turn around in Main Street from right to left, to go back to where you came from, it was legal to do it there. Don't recall anyone getting "pinched" for doing that. It also served as the dividing line on Main Street. On Wednesday and Saturday nights, especially, cars could park crossways in the street, lined up with the flagpole. This was when there was no parking space left on either side of the street.

One day we had an unheard-of accident, right by the legal town turnaround. Don Barber was driving north on the right side of the street when Lew Larson pulled out from in front of the Post Office, and decided to turn around the flagpole, making a right turn around said pole, instead of a left turn. You can guess what happened. Don, seeing what was going to happen, slowed way down, and BOOM! Lew ran into him, just like that! What a crying shame. But that wasn't the last of the episode. Lew got excited, backed away from Don and then got more excited, shifted gears again, and went forward and hit him a second time. Nothing like doing a good job. This time, Lew was done, and the cars were bumper to bumper. Lew told Don, "Well, I gotcha!" How right he was. But there is a good side to the story. The way today's cars are made, there would be a couple of thousand dollars of damage. Do you know what? There was no damage to either car. In those days, a bumper meant what it said, it was a bumper, not for looks, but to ward off approaching danger. Let me tell you they were solid, and built to stand a pretty good jolt.

When we were in the lower grades, we had a sad fatal accident. Jerry Bunday had a small shed located north of the schoolhouse, and several of us kids would climb up on the roof and jump or slide off. Darrel Warne, who was in my class, did this one time too many. Don't know what happened, but he busted something inside quiet, as the kids got the message to shape up – or else! After that they were more coy at letting each other know that they were in love.

Sig Peterson, one of our neighbors, used to raise skunks. Don't know what the object was. He had them in pens and had them fixed so they couldn't spray on us viewers. They would scratch their feet on the ground, but nothing happened. That was lucky for us! Pete Peterson was his dad, and got arrested for trapping out of season. Ma and I were going over to see his wife, who we called Peenie. Ma had me by the hand so I wouldn't fall, and just before we got to their house she told me, "Now don't say anything to Peenie about Pete getting pinched." That was real thoughtful of my Ma. I must not have heard the message right. I had to settle my curiosity, so the first thing I did when we got into the house was to politely ask, "Peenie, did Pete get pinched?" "Yes, Pete got pinched!" was her reply. I think Ma could have hung me out to dry.

Peenie always had the coffee pot sitting on the coal stove. When anyone came to visit, she would toss in another dose of fresh coffee and let it boil. She never dumped the coffee grounds until bedtime, so a new batch could be brewed in the morning and the same old process would start all over again. I don't have any idea how much coffee they bought in a month, and what kind it was. T-Berry Coffee was a popular brand in those early days. There wasn't the variety we can choose from now. Peenie's coffee must have had lots of caffeine in it.

One day Obbie Melstad was trying to saw off a little limb of a tree using an electric chain saw. I walked over to watch. The branch was about an inch thick, and here he was, pulling the saw back and forth as if he was using a handsaw. I offered to go home and get my handsaw, as he was making absolutely no progress cutting off the branch. All he was doing was working up a sweat, with me standing there cheering him on. (I think that cheering might be the right word, but on the other hand....) Finally, he gave it up, and I laid off giving him any encouragement. We got to looking over the saw chain, and it was put on backwards. Of course it wasn't his fault. "It must have been one of the Johnston kids that did that." I don't know how John or Jim would have done that, but of course it wasn't Obbie. I think he eventually got the branch off from the tree, but not with the chain going backwards.

In the early days of Hetland we had a newspaper, the *Hetland New Era*. It was started by my Uncle, George Clark, my mother's brother. It was a thriving newspaper, complete with ads and all of the local news stories. All of this for 25 cents a year. What a bargain. Uncle George even took eggs and milk from subscribers who couldn't afford the two-bit subscription. No wonder he and his family lived on a shoe string. We had a page of the paper on the wall in the blacksmith shop, showing a picture of a fancy phaeton horse buggy, complete with side curtains and all of the trimmings, for the whopping price of, now get this, $35.00, but that did NOT include the horses. If any prospective buyer of that buggy could afford paying 35 bucks for the buggy, he could surely afford a nice pair of horses to complement a ritzy outfit to show off his wealth.

Another ad I remember was about the Post Office hours, as well as train times. The PO was open from 7 AM to 6 PM, I believe it was, with incoming mail sorted and delivered twice a day, and outgoing mail sent out twice a day, morning and evening. Post cards were sent for a penny, and first class mail for two cents, and that price STAYED like that for years on end. We had four passenger trains a day, with a separate mail car, as well as a separate baggage car, included. A letter could be mailed from Hetland to the next town, sorted in the mail car, and a few minutes later it was delivered to the neighboring town, and the so called "big wigs" in Washington, DC, thought that they could improve on that service. What a farce.

Hetland didn't take the back seat when we were growing up. Starksen's store had the forerunner of the modern two story malls. In the west end of the store was an upstairs balcony, complete with stair steps and hand railings as well. On this balcony were all kinds of goods, clothes, etc. that any would-be traveler would be proud to try on. On the lower floor were dishes and silverware fit for a king as well as a Norwegian, as that was Charley (Deb) Starksen's heritage. There were so many different patterns on display that it would "boggle" the mind, trying to choose just the right dishes to accommodate any décor.

Today we buy bananas in bunches all cut off from the main vine, or whatever the big thing that they were hooked onto was called. Back when we were kids it was a different story. Screwed into the ceiling was a hook to hold a small rope block and tackle used to hoist the big clump of bananas to an upright position. They hung from the ceiling above the counter, just as I presume they grew when on a tree out in the "wilds." Then, to complete the whole deal, Debs had a sharp curved-bladed knife that was used to cut off as many bananas as a customer wanted. I can still see those delicious golden bananas waiting to be plucked for someone's grocery bag!

In those days the store clerk went around with the customer and picked the stuff from the shelves, and it was not called "self service." It was SERVICE with a smile, and if you charged the bill and paid it at the end of the month, there was always a candy treat when you paid your bill. If you paid cash all the time, no treats, which I could never figure out unless Debs was glad the credit customer paid his bill.

If you needed a tailor made suit that was also available, and it came direct from M. Born and Co. in Chicago. My wedding suit was from this esteemed company. Debs didn't measure me right the first time, or else I had changed dimensions. The coat didn't fit worth a hoot, so my girl friend (about to be bride) Eva put the kibosh on that. Debs re-measured me and sent it back for what today would be called alterations. It came back fitting better and passed the about-to-be bride's inspection. The wedding suit is still hanging upstairs but I can't wear it now as it has evidently shrunk through the years, having been made in 1937!

When Harry Tolzin bought out Starksens's store, he had some M. Born pants (all wool) that were 1/4 inch thick. He offered me one of them, size 50 for 50 cents. I put them right over my clothes that I was wearing. Then, having gotten such a good deal, I asked him if he had any more pants like that to be used for patching. Lo and behold he did, a size 54 for 50 cents. Imagine that, when a snowstorm was approaching how nice and warm those 1/4 inch thick pants felt. Then he had a pair of slippers that fit and cost me another 50 cents. Boy, was I decked out at a final cost of $1.50 and didn't have to pay sales tax either. I am not sure but those wool pants might be around the house somewhere, as they didn't wear out. I carried them in the trunk of the car for many years just in case of an emergency.

My veterinarian friend, Doc Askey, brought his electric golf cart over to the shop to get it repaired. I told him that I thought golfers went golfing to get the exercise. "We do," was his reply, "getting off and on the cart." That sounded logical to me, not being a golf pro myself.

Way back when there wasn't much expensive equipment to open the roads in the wintertime. To help out the farmers and to bring business to town, we would take a whole load of men with scoop shovels, load them into Barber and Johnson's old International truck and proceed out into the country to shovel snow. Can you imagine the backbreaking job of shoveling out drifts several feet deep in order to let a car go through? Some days we didn't get much done but we would enjoy the fellowship and doing something worthwhile to help out our farmer friends. After all, they patronized us so we could keep our business going.

Vi, Dale's daughter-in-law, searches eBay for anything referring to Hetland. As a result, she has accumulated a number of items, including postcards, dishes, and memorabilia of all kinds. Included in them were a Bean Pot and a Matchbox that were given by Hetland merchants to their customers. She asked Dad to give her some information on the businesses. Here are some of his comments.

An ode to a matchbox –

A matchbox specifically from Starksen's General store in Hetland, SD. This was a type of matchbox that was used in days gone by. At Christmas time, it was the usual practice of business places to give something to their customers as a token of appreciation for their patronage through the past year. This matchbox would hold a big box of "strike anywhere" matches as the match maker's slogan depicted, but they would NOT ignite under water.

The Diamond Match Company seemed to have a corner on these versatile matches. Whether they were better than other brands or not, I do not know.

A cardboard box with a hundred or more matches in it would be deposited in the top of this box. It was then pushed down to the bottom of the match box holder, which would generally be hung on the wall or sitting on a place where it was accessible. Some smart engineer (probably a Dane) concocted a way to hold the matches in place without spilling out of the original box when the box was placed into the matchbox. A one-inch wide piece of heavy paper was inserted into the top and bottom of the box to hold the matches in place while it was inserted into this matchbox. When the box hit bottom, the paper was pulled out of the holder, and Bingo! All of the matches were in place, ready to be plucked out of the bottom opening.

This matchbox has a safety device at the bottom opening, where there was a lift-up cover to prevent anything from igniting the matches inside – another smart invention. One of the favorite ways to ignite these "strike anywhere" matches was to lift a leg, so that the pants were extra tight on the back of the leg, then lean over and scratch the match with a quick motion. BINGO, the match was aflame, ready for action. Another way to get the match lit was to hold the match between the thumb and index finger. Then, if one was versatile, with a swift motion scratch the thumbnail across the tip of the match, and fire would erupt, just like that. A novice didn't have much luck with this deal, but Practice made Perfect.

By the way, Starksen's General Store meant just that. If you wanted groceries, they were provided, with a clerk to help you pick out what you needed. If you needed clothes to cover your body, anything you needed was available. If you wanted a new set of dishes or eating utensils, there was a ready choice of them available. This store was ahead of its time, as there was what is known today as a mezzanine that extended out over the dishware. Ladies could

Matchbox from Starksen Store

climb a flight of stairs, and come down the stairs with a complete wardrobe, even complete with any type of girdle that their frame desired.

Charles (Debs) his nickname, had anything a customer desired in his store, within reason, of course.

An ode to a high priced crockery pot —

Dear Vi,
Your valued possession came from the Farmers Union elevator, which was located at the west end of town, on the south side of the railroad tracks. This building would have been located straight south across the tracks, from the Morris Andersen abode. It was an Eagle Roller elevator before the Farmers Union bought it, and the Union stocked it with hardware, merchandise, coal and feed. I don't recall that they ever were in the grain buying business, as selling to them was better than buying grain. The other three grain elevators in town took care of the grain buying business.

When this pot was given away to customers at Christmas time, the elevator was managed by Charles Bryan. At one time his family resided in the house where Dale and Eva Andersen have raised their family, and which is still, at this writing, their home. At that time Charley Bryan was paid $25 a month to manage the joint. He was responsible for any bad bills, which would be deducted from his lucrative salary if they were not collected.

My brother, Clayton (Skinny), managed the place while Charley went on vacation. Skinny was told, in no uncertain terms, that he was NOT to charge anything to anyone, as Charley would be responsible for any unpaid bills. Lo and behold, while Skinny was on duty, a "big wheel" farmer from south of town bought some merchandise which totaled up to a little less than two bucks. The "wheel" told Skinny to charge it. Nothing doing, no charging, just cash. The farmer let my younger brother know that he was a director of the company. Director or not, he had to pay cash for the stuff, or NO sale. Skinny got the money, and the director went home mad, after digging up the cash.

All of this took place in the dirty thirties, of 1900s. Cash was as scarce as hens' teeth at that time. We used to razz Charley about one of his coal ads that he had listed in the paper, "Nothing but ashes from Great Heart coal." This coal had little stickers all stuck to the lumps of coal, portraying that it was indeed, Great Heart coal. Even though it was good coal, we would let him know that the ad was right, no heat either, just ashes.

The elevator has been long gone, being torn down, but there are still some artifacts left where the old building used to stand. That's it, with Love, from your relative and old mentor.

- Dad

Bean pot from Farmers Union Elevator

Chapter 12
In the BS Shop

Top: Dale and Morris... note the plow lays on the floor
Bottom: Dale, age 5, at the anvil

154 *BS Stands for Blacksmith*

Top: Dale at the forge
Bottom: Dale at his shop, 1986

In the BS Shop

When Pa bought the Blacksmith shop from Lynn Barber in 1907, it was east of the house we now live in. It was alongside the alley, facing south. Barber didn't want the shop on his property, so it was moved across the street, using pipes for rollers. I don't know how they did that, as the building had to be turned around and backed into place where it is now. Guess those older Danes had more insight on how to do that than I would have.

Lynn W. Barber

Pa had a reputation for being able to fix anything. Us kids used to brag that our dad could fix anything but a broken heart. He had good boasters, and didn't need a newspaper advertisement. He did a lot of boiler work on steam engines. I went out into the country with him one night while he worked on a leaking boiler. We didn't get home until 4 AM, but the engine was ready to go when the threshing crew got there in the morning. I remember one night somebody brought a steam engine to the shop for Pa to fix the next day. Holy smokes! About midnight there was the most awful noise that woke up the town. Someone had tied the whistle open on the steamer, and it was really screeching. Pa finally got up to disconnect the whistle so that people could get back to bed for their beauty sleep.

Morris in the shop

The story is often told that a blacksmith starves to death if he doesn't charge enough, or else has been pounding cold iron. Pa didn't charge enough and certainly didn't pound cold iron. I think that I fall into both categories. Back in the depression years of the 1930s there was a customer, Chris Miller, who came into the shop and wanted to know if we knew where he could get a disk, as his old one was "shot." Pa told him that we had an 8-footer that he could have for five dollars. Boy, that was great, but this Dane didn't have any money, and would try to pay for it later. That was fine, so the happy farmer took the disk home with him. In the fall, this honest Dane came and held out a $5 bill. Pa wanted to know what that was for. "To pay for the disk." Pa told him that it was only $2.50, as that was what he had paid for it, and he wasn't taking any more than that. Chris said he was satisfied with the $5, and why didn't Pa tell him that when he was only going to charge $2.50? Pa told him he figured that Chris would probably try to negotiate a lower price, so this way he could come down, if he needed to. Chris was more than satisfied with the deal, as he was a busted farmer like lots of our friends. Broke through no fault of theirs, with no rain and no decent price for their crops, there was no way to make both ends meet. This not only affected the farmer, but also took its toll on business places, too.

I remember one of the years in the shop, that Pa and I split $900 for the total year's work. That was all we had to show for a year of hard work, but that didn't give us very much money to put food on the table, etc. But – we survived. Lots of the farmers thought that we were charging too much for our work. After all, most anyone could be a blacksmith. All we had to do was fix stuff when the farmer was broken down. Most of the time, what we had repaired seemed to work, for which we were thankful. Anyway, one day I figured up how much was made in the shop in the last 30 years before I had to give up working. Now, these were the so-called "boom years" when everybody really made big money. We were an exception to that rule.

Over the past 30 years, our take-home pay amounted to $4,800 a year, which, according to my calculator, was $400 a month. At least we didn't go in the red like Uncle Sam has done for years. We didn't take Saturdays off, either, and worked from 7 AM until 6 PM, and lots of nights we were there until 9 or 10 PM, too. Today we would call a 60-hour work week a little bit excessive, and then several hours added on to that, working at night. I might add that this $4,800 figure included steel, bolts, etc. that we had sold and supposedly made a little profit on as well. How much profit we made, I didn't try to figure out. But at a mere 60 hours a week of labor we probably came out at $1 an hour or less. With the extra time figured in, it would have made the hourly wage even less. It wouldn't appear like we overcharged anyone. If anything, we probably were on the short end of the stick. I used to tell Eva that we weren't making anything, but that I was having a good time doing it. It was enjoyable work, and each day brought another challenge.

Morris and Dale

Nels Damsgaard, a Dane farmer from south of Arlington, could tell some pretty good tales. I wasn't too big when I was in the shop one day, and he and Pa were talking about windstorms back in the early days. Nels told about some guy that got caught out on the prairie when a tornado hit. There was no place to go, so he lay down on the ground and grabbed hold of the tall prairie grass to keep from getting blown away. Nels said the fellow wasn't a bit scared, and then he would look at me as I suppose I was looking really worried about that time. Then Nels said the wind took the guy off from the ground with his feet high in the air, but he still wasn't worried. But when this poor fellow heard the grass start to crack, then he got scared. By now he was really enjoying the look on my face. This guy must have had good hearing to hear the grass crack!

This same Nels had a good vocabulary, not only of good stuff, but sometimes not so good. One day he was in the shop and seemed to be more profane than usual. Might have had a fight with his wife. While he was wound up, our minister, Aaron Mickel, came into the shop. Pa tried to motion to Nels to lay off the nasty talking, but the more he motioned, the worse it got. Finally Aaron told Nels that he was a minister, and wasn't used to that kind of talk. Nels said, "I can't help it if you are a minister," but he went to the other end of the shop and walked around there until the preacher was gone. When he came up to the front, he asked Pa, "Why in the hell didn't you tell me he was a minister?" Pa told him that he had tried to motion to him to keep it cool. It was good enough that the preacher had heard his foul language, and now he would know better. The next time Nels came to the shop, he threw his cap in before he came in, and wanted to know if there were any preachers here. Luckily, there weren't. Then he said he had told his wife about the whole deal, and she didn't sympathize with him either. She told him that it was good enough for him, as he didn't need to talk like that.

Nels was a top-notch farmer, and always topped the market when he sold his cattle. He was a big feeder. He used to bring nice big beef roasts and steaks to us during wartime, and boy, they were prime. He wouldn't take anything for them, either. One time he brought in a big driver wheel from a tractor that was really busted up. It was so big that we used a block and tackle and hoisted it up toward the ceiling so that it could be worked on. I was ready to start the torch to weld the contraption when Pa came over and told me, "You aren't going to weld that, I am." Nels went over and tapped Pa on the shoulder and told him, "Dale is going to fix it." I got the job done, and it turned out to be a big job, and it was a success. Boy, Nels stood high with me, to let me tackle a big job like that, just being a young kid. I asked him how he dared to let me weld it. "I knew you could do it, and if not, your Dad could finish it." He was different from a knuckle headed farmer who came in with a broken piece from his binder, and asked me if it could be welded. I told him yes, and started for the welding room to weld it. Pa was busy, and it wasn't that big a deal. What do you suppose this character wanted to know? "Are you going to fix it? "Yes," was my reply. "I had better go uptown and buy a new one, then." He took it out of my hands and up to the IHC store he went, and bought a new one. I didn't have any time for this narrow-minded clown, before this deal, and to this day, even after he has left this earth, I wouldn't give him the time of day. The welding job would have cost 35 cents.

Every so often Charlie Starksen would bring something to the blacksmith shop to get fixed. He would always put it on top of the anvil. Pa would promptly pick it up and throw it out in the street. This would go on for two or 3 times. Then Pa would fix it. Debs would go back to the store and bring down a box of Copenhagen snuff and lay it on the anvil. This was all the pay Pa got for any job he fixed for Charlie. The snuff cost five or ten cents over the counter so Debs got it for less than that. No wonder times were tough in the BS shop with all that money coming in at one time.

Harry Starksen used to stop at the shop on his way home from school when Pa was shoeing horses. We had a hunting dog, an Irish Setter named Sport, who would be lying in the shop when I wasn't chasing after him with my walker. If Sport was in the house he would get behind the cook stove so he could get some rest without me chasing him. Anyway, Pa told Harry to quit calling Sport when he was shoeing a horse, as the dog would run out of the shop and get petted. He told him he would put Harry in the water barrel if he didn't quit. Harry of course, didn't quit. One day he hollered at Sport and the horse Pa was shoeing kicked him into the shoeing box. Pa picked himself up, went over to Harry, grabbed him by the seat of the pants and dropped him into the water, head first, until he nearly touched bottom. When Pa pulled Harry out he was black as the ace of spades, water dripping off from him and he was mad. However, it must have soaked in as Harry never tried to call Sport out of the shop again. Harry used to say, "The water was damn dirty too." I don't know if Harry, being a Lutheran at that time, had ever been "submersed." Later he became a Congregationalist.

Pa was giving Homer heck about something he had done. Homer said, "What can you expect, you are the one that taught me." That kind of fixed the whole deal.

When Eva and I were coming home to Hetland about midnight one night, there was a truck stopped down on the south end of town. I called him on the CB radio to see if he was okay or needed any help. He said he was okay and wanted to know who he was talking to. I told him "The old diddler." Then he wanted to know what I diddled in. I said "a BS Shop." It was all quiet and finally he said "Oh." Eva said "What did you do that for, a BS shop?" I told her there was nothing wrong with that, it was a Blacksmith Shop. Just keep your mind higher up and that is all it amounted to. She didn't agree with me.

I hope that you don't think that I'm picking on Lewis Crandall, because that would be far from the truth. Most of you who read about happenings here in Hetland wouldn't have known Lewis, but he was a dear old soul. He was never in a hurry and had some quaint sayings, but he was so gullible that it was a temptation for everybody to pull a fast one on him.

He and his wife, Rose, had been visiting in California. When he came to the shop after being out there, he was all steamed up about a gadget on a pad, that when the button was pushed, the garage door automatically opened. He told me that I should have seen it.

We have a big pedestal drill that we have bypassed the switch on, and have a pedal on the floor so we can start and turn off the drill by stepping on a floor switch. I told Lewis we had something that beat that door opener, and proceeded to show how our drill worked. I took hold of the lever and said, "Start," and lo and behold, it started. If you had known Crandall, you would automatically know that he would indulge in some cuss words. "When did you get that?" Then I told the machine to stop. More blue air. Finally I kept on, "Start, stop, etc." until he began to smell a rat. He looked, and saw the electric wire going under my foot, so I showed him the contraption and how it worked.

If I had stopped after the first demonstration, he would have gone uptown and told everyone what a wonderful outfit the blacksmith had. Start and stop – WOW, that would have been something to really crow about. It was a good thing I had told Lewis how the drill really worked to save him from embarrassment.

Inventions of Necessity –

Before WWII, Pa and I made a tractor that was appropriately called "Hitler." We used an old Fordson tractor rear end, tipped it upside down, and used a Nash engine for power. The engine knocked out a connecting rod in the car that it was in. When it broke, it went through the block. I welded up the hole in the block, we put in a new rod, and we had a good tractor motor. We hooked the motor and rear end together, and

"Hitler"

it really made a good tractor. During the war, there was a shortage of rubber tires. We had put rubber tires on the front wheels, and had two big tires to put on the back, but decided to give them to the government for the war effort. The original steel wheels we made are still intact. It still sits out in back of the blacksmith shop. When Homer and Elden used it for farming, it would run all day on five gallons of gas. It had lots of speed, too. An antique tractor collector wanted to buy it for his collection, but I told him he could buy it after I had departed this earth. He has gone to his reward, so he won't be around to bid on it.

Pete Peterson came over to the BS shop one day and told Pa that he had a brilliant idea how to split long logs in half. If Pa would make the device, Pete told him they would patent it and get rich. Pa looked over the plans and told Peter it wouldn't work. Pete kept after him, so finally Pa made the outfit as directed. Dynamite was supposed to supply the power to drive the "would be" wood splitter through the long log.

The big day came, and Pete came into the shop and told Pa everything was in place, and that Pa and I should come out behind the shop to see how the wedges that were going to make us rich worked. Nothing doing. Pa said it wouldn't work, so we stayed inside and kept on working. All at once, KER-BLAM, the dynamite went off, and we heard shattering glass. We couldn't stand the suspense, so we went out to see where the log went to, as long as the blast took out most of the window panes in the shop. Alas, the log still lay on the ground, and hadn't even moved. All of the force from the dynamite went up into the air, and headed for parts unknown. Pete spent some time putting in window panes. The rags to riches scheme went by the wayside, or maybe the idea went up in smoke. No patent was taken out, either.

A couple of fellows from Arlington came into the shop one day with something to fix. These two had been doing more than sniffing the bottle, as they were pretty well loaded. They still hadn't had enough to quench their thirst, as they wanted to know if we wanted a bottle of beer. We told them that there was no beer sold in town. That was no problem, they would go back to Arlington to get some. They came back with six bottles, and we popped the corks, and were going to cool off while the welding job cooled off. Boy, this was the blackest looking beer I had ever seen. Not being a connoisseur of drinks, who was I to know what good beer looked like? Well, I took a small swig of the stuff, and I thought my hair was going to stand up straight, and my eyebrows, too! Wow, talk about rotten tasting! I looked at these two gentlemen, and they were gulping this stuff down like they really enjoyed it.

Pa was looking cross-eyed at his bottle as though wondering what he was getting into. I sampled the stuff again, and all at once I got the brilliant idea that I had to go out in the back room to get rid of some Vitamin P. I took my time coming back, and by that time the beer was mixed with the Vitamin P, but they didn't go through me together. Pa finally finished his, but the two liquored-up boys finished theirs in a hurry. I thought they would finish up the other two bottles, but they had a better idea, we were to keep them for ourselves. OK, it wasn't polite to turn down such a good offer, so I took them into the house in case Pa wanted to treat the rest of his kids when they came to see the two of them. My three brothers and their wives were there one evening, and Pa was telling them about this beer. Of course, they had to sample a bottle. None of them could take it, so they poured it down the drain. Good riddance. However, there was still one bottle left, gracing the back of the refrigerator, waiting for someone to imbibe.

By now, I presume that you dear readers are wondering why I have wasted all of this space talking about beer? Well, here goes. Our good friend Nels Damsgaard came to the shop again with a breakdown of course, knowing a good place to get the job done, and done right. I might add that it was a really hot day, too. A good day to get rid of that lone bottle of beer. So, while we were waiting for the job to cool down so that Nels could go home, I asked him if he could drink a bottle of beer. You bet, that would be good. I told him we had one bottle left, and he could have it. Oh, no, he wouldn't do that, as Pa and I didn't have one too. I told him that was OK, as I'd go up to the store and get some pop for us. Well, he hated to take the last bottle, but under the circumstances he would drink it. I got the beer and the pop, and we all sat down like, I suppose, all drinking buddies do, popped the corks and started to imbibe.

Pa and I watched Nels take a big long swig to see what would happen. He didn't say a word, but proceeded to read the label and look the bottle over. Every time he took a drink, he would go through the same motions, even tipping the bottle up to look at the bottom, what for I don't know, although I think both Pa and I knew what our good friend was thinking. We could hardly keep a straight face after seeing the look on his face after each swig. Finally, after what seemed like a long time, the drinking spree was over, and we all settled down to relax and "chew the fat."

Curiosity got the best of me, so I asked our friend how the beer was. Of course, he wanted to be polite, as after all, he didn't want to say too much against the brew, as long as the beer had been given to him. He replied, "Well, it was different than most beers." Then I went about telling him the story about how we only had one bottle left. Then all Hell broke loose. "Damn you, why did you give me that stuff when you wouldn't drink it yourself?" I told him, "Pa drank his and I had a swig out of one of the other bottles, so we weren't giving you something we hadn't sampled, and besides that, you were the thirsty one, and knew what good beer tasted like." "What in Hell was it?" was his retort. We all had a good laugh over it, and I think by his manner that he was pleased that I had pulled a fast one on him. We were still good friends until he went home to his reward. It was the blackest and the foulest tasting stuff you could ever imagine.

Pa was watching the World Series and I was holding down the fort, working in the shop. However, every so often I would slip into his house to see how the game was going. If nobody came I would look at the TV and then go back to the kitchen and look out to see if anybody needed me. One time I looked and here came Bertal Gaard with his old Woods Brothers corn picker. So I went out to see what might be the problem, as it wasn't corn picking time yet. I asked him if he was in a big hurry to get home as I had been in the house looking at the World Series. "What do you mean, looking at it?" I told him that it was on TV and we were watching the game. "You mean you can see it?" "Yup, we can see it," so I told him to come on in and we would look at it as long as no one else came.

Nobody came to the shop, so the three of us sat down and took in the ball game. After it was over, I fixed the picker, and Bertal went home happy as could be, hardly believing what he had seen and his corn picker was fixed, too.

Dorene Starksen and her husband and family used to come out from Illinois to visit her folks, Harry and Florentine Starksen. Their three kids would be over on the schoolyard every morning before the Devil got shoes on. They would tell us that Virg's chickens woke them up when they started to crow as the sun came up. Maybe they were right. We got so we didn't notice the crowing as the birds were out north of the house. When the two boys would go by on the sidewalk across the street from the shop, I would holler at them, "How are you doing, girls?" "We ain't girls, we are boys," was their response. Then they would go home to tell the folks, year after year "He still calls us girls!" One day they came down to Grandpa Starksen's store to get some breakfast food. Out in front of our house there was a big puddle of water, mixed with mud. I saw them coming back, and what do you know: When they got to the puddle those little twerps sat down in it and then proceeded to cover the Post Toasties box with mud. They finally put the soggy box under their arm and took off to get something to eat. Dorene called me afterwards, and wanted to know what happened. These boys got a change of clothes and a bath, to boot! I didn't ask how the cereal turned out, whether it was edible or not. They always had a good time while they were here visiting.

Another time I had a binder in front of the shop and these boys had to play around on it. They found all of the greasy spots, and proceeded to wipe their hands off, using their clothes as towels. It was another time that Dorene called to ask, "What happened?" I didn't care about the grease, as there was more where that came from. The kids had fun, and so did I, watching them.

I did a lot of work for Doc Askey, the veterinarian in Arlington. We always got along great, and it was a pleasure to work for him. He would always go over to visit Pa when he came to the shop, and when it got so that Pa couldn't see who he was, he could tell by his voice. Doc would ask, "How are you, Mr. Andersen?" The answer, "It's that damn horse doctor," as Pa always called the vets. Doc would come back laughing, but they always had a good visit, and Pa and I both appreciated him taking the time to spread cheer to an older man, even though he was a "damn horse doctor." There was nothing derogatory about it, either.

Pa's first name was Morris, but he always signed checks, etc. with M, instead of Morris, probably to save time. He was always proud of his Danish ancestry, but he was more proud of being an American citizen and NEVER missed a chance to vote. The judges once even brought him a ballot so he could vote, even though he was at home, confined to bed. Some of today's non-voters should take a lesson from our Pa. He deemed it a privilege to Vote.

If some Dane came into the shop and started talking Danish, Pa would answer in English, and many a time have I heard, "What's the matter, why don't you talk Dane?" Pa's answer "These others can't understand Danish so I'm not talking Dane when others are around." I was always proud of him for his concern for others. Even though he had a gruff way about him, he had a warm heart. If no one was present Pa could talk fluent Dane, as well as English. By the way he talked, wrote and read, you would never know that he only went through the sixth grade in school. Sometimes when he was finished writing a letter to his Ma in Denmark, he would ask me, "How do you spell Europa?" "Oh, you mean Europe?" He hadn't switched over, from Dane to English.

An old Dane, Chris Brixen, would sometimes talk Dane to me. Finally realizing that I couldn't understand a word he said, he would say, "Oh by gos I hevn't switced ovur, yet." When he wanted oil for his car, he would tell the garage man, "I vant sum slip easy fer my enyine yoints." He got what he wanted.

I have been getting some static lately about the spelling on the sign on the front of the blacksmith shop, which is spelled AndersOn instead of AndersEn. What a misnomer! Let me assure you that this is NOT a typographical error, and the Norwegian who painted an O on the sign, instead of an E, got paid for it, and it was NOT in Danish money, either. The worst part of it is this: He got away with it. Pa didn't have the heart to make him correct the O to an E. Now me? I was just a seed in 1907 (having recently come over on a boat from the Old Country) when Pa bought the shop from Lynn Barber. If I had been around at that time so that I could have waved my arms into the air, something would have hit the fan on a deal like this, and the "O" would have gone down the drain, replaced with an "E." No ifs, ands or buts. Period.

Back in those early days, and even in today's world, the Norskes seem to think that they are the chosen people. The Danes once owned Norway. After centuries of trying to settle the Norwegians down, the Danes finally gave up on them, turned them loose on their own, and even sent a Dane king along with the deal to try and keep those Norskes in line. The 17th of May is their Independence Day, the anniversary of the Danes giving them the boot.

The Norwegians, (may they rest in peace), normally spelled their last name with an "O" if their name was Nelson, Peterson. Johnson, etc. The Danish names usually ended with an "sEn." Hetland was settled by a Norwegian majority who spelled their names with sOn, and by convention assumed that spelling was correct. That is the way Pa's misspelled sign came into existence. The original sign (and it is still there) read, M. ANDERSON, HORSESHOER AND

BS Shop sign... note the spelling of the name

BLACKSMITH. The letters were black, painted on a white background. Over the past 100 years the white weathered away, and the original letters are now raised, since the black paint was better, and did not weather as fast.

I have a different attitude about the spelling of our name, Andersen. When someone spells my last name with an O, watch out! Them iss fightin' words. Spell it with an E, or this Dane's ire is being agitated. Right is right and wrong is wrong, or so the old saying goes. When I was old enough to have a little say so in the shop, Skipper Peterson repainted the sign to read: M. ANDERSEN AND SON, BLACKSMITH. Skipper was a Norske and he and I were good friends. He did what I told him to do, and spelled it with an E. But alas, the first Norwegian painter had the last laugh. He is probably chuckling while sipping his beer, att da samme tyme tinkin, mi Blak paint vas mor bettor dan vat Skipper putt on, as Skipper's stuf hass dun gon Kaput, an mi painted letorrs R jus liik knew. HA HA an HOE HOE, dat iss ITT. Now you know what's what about the BS sign.

Chapter 13
Life Along the Railroad

Top: Hetland Depot (on the left) as it was originally built. Later it was lowered, remodeled, and the platform extended to the street. It was struck by lightning and burned down in 1919. To the right in the picture is a threshing rig on a flatcar.
Middle: Snow on the tracks, 1936
Bottom: Railroad snowplow, 1936

Life Along the Railroad

Hetland is one of the highest points for elevation on the local railroad. Formerly the Chicago and Northwestern, it is now the Dakota, Minnesota and Eastern Railroad. When steam engines were in use, and there were more than one engine on the train, they had to be synchronized in order to get the power needed to start them. Many times we would watch the two steam engines try to start when they were ready to leave town. There would be clattering and more clattering of the wheels while the engineers tried to get the engines to start together. There was an engineer and a fireman on each engine. Sometimes nothing worked, and the train would back west out of town to give it another try. It didn't help either to start, when sometimes some of our more ambitious citizens would put lard or axle grease on the rails, and then nothing moved. Boy, talk about slippery! That was something else. In case you might think that the devil in me was in on this, let me assure you that I was perfectly innocent – too messy.

We used to have four passenger trains a day through Hetland – two from the east and two from the west. Trains came from the east at about 6 AM and 7 PM. Trains from the west were scheduled at 9:45 AM and 10 PM.

We have had a few wrecks at the railroad crossing here in town. One day one of our customers, Oscar Omdalen, left the shop just before the 9:45 train was due from the west. I heard the engineer really laying on the whistle, (these were steam locomotives), like he was sent for, and couldn't come. Then I heard a CRASH, and I high tailed it for the depot. There was Oscar's car sitting across the track, right side up. It just so happened that Oscar was far enough across the tracks that the cowcatcher, as we called it on the front of the engine, crashed through the front door. There was Oscar, sitting behind the steering wheel, with blood running from several spots on his head, with the monstrous cowcatcher resting on the floor of the car, keeping the car from tipping over. The front end of the cowcatcher was nearly resting in Oscar's lap. Boy, was he LUCKY, as the rear wheels of the car slid along the depot platform, and that and the cowcatcher reposing on the floor boards kept the car upright. He said the reason the train hit him was because he was waving to the people on the platform and didn't look west to see if the way was clear. It wasn't!

He, being a full-blooded Norwegian and a really NICE fellow, and a good farmer, survived the wreck. Pa and I still had a valued customer for life, and we never had a complaint from him. He was as honest as the day was long. He never told us, like some of our customers did, that they would pay their bill when they sold their hogs. Boy, as of this writing, there are some OLD hogs that never made it to market.

We used to watch the trains and some of their maneuvers. One was called the "flying switch," used when they had a car that was supposed to go on the sidetrack to one of the elevators here in town. The boxcar to be left would be unhooked from the other cars behind it. The engineer would pull ahead beyond the switch, where the car would be unhooked, and a brakeman would get on it. Another brakeman would open the switch for the sidetrack. The engineer would get up speed backing up and pushing the cars. At the last minute, the engineer would let up on the throttle and the boxcar that had been uncoupled would go merrily on its way down the sidetrack. The brakeman on top of the uncoupled car would turn the wheel to put on the brakes to stop it at the right location. The brakeman at the switch would close it after the car had passed and before the train got to it, so the train could continue up the track to hook on to the rest of the cars that had been left. I don't recall ever seeing this done since diesel engines were put into service, but when steam engines were used, it was fun to watch.

One of the Stanglands was an engineer or fireman on some of the trains that went through Hetland. He let everyone know when he was on the engine, as he would start whistling long before they got to town, and hold the whistle open after the engine was through town. Nothing like letting the townspeople know that one of its "native sons" was helping keep the trains running. In later years, Verle Dutcher was an engineer on some of the trains, but he didn't lay on the whistle like Stangland.

In those days there were no walkie-talkies for the railroad crews to talk to each other or anyone else. When our depot agent had to get a message to the engineer on a through train, he would stand out beside the track with an outfit that looked like a big O with a long handle on it, holding it up as high as he could. There was a place to put the message that had come to him by telegraph. This was the only way to convey messages about other trains, etc. When the engineer saw the agent out by the track, he didn't slow down at all. He would lean out of the window as far as he could, put his arm out and try to put it through the big circle O that the agent held. Once in a while, they didn't make connections, but most of the time it worked. The engineer would take off the message and drop the outfit to the ground to be used another time. This was a good idea that someone, probably with a college degree, had thought up. Anyway, it was better than sending up smoke signals. As I think about it, those trains were probably going 35 or 40 miles per hour, so everything had to be timed perfectly for the engineer to "snare" the message.

In 1937 we had a doozey of a blizzard on the 21st or 22nd of April. Yes, I said April! Everything was at a standstill. Eva and I walked out east of town when we heard the train was coming with a snowplow to try to clear off the tracks. The "cuts" where the tracks went through were even with the tops of the telegraph poles. We sat on top of the poles east of town, and waited for the show to start. Here came the two locomotives with black smoke rolling out of their stacks pushing a big gondola car loaded with sand and with a V plow on its front. They were ready for action, and so were we. Half of the country seemed to be there as the weather was nice and warm as it should be in April.

Plowing the railroad, 1936

We had it all figured out that these two engines would hit the snow at breakneck speed. However, the engine crew knew more about moving snow than we novices did. They crept up to the monstrous snowbank, pushed the plow into the snow and of course they got stuck. We could have told the crew that, but no one asked us how to do it. The caboose carried a lot of men with shovels. They came out and began shoveling and finally got the train backed out. This went on for a few times, and finally the engineer figured they would never get to where they were supposed to be at this snail's pace. They must have had a meeting of the head honchos, because all at once the engineer meant business. Black smoke belched out like you wouldn't believe it, as the firemen must have really been shoveling in the coal. The whole outfit began to move, and all we could see from the top of the telegraph poles was black smoke and snow coming up over the side of the engine. Finally, after several hundred feet of this, we could see light at the end of the tunnel. The snowplow headed east and the track was clear. As we looked east, it looked like a tunnel without a top on it. The next train was cleared to head for Chicago.

Eva... snow by railroad

When the railroad demolition crew tore down the depot, I went down and bought some lumber. After I had paid the boss, he asked me, "Does that home run hitter still live here?" I asked who that was. His reply, "Mory Andersen." I was polite and wanted to know if he was a home run hitter. "Oh, man, when he came to bat we went back as far as we could go," was his reply. I told him, "I'm Mory Andersen." Out came his hand, and we shook hands as good old buddies should do. Then "Who are you?" was my question. He told me his name. I told him, "You must not have been worth a damn, as I don't remember you." We had a good laugh over that. Maurice Matson told me that was a poor way to repay a compliment. He was right.

Lewis Crandall was coming into town from the south one time as the morning passenger from the west was coming to a stop at the depot. The first thing Lewis knew, he saw the two big wheels (drivers) in front of him. Now, as Lewis would say, "Where did they come from?" He wasn't going very fast, and hit the engine in front of the ladder where the engineer and fireman crawled up into the cab. In some miraculous way, the step hooked onto his car and carried Lewis (who was still holding on to the steering wheel) across the road and unceremoniously dumped him and his car on the other side of the sidewalk. He was bruised and lost some blood, but otherwise he was all right. Besides that, the railroad paid him for running into their engine. We used to razz him about getting paid for running into the train.

A farmer who lived south of town hit a through freight train right on the ladder the brakemen used to crawl up on top of the cars. He hit this moving menace (ladder) just right. The train carried his car about 50 feet, and then the car dropped off from the ladder, right side up. But that wasn't the end of the fiasco. When each subsequent boxcar came past, its ladder step would hit the car. The car would bounce up in the air, and then start to come down when

WHAM, the next step hit the bouncing car. Martin Steffensen, who managed the elevator, saw the whole accident. He tore out to the car and managed to get the passenger side door open. The farmer was lying with his head on the floor, so Martin grabbed him by the neck, and got the poor guy out and laid on the ground. The freight cars kept on bouncing the car until there was no more car. If I remember right, the train stopped when the men in the caboose saw what happened. The fellow wasn't hurt, and I don't know if he sobered up in a quick hurry or not. We always figured that a sober man would have had a sad ending. He was a nice guy when he was sober. I felt sorry for him. He and I were friends, but not drinking buddies.

At night in the summertime when we had our windows open, we could sometimes hear the mournful yet peaceful sound of the steam whistle sounding the alarm at each mile line crossing that danger was approaching. It seems like only yesterday when I think of lying in bed and enjoying that peaceful sound, sometimes heard as far as five miles away.

Chapter 14
Tall Tales

Tall Tales

When we were kids our elders would have us running around town looking for doughnut stretchers, left hand monkey wrenches, sky hooks and striped paint. We finally decided their articles were something to be desired and mere antiques.

I should tell you about Baron Munchausen who we used to hear on the radio. Munchausen must have originated from a long line of liars, or else he was the granddaddy of all liars. I don't know. He would get wound up on some story that would make your hair stand on end, unless of course, you were bald headed - then?? They were not short stories, either! Oh-oh, I forgot to inform you that the old Baron had a sidekick whose name was Charley. He was the one who made the tall tales more vivid for the imagination. When the Baron finally got to the climax of his fantastic story, the sidekick, Charley, would politely tell the storyteller that the whole story couldn't be true. Baron would ask, "Vere you dere, Charley?" That made the story believable. Obbie Melstad couldn't hold a candle to this liar even though Obbie had another nickname, Baron, which we would sometimes call him when he got too far out on a limb with some wild tale.

Happy Larson and a bunch of the fellows were "shooting the breeze" about the bad storms we were having. Happy finally told about being out in a storm that was really bad. He looked up and saw a bolt of lightning coming at him so he stepped aside and it hit the ground where he had been standing. Everyone laughed in disbelief, of course. Happy turned to Obbie Melstad and said, "Ain't that right Obbie?" Not to be outdone, Obbie replied without batting an eye "You're damn right, I was there." That's what I call quick thinking, one liar backing up another!

Skipper Pederson's café was a hangout for the local whiz kids. They concocted a device where Obbie Melstad could cut in on a radio program and bring something special for Hetland. One day Nick Nelson came into the café. Obbie was out in the back room and suddenly interrupted the WNAX radio program with a special item for sale. Nick Nelson of Hetland had a blind horse for sale. Obbie poured it on how good the horse was and told anyone interested to contact Nick at Hetland. Nick stopped dead in his tracks when he heard this and exclaimed: "Now how did Yankton know about that horse being for sale?" No one told him so he figured news traveled fast in this little town.

On a nice, clear winter day, Mamie Crandall came into the café. Obbie butted in and cut out the regular broadcast from Yankton (which, by the way, was our favorite radio station). Obbie reported a big blizzard was up north of Hetland and headed south. It was up by Walt Crandall's farm and everyone should take shelter and stay inside, as it was a "big dooser" of a killer storm. Needless to say, Mamie got excited (and who wouldn't) and yelled "Where's Raymond and Cecil, we have to go home right away!" Obbie could really lay it on thick when he wanted to.

Pa told about the Streels in Norway who found a watch, and it was ticking. They called a big meeting to see what to do with this strange device. They decided to send out the smartest men to dispose of it in the ocean. The boatmen (not the Volga boatmen) took said watch out into the ocean. One of the brain trust was about to drop the watch into the water when another intellectual hollered, "Wait, let's mark the spot so we can find it later on if necessary." It was a good idea, so one of those smart Norskes took his knife and cut a V in the side of the boat, and then sent the watch down to Davey Jones' locker. Pa said they told this story in Denmark, and us kids believed that it should be true. Don't know if the watch ever needed to be found. (In later telling of this and similar stories, this question was raised: "How they could find it later if they used a different boat?" – ed.)

This story was told to us as kids, and we believed it, too. A Norwegian was driving a team of mules. All at once they stopped and wouldn't move. He did everything he could think of to get them going, but to no avail. A Dane watched the proceedings and told the Norske that he could get them going. Nope, they won't go. The Dane calmly walked up to one of the mules, took hold of his ear and whispered something to the four-legged beast. Lo and behold, the team took off on a trot and the problem was solved. The Norwegian wanted to know what his friend did to get the mules going. The sharp Dane told him that when he had the mule's attention, by holding him by the ear, he told him in no uncertain terms, "Get going or I'll beat the Hell out of you." Funny how a simple thing like that worked, when everything else failed. Do you believe in miracles?

I never could figure out how a woman would buy a girdle that was two or three sizes too small for her, and then wiggle and groan pulling it over the spots that were supposed to be smooth and make her figure look great. Back in the good old days, the girls were dressed and if the seams of their stockings weren't straight they were not well dressed. I don't know how a bow-legged girl decided if the seams were straight up and down, or followed the curve of her leg.

We always heard that a man who wore a belt and suspenders at the same time must have been a pessimist. He didn't want to get caught out in public with his pants down, if one or the other should break. This way, having both, he had a backup just in case he needed it. I don't know if the government spent any dollars to figure this out. From what I have read they could have done worse, especially since spending a half million dollars studying the sex life of a bullfrog in Mexico. I never have heard the outcome of this noble endeavor. Personally, I think the man wearing suspenders and a belt is an optimist. He is trying to keep the economy going by putting more hard earned money into circulation, especially if he is working in a clothing store, or owns it. Good for business.

Just in case you wondered how I got suspenders and a belt into this girdle deal, I'll have to explain how that came about. On the bottom of a girl's girdle were several elastic devices, on the order of a suspender for men. The girls would hook these to their hose in order to keep said hose up, and not slip down and make wrinkles. Besides, the seams might not follow the contour of the leg. You younger girls don't know what you missed, since now the nylons seem to go on any old way, as long as you put your foot where the opening is. Maurice Matson used to tell me that in Denmark on the bottom of a pop bottle was a notice: "Open the other end." Don't know if stockings had one that said, "Put foot in other end."

The favorite recipe for baking carp was to put the fish on a board, sprinkle on all of the ingredients and spices, and put it in the oven and bake for two hours at 400 degrees. After this, take out the board and the fish, throw the fish away and eat the board. Sounds like a good recipe? Some Dane must have thought it up.

Jerry Bunday, who ran the east elevator, stopped into the shop to show us how he had spent a dollar. An ad was in a magazine, advertising, "A sure kill for potato bugs or your money will be refunded." The potato plants always had bugs on them, called potato bugs. Don't have any idea what the scientific name of these bugs was, but they could surely raise hob with the potato leaves. We used to mix up a poison mixture of Paris Green to kill them. We would mix it in a pail and then we'd dip a paintbrush into the liquid and shake it over the plants. This wasn't a guaranteed process, either. Getting back to the invested buck: Jerry opened the package, and lo and behold, there were two flat pieces of wood about a foot long and two inches wide. On one board was a big red dot about the size of a quarter. Underneath it was posted an instruction on how to use this 50-cent instrument. It went as follows: "Place the bug on the red dot." Boy, that was an easy instruction to follow. On the other 50 cent investment was an even better and more scientific instruction: "Hit the bug with this board." All of us got a good laugh from this, including Jerry. By the way, he didn't try to get his buck back, because the killer device was a sure kill, when the directions were followed. Potato bugs - BEWARE! They would be dead as a doornail after getting squashed.

Around the stove in the hardware store, as it was around the stove in the BS shop, there were some pretty tall tales told. There was a salesman that came to the hardware store and Jim and Charlie called him Liar Hansen. We happened to be up there one day when this character was there. Boy, he was a polished liar. He was spinning a yarn about shooting a pheasant, and he had only winged it. The bird took off running, and Liar Hansen took after him. He told us he never saw a pheasant that could run that fast, but that he, Hansen, was gaining on the bird when a jack rabbit got up and started to run too. Hansen said he was going so fast that he gave that rabbit a kick in the butt and told him to get out of the road and let somebody (him) run who could run. We decided he was a pretty fast runner or maybe he was a liar. I suppose the bird lost the race, but Hansen never got that far with the story. Boy, was he windy, but interesting.

Old man Barber (Lynn) used to tell us kids that he had seen it so dry here that he could look up and see the rain coming, and it evaporated before it hit him on the head. Wow! That must have been dry weather. He also told us he had lived on this earth before. He was here as a jackass, and he had seen himself standing under a tree in order to shade himself. Could be - us kids didn't have any reason to doubt his word, as he was older and more mature than we were.

Chapter 15
Faithful Living
(Church stories)

Top: Church, ca 1940
Middle: Church, 1991
Bottom: Church and parsonage, ca 1907

Faithful Living

Through the years, the Lord has blessed us with some outstanding ministers who have been dedicated men of God. When our little church has been in a crisis, the Lord has stepped in and helped us overcome and take care of our needs. We sometimes think that the congregation solved the matter, but deep in our hearts we know that our Maker took care of it for us. We were only His tools.

When Rev. Hoare was here we had big, and I mean BIG Christmas pageants. We would practice for weeks learning the lines of our Christmas story. Then on Christmas Eve we would put on the Christmas story, the birth of Christ. We had a big tree that reached to the ceiling of the church and was beautifully decorated. However, in those days if one light burned out the rest went out too. We had a big ladder beside the tree and when this happened we would climb up and try to find the "dead" bulb so the rest would work. This program was something to behold and there was only standing room in the church. Everyone brought what presents they had and put them under the tree. There was a big pile there and then you hauled them home again. There were always presents for the preacher and SS teacher. Some of the presents were opened there, some brought back to open at home.

Rev. Hoare used to remark that he could use the Andersen boys anywhere in the Christmas program, but he never tried to make angels out of us. I never knew why. He once commented something about my roly-poly brother Clayton and referred to him as that little "Skinny boy." That's how he got the nickname "Skinny."

Sunday School playground

The preacher and his wife, with help from volunteers put on six weeks of Bible School for us kids. At that time we had 120 in Sunday School. Behind the church the men in town had built swings, a merry-go-round, a chinning bar, a slide about 12 feet high, and then a big Ferris wheel. At first manpower was used to turn it but then Pa and some others put a gas engine on it to furnish the power. Boy, that was something.

To finish off Bible School we would have a croquet elimination and then get it down to 8 players to see who was champion. It was the same for double partners. One year I was in the finals and 3 or 4 of the finalists got in the first arch and wouldn't let me get through. Then somebody goofed and left a hole so I got through the first arch. It ended up I got to the last 2 arches and the stake and the rest of them came down and hit my ball and knocked it down to the south end of the church lawn. I'd come back again, they would hit my ball back south again but finally I won the tournament. The preacher's sister-in-law and I teamed up for doubles and we won that too. Must have been luck connected with it.

Rev. Hoare asked us how many were good Americans. Everyone raised their hands except me. He wanted to know if I wasn't a good American. I replied "I'm a Dane." Boy, how he laughed. When I got home I asked my Ma if I should have raised my hand. Would you call me dumb, ignorant, or proud of my Danish blood? That's a good question!

Jessie Hurd was teaching our class of little folks in Sunday School. Somehow she got to telling about David killing Goliath and said that David shot at random. I piped up for some unknown reason with "Was he there too?" Needless to say, she never let me forget it. So far I haven't found out anything about random in the Bible.

Our kids would have Sunday School at Earl Dutcher's home. Anna Dutcher would teach the class. Dutchers had Grandpa Barber's parrot, Jack Sprat, and that old bird could swear as well as say some other things. The kids came home laughing one day, telling that Jack Sprat would say the Lord's Prayer along with the class. I suppose he heard it enough so that he got the gist of it.

Aaron Meckel, one of our preachers, was going with Miss Schadde, one of the High School teachers. Let me assure you that he was single and had never been married, as far as we knew. One night, several of us kids saw him go up to Bunday's home where the teacher stayed. Well, we didn't have anything better to do, so we decided to check this out. The house had a big bay window facing Park Avenue. Now, lest you get any idea that we were "peeping toms," we were not. We didn't have anybody in our group named Tom. We boys, there were no girls present, ambled up the street and slowed down and finally stopped in front of the bay window. We were out on the sidewalk of course, which wasn't private property. The only reason we stopped was because we saw our preacher and his girl friend, the teacher, in the living room all by themselves. This was interesting, so we decided to take in the proceedings. She sat on the davenport and our preacher got down on his knee. Now, we thought that was odd, so we moved closer to get a better look. We figured that he should be on the davenport beside her instead of on his knees. We had a quick discussion to see what was going on here. We had it! The preacher was asking the teacher to marry him! We had heard or read about such romantic events. Sure enough, old Sherlock Holmes would have been proud of us kids. The two were getting married and we "scooped" the rest of the town that the girl said, "YES." The marriage hung together and he went on to be a famous Congregational minister in several churches in the East, as well as a writer of many Christian books.

The finances of the church used to be in such dire straits that the elected treasurer at one time wouldn't take the job, because the church had no funds to pay the bills, and he didn't want to face those who had money coming from the church.

The Lord has really blessed us in the last several years, as several of our friends and former parishioners have left us money in their wills to help us keep their, and our, church as a loving and caring beacon in our little community. Some of these benefactors had been gone from here for more than 70 years, but they still remembered what the Congregational Church in Hetland meant to them.

When Eva was preaching in Hetland, services were scheduled from 11:30 to 12:30. One Sunday she got wound up and didn't seem to know when to quit. She would look at her watch, and then go at it again. Several more times she would look at her watch. Margaret Karban was the pianist at the time, and needed to catch the bus to return to college. Finally, at 12:45, Margaret left to catch the bus. Mom looked kind of funny, looked at her watch again, and do you know what? It had stopped, so no wonder she wasn't concerned about preaching overtime. I don't know what the sermon was about, (I don't think it was hellfire and damnation) but she always had a good service, even though I might be a little prejudiced.

Eva was preaching a sermon about giving to the church. She told a story about a widow who didn't have much of anything to give, so she laid an egg on the altar. After she said that, she wondered if any of the flock would catch the way it sounded. She didn't need to worry, as no one even commented on how it sounded.

One Sunday after Eva finished preaching at the Hetland service, we were to go back to Badger for a church dinner. We were all ready to go but couldn't find Virgil. Different ones in town had seen him, but no one knew where he was. Most of the town was out looking for him, checking cisterns and all out of the way places. We were about frantic, not knowing what had become of him. Finally we came home and went upstairs, and there he was, sound asleep on his bed. He was tired, and the bed looked good to him. We thanked God that the lost boy was found safe and sound. We got to Badger and had dinner, even though we were late.

Myrna got an early start playing for church. During World War II we didn't have a minister, so Eva preached in the Hetland and Badger Congregational Churches for eight years. Sometimes Eva used to play the piano and preach

Virg, Myrna, and Eva

too, rotating from the pulpit to the piano. When Myrna was about nine, her mom had taught her to play for church, so at last we had a church pianist. Myrna did the Lord's work, being in charge of the music for a Lutheran church in Galesburg, Illinois. She retired in 2004, having served there for 36 years, teaching one generation of kids, their kids, and their grandkids, too. She takes after her mom in inspiring everyone to do his or her best to further God's kingdom here on earth.

Virg and Vi have done much the same in their UCC Church in Sioux Falls. Virg directed the choir for several years, and both still sing in it. Melanie and Elaine, their kids, said that their dad did the driving of the choir, as well as the directing, and mom did the pushing. They too are following in Eva's footsteps. They don't get it from me.

On one occasion, we had first hand evidence that there was at least one Norske who got trigger happy with an air gun. We were having a Congregational Church meeting at our house one evening when BANG! somebody shot through our dining room window. Glass splattered, but no one was hurt, for which we were thankful. After all, it was a church meeting and should have been a safe place to be. Alas, it wasn't. I ran to the back door to see what the ruckus was all about. I saw two kids out in the street. One had a gun and was ready to shoot out another window, and perhaps annihilate one of the church flock.

I hit the ground running at full speed to stop the slaughter. The two kids had a head start on me, and got to the cornfield before I did. If I had caught them, especially the one with the gun, he might have met his "Waterloo" right here in Hetland! I heard afterwards by the grapevine that these two culprits remarked that the "old fart" could really run. I must have been in better shape than I am now.

The next day, we found out the kid with the gun had shot out the windows in the girls' dorm, so we got by with only one gone. Mayor Crandall vowed that when they caught the fugitives that the town would "throw the book" at them. After careful scientific research, the "wheels" covering the investigation found out who the would-be Jesse James was. But I have bad news to report. The Mayor came down to the BS Shop and told me who the sharpshooter was. He also told me they couldn't do anything to him because he came from a "good" family. I don't know what "good" meant in a case like this, but I assumed that if the shooter was from a "poor" family they probably would have thrown the book at him. Case was closed, and I guess the window glasses were put in. Don't know who paid for them. Incidentally, those kids lived in "The Holy Land."

I must tell you what the Holy Land and the Holy City are. I didn't know either where this sacred ground was until some of my friends told me. It seems as though there were a lot of Norwegian Streels and Stavangers who settled in an area called North Preston. From what I could gather, this area was the Holy Land, and where the North Preston Lutheran Church was located naturally had to be the Holy City. I don't recall seeing this on the county map, but I presumed this to be true. We had a lot of kids from the Holy Land that went to school here. They seemed to be good kids too, just like the kids here who lived on ordinary Terra Firma (ground).

Eva preached in Badger as well as in Hetland. The Badger church had a small choir, which she directed, and of course, sang for church. One year, before Easter, she realized that with only 60 piano students she still had some free time – when, I don't know. Anyway, she talked to the choir members who decided that it would be nice to invite other church singers to get together and have an inter-community choir for Easter. We had about 50 to 60 singers, and it went over

Intercommunity choir, ca 1957

great! We practiced for weeks on end to put on a cantata about the Risen Lord. We had singers from all around – Hetland, Badger, Arlington, Volga, Lake Norden, North Preston, and De-Smet, and performed concerts at least three or four times at Easter in various churches.

We had good cooperation from most congregations, except some of the Norwegian preachers told their flock not to sing with Eva's choir. After all, we had Congregationalists, Methodists, Covenant, Lutheran, Dutch Reformed, Presbyterians, Baptists, and even Marius Krog, the Danish Lutheran preacher from Badger, singing with the group. A sprinkling of brave souls, most of them Danes, defied the edict of their preacher and sang anyway. After all, we were singing to the glory of God who is Father to all of us.

The preacher from the Holy Land didn't give such an edict. We had several from there who had gone to school here, and knew that Eva, their ex-teacher and music director, didn't have horns on her head. We had this choir for about eight years. It was a lot of enjoyable work, fun and fellowship. The women made choir robes for each member, so you can see the dedication that went into the joy of proclaiming the resurrection of Christ.

One year we were to sing in the North Preston church, but alas, the preacher they had then put thumbs down on it. No concert in his church. We were devastated, as a good number of our singers were members there. After all, most of the Intercommunity Choir members were not Lutherans. Besides that, there were several of us who were members of the Masonic Lodge. I can see where this preacher, as a leader of his flock, put thumbs down on having all of us in his church.

One morning, out of the clear blue sky, I think it was blue, or would be, Eva wanted to know if I would take her to Lake Preston. She was going to give the North Preston preacher a piece of her mind, and let him know what she thought of his childish antics. I was happy to take her and was ready to add some of my philosophy to back her up. We were getting ready to leave when the phone rang with good news. The singing problem was solved. Some of the "powers that be" in the Holy City had a big pow-wow and decided that as long as we were singing about the resurrection of Christ, that it would be OK to let us into the church. Praise the Lord!

The big night for the concert came. Lo and behold, the church was packed to capacity. It had been dry all spring, and at the time the ground was begging for rain and the crops were suffering. We were all on our best behavior, and Eva lifted her arms to give us the sign to start to sing, when "BANG" there was a flash of lightning and thunder, and it started to pour! Probably not like Noah's flood, but it poured and kept on pouring! We really had to lift our voices to compete with the vicious storm. We came to the song about the crucified Christ calling out in a loud voice "It is finished." BANG! There was lightning and a loud clap of thunder. The "veil of the temple was rent" brought another loud BANG! and rolling of thunder, then there was the earthquake and the stone was rolled away, accompanied by "BANG! BANG! and more BANGS!" Christ had risen!

Just that quickly, the storm was over, with no more lightning and thunder, just the drops of water coming off of the eaves – a deathly silence that was almost frightening. We kept singing and when we came to the part on the road to Emmaus after the resurrection, it was so quiet outside that it was almost eerie. We had the feeling that God, in his own way, had punctuated the Easter story for us. A wild replay of what it must have been like when Christ was crucified for our sins and then raised from the grave, when the stone was rolled away so that we might have eternal life.

Myrna and Virgil were too small at the time to sing in the choir, but did sing a few years later. Bessie Damm was seated between the kids, and asked Myrna if the church had lighting rods on it, the way the lightning was flashing. Myrna didn't know, but told her we didn't have any on our house either, so she must have figured one place was as safe as the other.

When we were ready to go home, the stars were brilliant and the earth soaked with three inches of rain. The crops, which only a few hours before had been begging for rain to keep them alive, now had a new lease on life. If the fields of grain could sing (and maybe they can) they would be singing thanks for the much-needed rain that in an hour's time had changed a parched land into a Garden of Eden. Who knows? The Lord could have been patting Eva on the back to show that He appreciated her vision in getting a choir like this together to help proclaim Christ's mission on earth. I'm sure that each member of the choir pleased the Lord also, and felt it in their hearts. End of the sermon, I'm no preacher, just an old blacksmith.

Del Horsted, a blacksmith from DeSmet wanted to sing in the Inter-Community Choir. That was good, as we were always looking for gifted singers. Del wasn't short on self-esteem. Found out later that he was at least part Danish. Don't know if that had anything to do with his esteem or not. Eva wanted to know what he sang. His answer, "What do you need?" She checked him out and found out where he belonged, which was not in the women's section. That wasn't so bad, but then Del decided that he had better tell Eva how one particular piece in the cantata should be sung. Having lived with this director for several years, I knew she could have "told him off." Instead, she politely told him that she was doing the directing, and if the concert sounded good the singers got the credit, and if it wasn't good, she would take the blame. He didn't question any of her decisions after that, and became a loyal and enthusiastic member of the choir. Tact worked again.

One Sunday we were to be gone, so I called Esther Warne to see if she and her husband Clare would host pastor John Johnston for

Sunday dinner. She said that would be OK with them. Then she got to worrying what to feed the preacher. She called me and wanted to know if John would be offended if she had baked potatoes for dinner. I told her baked spuds were the best there were, as far as I was concerned, and that he wouldn't object, as he ate anything that Eva served us. These two good friends were so nervous about having a preacher over for dinner that they didn't even go to church, but stayed home waiting for church to be over. These two never missed church unless they had a good reason, so I suppose Father John was a good reason to stay home.

John and another pastor, Chris Klug never minded what Eva cooked, and ate to their hearts' content, which is what any good cook appreciates. Eva was really a good cook, and we never suffered for a good home-cooked meal. I used to tell some of the fellows that it was no treat for me to go out and eat, as I was spoiled with such a good cook at home. I meant it then, and still do. Eva's cooking rubbed off on Myrna and Virgil, but I just tagged along, although I can boil water without burning it.

All through the years, the Hetland Ladies Aid has been the backbone of the Church. Without these dedicated Christian women, the church would never have survived all these years. The ladies did everything imaginable to try to make some money to help pay the operating expenses of the church. Time and time again when the local church was "flat broke," the Ladies Aid somehow came to the rescue with much needed finances. These ladies, through the years, have never taken the back seat for anyone when it comes to cooking and for getting things done with wonderful planning skills.

I can't begin to tell of all the different things the ladies did to raise money for the Lord's work. They had ice cream socials, basket socials, bake sales, chicken suppers, regular suppers, strawberry socials, plays and lunches. I can remember

Ladies Aid Hat Social

when it cost 15 cents, and then later on a quarter for a full course chicken supper. Ice cream socials were 10 cents each.

It was comical when they had basket socials and some girl would bring a fancy basket, and if she had a boy friend, he was supposed to buy it – or else. It was great sport when someone else would bid up the basket, and the poor boy friend would have to "pay through the nose" in order to stay on dating terms with his girl.

Quite often in later years the ladies would have lunches and bake sales in Barber-Johnson Hardware. Eva would bake several batches of cream puffs, and they would be gone in no time. She would tear home to bake several more batches in order to accommodate those who knew her cream puffs were good – and they were really good! People still talk about her good cream puffs, and many say they were the best they had ever eaten. I could vouch for that, as we have had our share of them in our family. They were tops.

Back in 1988 the Hetland Congregational Church was ready to fall into the basement. We were pumping 6000 gallons of water an hour out of the basement. It got so the church wasn't safe to have anything going on except church services. Margaret Karban Decker and her husband Herman decided something had to be done. They gave the church $1,000 to see if it could be blocked up. We tried to block it up and there were no footings or anything to hold it up. Then Chuck Starksen took ahold of the project and sent out letters for donations to see about moving it. Red Stangland and a Shriner friend of his from Sioux Falls who was a contractor came up and told us there was nothing to do but move it. Enough money came in from people who used to go to church here and some that never did go to church so that we could move it.

In the renovation deal we found a cornerstone. In that box was all kinds of stuff from 100 years before. There were newspapers from around the county, a scroll from China and all kinds of information about work in the church. Rev. Smith was the one who was mainly responsible for having the church built. It cost $5,000 to move the church east about 50 feet and put it on a foundation level with the ground. When they lifted the church up off the foundation you could push the walls into the basement. The 8 x 8s that held the church up could be pushed over too. So, the church was there by faith and that was it, as far as the foundation holding it up. Nothing there except Divine Grace. During the Hetland Centennial in 1988 we had a monstrous crowd at church on Sunday. What a glorious way to celebrate the way the Lord took care of our little church! Thanks to the volunteers for seeing to it that in the year 2007 we still have a church, even though we are few in numbers.

By the way, the original church building cost $1,500 in 1915, and in 2004 we spent $8,500 to put a new roof on it. Times have changed!

The Hetland church is one of the only Congregational churches left in South Dakota. Nearly all of the others joined with the Evangelical and Reformed Church in 1957 to create The United Church of Christ. We didn't join, although Eva and I voted for it. The Lord has blessed us through the years in giving us good ministers. Not all of the members were always satisfied with the preacher, but we all can't please everybody all the time.

When one of our ministers left, we didn't have any idea who we could get to replace him. I called around to friends we had and got a lead on Chris Klug, a young man in Brookings who had just come from Chicago to help out a peace group. I called him, and Eva and I went to meet him at McDonalds. I told him what color shirt I'd be wearing, and he told us what he would have on. When we came into the restaurant, lo and behold, here was a nice looking young man with a nice smile on his face, so we decided he must be the one we were looking for, and he was.

We visited for about two hours, and when we left him it was like the three of us had been friends for years. He came over here the next Sunday and preached, and stayed to serve us for 4 1/2 years. He is like one of our family, as we had him over for dinner every Sunday after services. He always said that he had one good meal a week with Eva's cooking. He and his charming wife, Bev, live in Iowa and still get out to Hetland to visit and we talk over the phone on a regular basis.

When Chris left to go to another job on the east coast, he saw to it that we were well taken care of, as he had talked to Floyd and Norma Mills, who lived in Huron, to take over his position. The two of them took care of our little flock for a number of years, and are really dedicated and caring people. After they retired and moved to the Black Hills, Marilyn Jones assumed the pastoral role. Bob Kallesen, is our organist. Little did we dream that when little Bob started taking his first piano lessons from Eva umpteen years ago, he would be using his musical talents today in our little church. Again, our cup runneth over.

I like to think that God in His wisdom had a big part in the love that radiated from the church to those who never forget how much their church meant to them through the years. We praise God for His loving care. He still works in mysterious ways.

Chapter 16
Reading, Writing, and Arithmetic

Top: Schoolhouse, 1917
Bottom: Schoolhouse, ca 1990

Reading, Writing, and Arithmetic

I never went to college but did manage to graduate from the best high school in the state, a school that was known for the Hetland Broncos, with red and black as the team colors. These Broncos were the scourge of the county when they got in action, even though they had to compete with all the big towns in the state. There was only one class of school and that included Sioux Falls, Rapid City, etc.

The first day I went to school was something else! In the first place, I didn't want to go, so Ma took me by the hand and led me up to the primary room. Of course, I was crying crocodile tears all the time and scared spitless. Then, to top it off, Superintendent Korstad came down and patted me on the head and said: "Don't cry, little boy, you have 12 more years of this!" If I could have I would have kicked him in the shins, but after all I was just starting grade one! No justice at all!

Pa used to tell us that if we got a licking in school, we would get a worse one when we got home. We never got licked in school. In grade school, we had a teacher who didn't spare the rod when she needed to use it. She whacked one kid over the head and then grabbed him by the hand and swatted him on the hand. That was a mistake. This kid grabbed the ruler, and held on so she couldn't hit him again. Another time one of the girls was acting up, and the teacher grabbed her, gave her a shaking, and asked, "Just who do you think you are?" "I'm Clara Mae Weidenkopf, and who do you think you are?" Wow!

One Halloween some jokers put a cow upstairs in the east assembly of the schoolhouse. Guess they nearly had to kill the critter before they got her down the stairs. Besides that, she was scared of being "in school" and the floor was pretty slippery from all the excitement. Don't get any idea that I was in on this because I was too small when this happened. It even made the editorial section of the *Hetland New Era* newspaper.

I never heard how the school officials got the cow down the stairs. It still puzzles me, how that poor cow felt, starting school in high school, of all things. Nothing like starting at the top, or so I have been told. But with me, I had to start in grade one and twelve years later the teachers decided they'd had enough of me. I got the "boot" with a piece of paper to show that the booting was on the up and up, and my school days were all behind me. The war was about to begin and also the schooling known as, "hard knocks"! Ah well, they haven't been too bad, over the years. The best knocks have gotten the better of the "worst hard knocks."

We used to have two toilets out west of the schoolhouse – segregated, of course. They were big, with three or four holes so the waiting line wouldn't be too long. Had big four foot sidewalks leading to the doors, and the sidewalks are still there, even though the "cans" are gone. The one us boys used is now behind the city hall and is not in very good shape anymore. The girls' toilet had only one door. The boys' had two doors, on the east and the west ends, and with a wall in the center, which resulted in the boys having two private toilets instead of one multi-holer like the girls. Probably was a Norwegian that figured this out to save lumber and space, and having to excavate only one hole for the pit

If I remember right, some of the sidewalk had little pockmarks or ridges in the cement. I never did know what these were for, but after careful study, I have come to the startling conclusion that they were put there on purpose! The brilliant idea crossed my mind that in case of an ice storm, this would make the walk less slippery if one of the students was "high tailing it" in a great hurry to get to the toilet in the event that nature was calling. It would have been a crying shame not to have made it by slipping on the ice. Any better ideas?

Getting back to the girls' outhouse. On rare occasions in the winter we would get the girls "holed up" in their abode. We would keep them bottled up by throwing snowballs at them when the door was opened. They knew that we wouldn't hurt them, but they liked the excitement of being chased (I think!). One day we had several girls who were afraid to venture out, and we were having a field day making and throwing snowballs. We would hit the "can" with them to let the girls know we were still there, without opening the door. One day the superintendent, Pop Wallace, looked out the window and finally, by putting two and two together, figured out what was going on. Boy, we got called into the office right now! I just happened to be in on this deal – why I don't know, but that's a different story. Pop Wallace really let us know what he thought of the way we were treating our fellow (girl) students. He had a three-foot rubber hose lying on his desk, and while he was pouring it on to us he picked it up said hose and was caressing it like he was about to use it on us. Lyle Scherkenback got to bawling, and I think Pop liked to hear that, as he knew he was getting through to at least one kid. He finally laid the hose down and made us stay after school for a week. I think he didn't make too much of an impression upon us, as we still on occasion, kept the girls inside the outhouse.

After some of us graduated, the school board must have decided it was too much of a strain on the younger students to go outside to take care of nature's needs, especially in the middle of the winter. They put in indoor toilets that were something to behold. I've never been to the Waldorf Astoria Hotel, but doubt if they had anything better than this. A monster septic tank was put in east of the schoolhouse, and the drain field was nearly a mile long, ending up out west in the dump ground. I never did find out if this elaborate system worked any better than what us hardy pioneers had to put up with. Both served the same purpose, I presume. At least there were no snowballs downstairs, to throw at the "fairer sex." That was a plus.

I think that I used to be a pretty good writer, having spent all my school years going to the Hetland School. At least I should have been until I got fouled up again with one of my teachers, Winnie Burcham (later Stangland). It seems as though she had a rule that if a pupil got caught whispering once that the poor kid had to stay after school and write, "I whispered" 500 times. I must not have been too smart, as I generally got in the doghouse and wrote "I whispered" 1000 times. I think the teacher had eyes in the back of her head to catch me as often as she did. On the other hand, maybe she was lonesome, as she waited until school was out to get married. Anyway, I got so I could write, "I whispered" going at full speed so I could be outside with the rest of the kids who didn't get caught. I was a better writer before this writing disaster hit me.

After all we had something I think they called the "Palmer Method" in writing. I never could figure out why anyone named Palmer would want their name on such a "no win" method of writing.

One day during recess when we were in the lower grades, Bill Nordemeyer, the storekeeper's kid, and Pete Mauch, the banker's kid, were matching nickels. I don't know where Bill got any money, but Pete, being the banker's kid, had some coins. I watched them as I came around the corner, and come to find out, Bill was matching, "heads I win, tails you lose!" Poor Pete was mentally retarded, and ended up in the Redfield state school, and didn't know what was going on. I told him, "Pete, you can't win that way, so quit playing." "All right, if you say so," he said. I gave Bill the devil for cheating and told him to play it square or else. He got the message.

Fifty years later, a fellow came into the shop and wanted to know if I was Dale. Of course, that was me. "I'm Bill Nordemeyer," he told me. "The heck you are. Are you still missing the end of your finger?" I asked. He was, but he wanted to know how I remembered that, as we used to razz him that he wouldn't have to go to war, as the end of his trigger finger was gone.

Ma used to laugh about the time we had a heck of a snowstorm, and we came from school for dinner. We had Bill with us, and asked Ma if Bill could stay for dinner, as it was too bad outside for him to go home. That was all right with her, if it was OK with his dad, Fred. We would find out, so we went out into the storm and drifts, to go up to the store to see if he could eat with us. Fred thought that was OK. What Ma would laugh about, was that Bill was nearly home when he got uptown, but still the weather was too bad for him to go any further. After all, what are good friends for? He was our friend, and we took him in, as the Good Book says.

When Kai Rasmussen came to school one year he could hardly talk English. He was from a Dane family, and they always talked Dane at home. All of the kids were picking on him because of this. I didn't, and felt sorry for him. I finally told the other kids to "lay off" teasing him, as he was a Dane. Guess they must have known that us Danes were sticking together, and I meant business! I suppose if he had been Norwegian, I would have picked on him too.

About forty or more years later, a fellow came into the shop, and Pa wanted to know if I knew him. He had lived in California all those years. I sure did, as he looked like a genuine Dane. Then Kai told Pa he never forgot how I had stuck up for him when he first came to school and could barely talk English. Must have made a good impression on him, and I remember the occasion as though it was yesterday.

Tillie Scherkenback had to stay after school one night when he was in the first grade. He was scared out of his wits, so when the teacher was out in the hall helping the other kids get their coats on, Tillie climbed up on the open window sill and dropped down over six feet to the ground. Luckily, he landed on his feet, because he was just a little guy and could have broken his neck on that high a drop. He was OK, and ran out south of the schoolhouse heading for their farm a mile southwest of town. When the teacher came back into the room, Eileen Johnson, the school tattle tale, raised her hand, swinging it wildly to get the teacher's attention, at the same time hollering, "Teacher, teacher, Tillie went out the window!" The old girl went to the window and Tillie was streaking toward home as fast as his little legs would go.

Thirty or forty years later, there were some people over to the schoolhouse with a California licensed car. I happened to be out in the yard, and one of the fellows came over and told me who he was. Then he wanted to know if I knew which high window that his grandpa Mildren Scherkenback had jumped out of. I went over and showed them the window, as I was there and witnessed the whole affair. Boy, they were excited, and took several pictures of that old window in the Hetland School to show all the clan relatives where grandpa Tillie took his leap. Oh, by the way, Eileen Johnson was still the tattletale until she graduated from high school. Squealing on somebody must have been born in her.

Ralph Mauch always called his dad Henry. One day Ralph brought home his report card to show Henry. His dad looked it over and said it looked pretty good but how about that one subject—deportment, which had a low grade. Ralph looked at it and said, "Well, I tell you Henry, I have a good notion to drop that subject." Good idea, don't you think? He didn't get the job done!

The Buhn family had a long legged kid named Millard. He was left handed, and when he had to write, "I whispered" a few hundred times, he would try to get done quicker by writing with both hands. Anyway, it seems like several times we had a good reason to chase Millard home after school. We couldn't quite catch him, as he would take the steps into their house in two jumps, just as we were about to nab him. In other words, he was in a hurry to get out of harm's way – we being his friends ready to teach him a lesson or two. His ma would have the door open if she saw him coming, so he had it made. After they had moved to Brookings, he set the record in the state for the mile run. We, his friends, always took the credit for his running ability, as the track coach didn't need to tell him how to run. We had taken care of that before he even got to school in Brookings.

Debs Starksen had a grandson, Donald (Starky) who could soak up more water in a shower than any kid in school. After basketball practice, he would be the first one ready for a shower. He would just stand in the shower and let it run full blast. When the hot water was gone, he was too, and the rest of us took a cool shower in Hetland water. More than once we chased him home with our sling shots loaded with a stone, something like David had, according to the Bible, when he proceeded to let the giant Goliath know who was the boss, and sent him back to his maker. We didn't try anything like that on Starky, because most of the time we got along OK. However when he escaped from us and managed to get into his house, he would come back outside, armed with his BB gun. But he still stayed on the top step so he could get inside if we decided to launch an attack on him. He never took a shot at us, but more than once held the gun like he intended to use it.

One teacher would take us out to Mayflower Hill (west of Myrum Matson's) to pick mayflowers. It was a mile walk. We would roast wieners and marshmallows and then head back home. In 1928, we were out in Widenkopf's grove for the last day of school for a picnic. We walked out there and had plenty of stuff to eat. We just nicely got home when it started to get black. Clouds came up and we had a windstorm. It blew down tents and all kinds of stuff on the railroad right of way. The tents were there because they were gravelling Highway 14. Jerry Bundy, who ran the elevator, was trying to get home. He got by the schoolhouse and was hanging onto a tree. All at once, the basketball bangboard came flying right by his head. Then he was really scared. The church east of Badger, by Lake Thisted, had faced west before the storm, but faced north after the wind turned it around.

When we were freshmen, the senior class took us into the gym to initiate us. We put a stop to that, as we had more boys than they did, so we took them down and sat on them. I don't think the girls had any part of this. Anyway, the plans they had for us went up in smoke. Until our senior year in high school, we only had one girl in our class. In the 12th grade, we had two girls and ten boys. Boy – today wouldn't the "chicks" like that ratio – two girls to ten boys! Didn't bother us a bit; we went to school to learn what the books had to offer and get a signed diploma.

When I was a freshman in high school, the teacher, Harold Gange, asked for anyone who knew the answer to one of the questions to raise their hand. I raised mine, as I knew the answer. He didn't call on me as he probably thought I didn't know the answer anyway. That was it. I had enough of raising my hand. When I got home that afternoon I told Ma about the episode and informed her that I was done raising my hand. I stuck to my word and didn't raise my hand in class the rest of the four years in high school! Yes, they let me out after 4 years with a signed diploma. More than once, when the teacher would ask for a show of hands, the teacher would say: "All right, Dale, what is the answer?" Of course, sometimes I knew the answer! I remember one in particular. We were studying English Literature and Mary Ward, the teacher, wanted the name of some book. No one knew it so she said to me "What's the answer Dale?" (The answer was "She Stoops to Conquer.") I told Mary I didn't know all of it but it was "She Stoops to Something." I couldn't remember "Conquer." She laughed so hard I thought she would split and the rest of the Senior Class would too. Don't know if she gave me an "F" on that or not.

One day Myrna and Virgil found my old report cards at grandpa and grandma's house and they suspected that I had been "feeding them a line," something that I wouldn't think of doing intentionally. On the other hand, maybe I would do that on certain occasions. I always told them that when we went to school the grading was different than when they went. An "A" was awful, "D" was dandy and "F" was fancy.

Henry and Lily Cleveland had our basketball team out to their place for supper one night. At that time, there were about six or eight telephone customers all on the same line, no private lines. If somebody heard their neighbor's ring they lifted the receiver when the neighbor answered. This was a good way to get all of the news, only you would have to wait until the right neighbor answered the call. Then the receivers would start to drop and there were lots of eager listeners. We were sitting around the table and the phone rang for somebody else out in the country. Somebody (not me) lifted the receiver and then about ten of us would holler "HELLO!" The person on the other end hung up. What was all that ruckus? The phone rang again, same thing. Finally, no more rings. Something was wrong, so the would-be talker gave up trying to visit with the would-be talkee. What a shame. There might have been some juicy gossip to spread around the countryside.

Russell Eidsmoe and his charming wife, Beulah were here for two years. This was the first teaching job for both of them after graduating from Yankton College. "Gus" always told me that it was the best place they lived, as everyone was their friend, regardless of how old the other person was. I kept in touch with these dear friends all through the years, until they passed away near the end of the century, both in their '90s. I have met and visited with their son, Bob. He told me that he has a certificate from the Hetland Congregational Church showing that he was on the cradle roll at six months. I believe he is still a Congregationalist.

These two dear people thought enough of the Hetland church to remember us in their wills, and left the church a sizable sum of money after they went home to their Maker. They left here in 1932, so they had good memories of what the church here meant to them when they were just young kids starting out in life. Gus told me that they stopped on the hill south of town before school started and wondered aloud if that was where they really wanted to be. He said they never questioned it later, as this little town meant more to them than they ever could imagine it would.

A few years ago I saw a picture on TV of a Beresford graduating class celebrating the 70th anniversary of their high school graduation. Lo and behold, there was Eidsmoe and a couple of others who were the only ones left from that class. I about flipped over that, and then to top it off, here was a big write-up and pictures of the Beresford class in the Sioux Falls Argus-Leader showing how they looked both now and then. "Gus" was so small that they had to have a football suit and helmet tailor-made in order to fit him. I knew that "Gus" had graduated from Beresford High. I also knew that Senator Bulow, one of our senators in DC, was from Beresford, and always called him "Gus," his nickname in his hometown.

The next day I called down to Sioux City, where they had retired after finishing out his teaching career at Morningside College. "Gus" answered the phone. (Me) "How much did you pay to get your picture on TV and then a big write-up in the Argus, as well as more pictures?" (Gus) "Who is this?" (Me) "Mory Andersen." "That's what I thought," was his reply. "Well, how much did it cost you?" "Didn't pay anything, as they came and interviewed those of us who were still alive," he said. After "Gus" had passed away we still corresponded with Beulah at Christmas time.

Vi, our daughter-in-law, was a surgical nurse at Sioux Valley Hospital in Sioux Falls. After work one of her nursing friends who drove from Sioux City to work in Sioux Falls told her she had found out a lot about her family. Vi wanted to know how that could be. Come to find out, this girl helped take care of Beulah Eidsmoe and had read my Christmas letter to her when she couldn't see to read. What a small world we live in.

Eidsmoe recited a poem to us in one of his classes. When he started it out, we thought it was about Paul Revere and his famous ride in the Revolutionary War. We had just written an essay on it, and Eidsmoe read a part of what happened on Revere's famous ride, as one of our class saw it or tried to explain what happened. He wrote as follows: "Paul Revere rode down the street yelling 'two arms, two arms." After Gus read this much and spelled out TWO arms, we all laughed, but not the smart kid who didn't know that the spelling should have been TO, and not TWO as Gus read it. Then Gus went on to recite a different version of the famous ride. It went as follows:

"Listen my children, and you shall hear of the Midnight ride of a bottle of beer.
Up the hill and down the road, ran the man with his light load.
Into a dark and deserted shed and there he gurgled and drank his fill,
The beer that cost him a dollar bill."

This was during the time of prohibition. None of us had heard that one before, and when we got out of class everyone was trying to remember how it went. I was reciting it to the rest of the class when Gus came out and wanted to know if I had heard it before. I told him that I hadn't, and Gus just shook his head and walked away. It's rather odd that I can remember such famous words, especially when it has the original form of Revere's famous ride that the British were on the move, and coming to do battle. It's a good thing that we had such staunch patriots as Paul Revere, or we would still be paying duty to the King of England.

By the way, Revere was a Master Mason and Past Master of his Masonic Lodge, as were Brother George Washington and most of the Revolutionary War generals. They could trust each other and knew the high ideals that they all had in common. I am glad that Virgil and I have something in common with these staunch patriots, we too being Master Masons, and proud of it.

When I was in high school we had carnivals in order to raise money to help pay school expenses. We ordered trinkets from an outfit in Minnesota. Russell Eidsmoe was our superintendent at that time and when we ordered the novelties we always managed to order a dozen or two rings for the boys in high school. They cost ten cents and we sold them for fifty cents and they were worth it, not for the ring itself but for what came with it. On the side of the stone was a "peep hole." Look in the hole and you saw a scantily clothed, good-looking girl staring you right in the eye. This must have been a preview of the modern peep show. We didn't think Eidsmoe knew about it but he had to pay the invoice so I'm sure he knew about it but never let on.

When I was a junior in high school, our mothers served the senior banquet in the church basement. Money was scarce, so they decided this was one way for them to "toast" the senior class. They had a wonderful meal, and we had our program all laid out for the senior class. Didn't have to have an after prom schedule when they got their diplomas at the town hall. The next year when we graduated, the junior class mothers didn't volunteer to serve our banquet, so we went to Brookings and had our meal at one of the hotels, the Clarinda, I believe it was called.

To show that I used to like to argue, I'll tell about a time in ancient history class when the teacher, Borghild Johnson, and I went toe to toe to prove our point. We were studying about Rome, and that the Huns had captured the city. She proceeded to tell the class about this historic defeat suffered by the Roman army. In the history book it said the Huns were unable to take Citadel Hill, and finally gave up the battle for it, with the Roman soldiers still holding the hill. I politely (I think I was polite) asked her how could the Huns claim to have captured the city and not Citadel Hill? They captured most of the city, and I based my profound thinking on that argument. We didn't agree, and soon it became apparent she wasn't going to change my mind, and I was sure she wouldn't change hers. Finally, in desperation she pointed her longest finger at me and said, "Dale, shut up!" Of course I shut up, but about ten minutes of class time were gone, so we didn't have to spend any extra time answering questions, which the rest of the class thought was OK. It never dawned on me that she would pull rank on me, and win the argument by telling me to shut up. Ironically, I never did get any better grade from her regardless of how hard I studied or didn't study. She said she graded on the curve, whatever that was, and I think I must have missed the turn, and proceeded to end up in the corner of a right angle. However I did pass, but not with flying colors. Enough said.

We didn't get back to school in time once when we were hunting pheasants over the noon hour. We got called into the office, and were going to get dressed down when we told the superintendent that we had a good excuse for being late. There were some fellows hunting in the slough where we were, on the other side of the fence. All at once we heard a gun go off, and then a fellow started hollering as loud as he could. He was shaking his arm, and holding on to it for dear life. We tore over there and come to find out, he had accidentally stuck his gun barrel into the mud. He put his finger in the barrel, when BOOM, the gun went off and the finger went someplace up in the air, and that was why we were late, helping get him to his car to see the doctor. We must have presented a pretty good story, as we didn't have to do any time for being late. Incidentally, in the winter this fellow's finger was always cold. There was no finger there, but it was still cold. Hard to imagine such a thing being possible.

When we were seniors in high school, we had a teacher, Mary Ward, who was a granddaughter of the founder of Yankton College, Joseph Ward. She was an expert shot with a rifle, and had competed in the DeWar shooting matches. She had all of the equipment with her and we had a chance to go out by the dump ground and watch her shoot at targets. We had a chance to try out the guns, too. She didn't use regular .22 shells, as she had to use some that were special, called match ammunition. Didn't seem to help us to hit the bull's eye, but she surely could.

Since 2004 I have been in contact via e-mail with Mary's daughter, and her nephew, Joe Ward. Virg and Myrna attended Yankton College with Joe, and he and Virg are both YC trustees. Her daughter told me Mary Ward died at the age of 52. She didn't know her mother had taught school here, so I was happy to fill her in on some of the things that went on while I was her student.

One day as I sat in the back row in the east assembly room, Delbert Roderick decided to shoot me with a paper wad. Why, I don't know. I was studying when this happened and hadn't even tweaked my ears at him, so I couldn't see where he had any reason to try to commit mayhem on me as I minded my own business. This was a <u>bad</u> mistake on his part. I had a rubber band in my pocket and tea lead (this was a forerunner of aluminum foil) besides. Now, before you get any mistaken ideas about me having these weapons in my pocket, let me assure you they were there only for me to use if somebody should attack me. In other words, they were for defensive measures only. However this called for serious deliberation. Delbert had inflicted damage to my anatomy, as well as picking on someone bigger than he was, and an upper class man at that! This called for decisive action at once!

I sized up the situation, and decided what was the best way to retaliate. The teacher, Mae Foote, was standing at the blackboard writing something, so now was the time to teach that upstart a "stinging" lesson. I proceeded to load up a nice big fat tea lead on to my rubber band, walked up to Mr. Roderick and with said weapon six inches from his cheek, let him have it. Pow! There was a big red welt where the lead hit his face, and his hand was there in a flash to try to deaden the pain of the impact. I started to walk back to my seat when lo and behold, Kenwood Cleveland in the other row of seats was up from his seat in a semi-crouch, aiming his rubber band and paper wad at me. Guess he was taking sides, and decided Roderick needed help. He didn't get to let me have it, as Miss Foote looked around and saw him ready for the attack. She hollered at Kenwood to give her the rubber band, and to sit down. She had no idea what had been going on until I told her a few days later. She told me she knew I was up to something, but she didn't know what.

This took place in 1932. I never could understand why Kenwood would even think about taking a "pot shot" at me. We were good friends at that time, and we still are. I don't hold any grudge against him after all of these years. Incidentally, in September 2000, Delbert, his wife and daughter came to Hetland and we had a good visit. He didn't remember me chastising him, as he never shot me again. He was a smart kid, and worked as a scientist with the big wheels perfecting the atom bomb that was dropped on Japan.

When we had our meeting to see what our class colors and motto were going to be, we didn't all see eye to eye. Some of the mavericks (I was one of them) suggested that we have for a motto, "We have come to the edge – we're going to jump off." We were probably lucky that cooler heads outvoted us, but to tell the truth, I don't know what our motto was. Seems rather odd that I can remember what it could have been.

Idor Hesby and I temporarily stopped the east assembly high school kids from getting out at noon to have dinner. Seems as though we got out first and decided to shut the door on the rest of the tribe. We took hold of the doorknob and braced ourselves against the door to keep the rest from getting out. Don't ask me how we concocted this plan, as I can assure you it wasn't planned in advance. Let's put it this way – it must have been on the spur of the moment. Anyway, I was holding onto the doorknob and must have had more strength in my fingers (being a Dane, I suppose) and working in the blacksmith shop. I was able to keep anyone on the other side from turning the knob to unlatch the door. Idor was braced against the door with his feet braced on the stair rail post, just in case we couldn't hold the fort, and the other side rolled over us. You should have heard all the hollering and beating on the door. "Let us out, let us out!" They didn't need to tell us that, we knew that was what they wanted, without being so upset about it. All at once, everything was calm. Now what? Our instincts knew that something must have been transpiring on the other side of that closed door. Deathly silence! Then we had a rude awakening. "Open that door!" Eidsmoe was on the other side, and didn't even have to take hold of the doorknob. The door opened by itself, or I should say, with help from us. He didn't say a word to the two of us, but gave us a look that should have killed, and then just shook his head. I think he had a twinkle in his eye, so maybe he had been involved in stuff like that before he started to teach school. We didn't do that again – must have learned our lesson.

When we were in high school we didn't get a chance to listen to the World Series on the radio, as we were in school to learn and not listen to the radio. After all, it was just a ball game. However, we got around that as my Ma, Ruby, would put a paper up in the west window of our house if one team was ahead. And in the north window if the other one was ahead. One of us would go and close the assembly room window to see who was ahead. Then someone else would go and open the window to see who was ahead. This would go on several times while the game was on to see which team was winning. We had really smart teachers, but don't know if they knew why the window had to go up and down as often as it did. We thought that was a neat way to find something out and it was better than sending up "smoke signals" and not so "smelly" either. Where there's a will there's a way. After all, we were going to Hetland High School to learn and to improvise without modern technology.

We always had the high school baccalaureate in the local Congregational Church. One year, several kids from the Holy Land were in the graduating class. There must have been some kids or their folks whose ears rubbed together or else didn't have much between them. They served notice on the school board that their kids couldn't go to our church for baccalaureate, as it had to be in the town hall. When we got to the service in the hall, lo and behold, the Lutheran preacher was preaching from the Congregational Church pulpit! How did that get there? Some of the class had gone to the church, loaded it up and put it in the hall. It was returned before our next service. Our minister was so hurt that he resigned at once. I put up a squawk, and let it be known that this was a low blow, and pretty narrow-minded.

The next year at graduation, the would-be "pulpit snatchers" must have gotten the message as to what I thought about the last year's fiasco. Whoever they were, they sent one of the teachers over here to see if the pulpit could be brought to the hall for baccalaureate. I was sitting in the living room when the teacher broached the subject to Eva who was in the kitchen. About that time I hit the floor, and not in the kindest tone, advised the go-between teacher where the pulpit stayed – in the church! I told him if the Congregational Church wasn't good enough for the Lutherans, the pulpit wasn't good enough for them either, and the pulpit would stay in the church. Their preacher used a table to expound on whatever he wanted to talk about, and it wasn't about Christians loving each other, either. Eva was embarrassed about the way I talked to the poor teacher who was only doing what he was asked to do. I told Eva there was no use "beating around the bush." This way they knew what the answer was, NO, in no uncertain terms! End of dialogue. At my age I would do the same as I did many years ago. I must not have mellowed too much.

Charley Johnson was Chairman of the School Board, and was giving a short talk at graduation in the hall when someone knocked over a tin cup and it banged on the floor. Charley said he heard the gong, so his speech was ended. At least he didn't get the chance to be long-winded when he figured it was time to quit talking.

When I was a senior in High School, Superintendent Eidsmoe got me an appointment to the Naval Academy at Annapolis. Eidsmoe was a good friend of Senator Bulow, and he was the one that gave me the appointment. All but one of the would-be admirals flunked the written exams. The one that passed flunked out of the physical exam – flat feet. There was no war, and lots of officers were left over from WWI, so the navy didn't need anyone from South Dakota. I didn't take any classes for the last semester, as I was studying for the naval exam.

Dale's High School graduation, 1932

Shortly after we had graduated from high school, we went to some doings in the schoolhouse. Afterwards, when most of the crowd had left, one of the high school girls suggested that those of us left should play a game of poker. Wow! Not me. I had never, never played poker and I wasn't about to get into this poker game, because of all things, she wanted it to be strip poker! That's what it ended up being. This girl (name omitted) must have been up to stripping men before, as she was the only girl in the game, and she had most of the men fairly well denuded of clothes. I couldn't leave watching the game, although it was getting late, and I supposed the folks were wondering what was keeping me out so late. Finally, when the chick had most of the clothes off of the gents, one of them looked at his watch and said, "Oh my gosh, I'd better get home, as I have to work tomorrow!" They all agreed and the would-be winner, after protesting about quitting so soon, gave back the clothes they had "ditched" and the game was over. I never heard if there were any other such games after this one.

Back in the dirty '30s and depression years, the Hetland school board did something unique that no other school did, that we knew of. They started dormitories for high school boys and girls. Back in those old fashioned days, the boys and girls had separate dorms – no shacking up in a single dorm. I guess they called that segregation, and had nothing to do with color or race, just sex.

Hetland High School dormitory dining room

No one had a car or even a private room. They lived five or six kids in a room, and they didn't complain about being too crowded for lack of sleeping room. There was only one bathroom for each dormitory, too. I don't think the kids in those days wasted time getting all shined up like they do now, or they wouldn't have made it to school on time. Everyone was served in the dining room, and had breakfast, dinner and supper five days a week for a total cost of $1.00 per student. They got a good education, besides. All of those kids appreciated this outstanding example of how badly the folks in Hetland wanted their friends from the country to get an education. Several of those that came here wouldn't have gone to high school, as their folks couldn't afford to send them. Two cooks, Mrs. Mae Greathouse and Mrs. Tina Peterson, took good care of getting the meals on time, and being of Norwegian stock, served well balanced meals.

This operation went on for several years, and the kids that shared this dormitory experience are still loyal to Hetland, and what the school did for them to help give them a good education. As I look back I marvel at how well everything clicked, with all the planning and getting good dorm deans, who functioned as Moms and Dads for the kids. Some of the deans were Floyd Waby, Rev. Arthur Green, Gerald and Adeline Dutcher, and Mrs. Sadie York. I hear rumors that the boys at least had some good times together, and that it wasn't all just eating and sleeping. Some of the boys could tell me if I asked them, but I won't stretch their memory after all those years of silence.

I told about having trophies for sports in high school, but didn't mention all the trophies we won for music. Until Eva Guptill (who became my wife) came to teach here, Hetland had the honor of being on the bottom of the "totem pole" in the music contests. We knew that we would be last, in other words, an "also sang" school.

When Eva started teaching music and English, she had all the school kids try out for singing. Some were scared spitless, and some of the louder ones had stage fright so bad their knees even shook. She found out most of them could sing, and promptly set to work to better Hetland's record of being last in every contest. She certainly succeeded, as Hetland got the reputation of being #1 in all contests, and took the state contest for class C schools which was held in Aberdeen. The winners were in all categories – soloist, glee club, small ensemble, quartets, etc. You name it, and they could sing it!

The school kids - boys and girls - even came to Springfield and sang at our wedding in 1937. The next day they went to Yankton and sang on WNAX radio by invitation. That was a JOY for us, that they helped us "tie the knot" that still holds us to this day.

Anyway, the trophy case has many first place trophies to recognize the achievements of the Hetland singers. They had a teacher who was interested in sharing her talents so that they and others could enjoy music as well.

To show you what kind of school kids we had in Hetland through the years, I would like to tell you about one example. In the Dirty 30s, nobody had any "surplus money" but the girls glee club bought pretty blue dresses from Montgomery Ward for a dollar apiece. Can you imagine a dress for a buck? Shortly before the regional contest, Bennie and Cora Williams' house burned to the ground. Nothing was saved, as the family wasn't home at the time. The Williams girls' nice blue dresses were burned up. I believe three of the girls were in the glee club at that time. Eva got busy, and she and the rest of the girls took up a collection to get three dollars plus postage to order three more dresses. I remember Eva "sweating it out," hoping that Montgomery Ward had three more dresses that would match the other dresses. When the package came, there was excitement as the girls opened it, and believe it or not, the dresses all matched! This was one example of how the Hetland family looked out for each other.

My brother Elden played the violin, or maybe I should say he moved the bow across the strings, occasionally. Before one contest, the teacher told him to have his bow up when the rest did, and to have it down when the rest did. Elden said he got off the notes when the rest of the violins made a fairly short note and then he couldn't keep up with the rest. I think after that he decided he would never make a "mistake" in the orchestra.

Homer played the trombone, but all I ever heard him blow was "toot toot," so he quit too. I played the drums one PM, but all I did was hit the drum when I thought it was time to. The teacher wanted to know if I wanted to keep the job, but I told her I would rather read a book. Why should I keep spoiling the music?

One of the earlier Hetland High School boys' quartets used to sing a couple of songs that brought down the house when we had school plays. I won't go into all the verses, but just a few lines to let you decide whether we had high class music or not:

> Bohunkas was the name of one, Josephus
>   was the other
> Bohunkas of the cholera died, Josephus by
>   request.
> Now these two boys are dead and gone, Long
>   may their ashes rest.
> Bohunkas went to heaven, Josephus went to
>   - - Arlington.

The crowd would go wild!
Another of their famous songs:

> Oh, Mr. Dunderback, how could you be so
>   mean,
> How long tailed rats and pussycats would
>   never more be seen?
> For he would grind them up into sausage
>   meat in Dunderback's machine.

*Something was the matter, the machine it
   wouldn't go,
So Dunderback he crawled inside to find it
   out you know,
His wife she got the nightmare, she walked
   around in her sleep.
She gave the crank a - - - terrible yank and
   Dunderback was meat!*

Great stuff, and enlightening music, besides. Elvis made more money than the Hetland singers did, with his so-called music. Oh well, our boys were ahead of their time, perhaps. These were NOT Eva's singers. Heaven forbid!

One spring, Blanche Calvet was driving a carload of kids to the music contest in Brookings. The roads were icy, and they met a truck west of Brookings. The suction threw the Calvet car over on its side. Luckily, no one was hurt. Harold Ashbaugh, the band director from Lake Preston, was right behind them. Eva and the kids had crawled out of the windows of the car, glad that no one was hurt. Harold wanted to know if anyone had to be on stage early. Eva said Helen Neilson had to be on at 8. She and Helen piled into Ashbaugh's car, and got to Brookings in time for Helen to sing her solo. The wreck didn't bother Helen or her pianist, Eva, as Helen calmly sang her solo and got a superior.

Eva also taught English. She must have done a good job, as the freshmen that went to South Dakota State had to take an exam in English before getting into college. It got so that when the kids said they had graduated from Hetland, they were told not to bother with the test.

When I was a senior, we won the District basketball tournament and went on the Regional in Brookings. At that time there was no classification and Watertown, Brookings, Chester and Hetland were in the Regional tournament. We drew Chester and beat them bad. They had one guy who had scored more points than all the rest of the team put together. The consolation was between Chester and Watertown. Chester beat them and we played Brookings for the championship. We had them beat with four or five seconds left. The referee, who was from Sioux Falls, called a foul on Del Barber who was lying on the floor at the time. Somebody had knocked him down or something. They made the free throw and then we played two or three overtimes before they finally beat us. And even Brookings was mad to think the referee was that crooked. Anyway, we thought he was crooked. We asked the referee afterward and he said he thought he fouled. So, Brookings went to State instead of Hetland.

After we graduated, the basketball players in school didn't have anyone to scrimmage with. So, those of us who graduated the year before went up and scrimmaged with them. We didn't treat them very nice part of the time. One time somebody had to shoot a free throw. I had my foot on top of my brother Homer's foot. When the fellow shot I stepped down on Homer's foot. He went to jump and never left the floor. Ended up flat on his back. He was about ready to clean me! With our practice help, the Hetland team won the District and went to the Regional in Watertown, but they didn't win. They were all pooped out from an afternoon of bowling. At least that's what we heard.

Madge Dietz, a high school teacher from Sioux Falls, was quite gullible, having lived in the big city all her life. One dark night some of the fellows in town talked her into going out west of Boyd's slough to hunt "hodangs." They gave her a big sack and told her where to sit and how to keep the sack open and wait for the "creatures" while they scared them over to her. These "friends" went to town and left her holding the sack. Sometime later after a couple of hours had passed Crandall heard about the "ruse" and went out and picked her up. Needless to say, the sack was empty, as none of the varmits had come that way. If it hadn't been for Lewis being a Good Samaritan she might have been there yet. At my age, I still haven't found out what a "hodang" is. Webster doesn't list it yet.

Madge's Ford car was low on alcohol antifreeze. It was below zero weather when the head on the car really froze up. Broke the head the full length. The kids in school had to kid her about breaking her head and Mory had to weld it.

One day, Madge and Leon Rustad, another teacher, were on the way to Sioux Falls when they smelled a skunk. Madge said, "Fresh coffee." Rustad about split, and told Eva about it when they got home. Skunk smell – fresh coffee – my, my, no wonder that I stopped drinking the stuff.

Another time, Madge went to Brookings in a rainstorm. She told me that the road was covered with frogs, and she had a hard time trying not to run over them.

Madge Dietz

I was president of the PTA (Parent Teachers Association) for a year, I believe. Anyway, Eva decided that I needed a new suit to wear when I presided over such an elite gathering in the school gym. All of the other men presidents had been older than I was, and they probably wore a suit and tie. I - or I should say we - went to Brookings to see about a suit. As far as I was concerned, this was under protest. We hadn't been married too long, or I would have seen the light and squarely forced the issue. I needed a new suit, but didn't know why. She decided which suit showed me off the best, but it needed alterations. Before paying the bill, I asked the salesman if I could get it done so I could take it home with me that day. We had a PTA meeting that night, and I wanted to look important or sharp, whichever the case might be. He let me know in no uncertain terms that it was impossible for the seamstress to get it that day, as she was extremely busy. However, he was polite enough to advise us that he would go back and check it out.

When he came back, the busy seamstress followed him. She came up and shook hands with me, and just about bowled me over when she asked, "Are you Dale?" I told her I was, but that I didn't know who she was. "Oh yes you do," she replied. "I'm Mrs. Snort Buhn." I told her that we took the credit for making a track miler out of her kid. Do you know what? We got the suit home with us, and I showed it off at PTA. I had a good notion to pin a sign on it: "Just bought this outfit." This was just another example of "it's not what you know, it's who you know." We were still friends.

Before the high school closed we had a Superintendent who liked to "nip" on the bottle. At noon, Virgil's mom would tell him to go over to the shop and get dad. As was the case most of the time, my little finger was the cleanest, so he would take my finger in his little hand and walk home with me. One noon we were out in the middle of the street and we met the superintendent. Virgil must have had big ears sometime as out of the clear sky he said "Say —, I hear you drink whiskey." To this day I don't know what his reply was as I was in a big hurry to get home. Eva was out in the yard hanging up clothes and was looking for a place to hide. I guess that was one of the times when it would have been proper to say "out of the mouths of babes." Anyway, Virgil grew up to be more diplomatic as he grew older. Takes after his mom!

Chapter 17
Team Efforts
(Sport stories)

Hetland Broncos 1932 District Champions. Back row: Lyle Cleveland, Charles Johnson, Homer Andersen, Telmer Peterson, Gerald Dutcher, Donald Starksen, Coach Russell Eidsmoe, Front Row: Roy Wilson, Delbert Barber, Idor Hesby, Wilbur Stangland, Dale Andersen, and Verle Dutcher

Team Efforts

We had a ball team when we were kids in grade school, but never played any other town – we just played among ourselves. Bob Roberts, who managed the Eagle Roller Elevator wanted to be our manager. That was a mistake, when we let him take over the reins of the team! He booked a game for us with Lake Norden (this was baseball). Our ball diamond was out north of the corner in Melstad's pasture. We didn't use cow pies for bases, but had to play around them. 2 PM came for the big day of our first – and I might add only – game under our present manager. Lake Norden brought Finns and Danes to play ball who were in high school or who had graduated. Here we were, 9 and 10 year olds, and supposed to play against that outfit. Well, anyway, they got to bat first as they were the visitors. We finally got the third out and kept on playing. In the third inning, it was 40 to 4 (not in our favor) when we called off the game by forfeit, because the way the game was going, it would have been called because of darkness, anyway. We fired the manager!

When we were kids we would finally get enough money to buy a ball and get to play ball. It was too bad if someone hit the baseball and broke the bat because we didn't have another one. We would sometimes find foul balls that had been lost so this helped the ball situation.

Sometimes I would be pitching hour after hour and my arm would get sore. Some kid would go home and get some Sloan's Liniment. I would lie on the ground and they would give me a good rubdown on my sunburned arm. It must have helped because I would get up and start pitching again and my arm was as good as new. Thanks to Sloan's Liniment. I don't know if they ever advertised it was good for that but it sure worked for me.

As we got older we would give John Cleveland a nickel apiece to buy gas for his old stock truck. We would all ride to play kitten ball as far as Huron, Watertown and Brookings. Didn't worry about the wind as we would lie on the floor or sit on benches. It was great sport too.

One time we played in Watertown and went 17 innings before we finally beat them, 4 to 3. About the 7th inning I broke out with chicken pox. I was playing 1st base. I wanted to quit but Tom Anderson the manager wouldn't let me. In the 17th inning Kenwood Cleveland got on and I got a hit to bring him in. Then we told the Watertown guys that the only reason they got beat was that they were afraid of going to first base for fear they would get the chicken pox.

Another time we were playing on the 4th of July out in Max Neilson's grove. I hadn't done a thing all day as far as hitting a ball. Everyone was really working me over. That evening we were playing the finals of the tournament. The umpire lived at Estelline and used to manage our Legion team in Lake Preston. At the tail end of the game we were behind and had a couple men on base. I came to bat and the umpire came out from behind the plate and tapped me on the shoulder and said "hit it out of here, Mory." So, I put it out over the center field fence. I came around 3rd base and here was the umpire out in front of the plate and he shook my hand as I crossed the plate. Glenn Nelson said "Yeah, that looked pretty good to have the umpire shaking your hand because you hit a home run." Especially because the whole crowd had been needling me because I couldn't hit anything all day. It was a good way to finish up the 4th.

We used to have a salaried ball team, and they played on a ball diamond located out west of town on a hill above where the dump ground is. We used to help out on the expenses, as we would chase down foul balls and any home run balls we could find. One of the salaried players got to going with one of the local girls, and that didn't go good with the businessmen who were paying to have a team in town. They quit shelling out the cash, so no more ball team. Don't think the players were worth a hoot, but that's just my opinion. I was pretty young to know much about baseball.

I played with the Arlington team one time in a donkey ball game. They wanted me to play with them, and dumb me; I didn't know what I was getting into. The first time I got a hit, I crawled up on this little fella (donkey) and my feet nearly touched the ground. I told him to git up, or something like that. That little critter didn't even bat an eye or move a muscle. I didn't have spurs on my shoes, but I tried to fracture his ribs, but to no avail. He was dug in at home plate, and I could do nothing about it. Whoa, wait a minute. The guy that ran the show must have stuck this little devil with a pin or something, as all H*** broke loose! Both hind feet left the ground, and at the same time there was daylight between his rawboned back and me. I thought I was airborne, but that was not to be. I came down like a bolt of lighting and lit sideways on that bone that held him together. Boy, I thought I had had it, but I still held on and we took off for first base. We never made it, as that little brute had other ideas where he wanted to go.

After a few weeks of pain, I went over to Arlington to see Dr. Grove, to see if I was still all in one piece. He didn't have any pity for me, and told me that I would survive, but it would take time. Boy, I was glad for that diagnosis, as I thought I might be done in for life! Oh, by the way, I didn't play any more donkey ball. I didn't know if the owner of the donkey talked to that critter before he and I parted company, or not.

We played basketball against the Arlington town team one night and they weren't playing as clean a game as we were used to. We were playing with some of our older players and they knew more about retaliation than us younger folks did. They had one kid who was bigger than usual, and who liked to shove his weight around. At the half, Charley Ballou, who was pretty stocky, suggested that we "get him," and we knew what he meant. The chance came after the second half started. Here came their big guy dribbling the ball, with Charley tearing right behind him. There was no one between the hoop and this guy but me. I was the standing guard, so didn't move around much. The way this guy was coming, I quickly decided that maybe I should forget about being a standing guard, and be a jumping one instead. I knew I wouldn't leave the floor too far behind and might come down on my feet or on my back, as I deduced what Charley had in mind. Quick thinking, I think that would be called. As the would-be basket shooter left the floor, so did I, and at the same time Charley hit this guy from behind, I nailed him from the front. Wow! Down on the floor went the shooter, just like a limp rag. I was kind enough to take the foul and still stayed right side up. Do you know what? We made a believer out of that Norske, as he didn't bother playing dirty for the rest of the game. He knew that there would be another day coming, to revert to all of his old tricks.

To this day, I don't see how the coaches let me play in a game, occasionally. I was no good at making a basket, was slow on my feet, couldn't get off the ground very far, not agile, and just seemed like all I was in the game for was to take up space. Hetland wouldn't have even won a game if they were to depend on me. Maybe, just maybe, that the coach figured I was big enough to intimidate some of the smaller players. Who knows?

Arlington wasn't known for being good sports in basketball, baseball, etc. In 1932, the year we were seniors, the dopesters had it figured out that Arlington and Hetland would play in the finals of the district tournament, which was to be held in Arlington, and that Arlington would win and go on to the regional tournament in Brookings. Incidentally, these so-called dopesters were from Arlington, so they were probably prejudiced. No one from Hetland had any such crazy ideas, as we had shown them (Arlington) that we had no trouble in subduing their team on the basketball court. Two out of two times, to be exact, that year. In the Hetland school we called that a thousand point average, which wasn't too bad for an upstart team from our little town. Oh, yes, I might add that in those days, other towns could recruit anyone they wanted to, and we had it happen that Arlington and Lake Preston took some of our ball players away from us, so they could supposedly bolster their team. Not many left here, and some of them that did had a tough time staying on our team, because we had tough academic standards to meet, or KA-BOOM, off the team went the player, whether he was good or not. A couple that come to mind barely could make the grade in school here, but in the other towns they improved enough to nearly make the honor roll, even though they thought that 2+2=5. Wonders never cease!

Oh yeah, getting back to the tournament. One root-n-tootin' family in "Ghost Town" (as Obbie Melstad called Arlington) was so sure the locals were going to the Region, that they had already ordered nice big juicy steaks from the meat market so the local players could enjoy the fruits of their labor, or in this case, ball playing ability, after they had won the tournament. However, the dopesters' plans didn't pan out, as the little town of Erwin derailed the "super" team. Boy - talk about bawling and shedding tears. One would have thought the world was coming to an end, just over losing a ball game. It was a good thing the crowd was in the bleachers, or else the gym floor would have needed to be mopped to get rid of all that Arlington water before any other game started!

There were eight teams in the county, and seven of them were rooting for the little town of Erwin. They were the underdogs, of course, when they played Arlington. The big title game finally got started - Hetland vs. Erwin. What a disaster, two little towns in the finals, and all of the bigger ones - Arlington, DeSmet, Lake Preston, Oldham and Iroquois - sitting on the sidelines. That didn't hurt our feelings one bit.

The game got started, and just like that, BOOM! BOOM! Erwin had us 6 to 0, so fast that we wondered what was going on! Enough of that! We called time out. In those days the coach couldn't get in on a time out, he had to send up "smoke signals" to tell us what to do, or send in another player to give us the message. I don't know what we decided to do after the time out, but whatever it was, it worked. We beat Erwin and didn't try to overdo it by running up a big score. We went on to win the game and the district tourney. Erwin, as always, were good sports, and came and congratulated us as usual. They had one player who was built like a "steam roller" and seemed older than most of us. His nickname was "grandpa," and derogatory, but Howard Walkow and I were good friends, and I never, ever called him that. He never let it bother him, either.

As I look back on my basketball career, or lack of it, I think the first coach we had was a pain in the neck, and that's being polite. I didn't think he had too much between his ears, but of course that was just one kid's opinion. I couldn't stand his big "I" and swagger, and no doubt he wouldn't have had to know too much to figure that out. At least I didn't do like Charley Ballou did, when he was riding the bench, and didn't get to play. Back in those days each team could only have eight players. One night Hetland was involved in a game, and three players fouled out (must have been a crooked referee). The coach looked down the row of players (as if he didn't already know who was there) and lo and behold, there was only one player left who hadn't played yet. The team was in luck, after all. "Charley, go in," the coach told him. "Go to Hell!" was the retort, so Hetland finished the game with only four players. After that, Charley got in and played regularly. Guess he knew how to convince the coach that he didn't think much of riding the bench. He turned out to be a good player, but could get nasty when he wanted to.

In 1930, our basketball team rode in the baggage car on the train to play in the district tournament in Arlington. All the roads were blocked with snow. The train was loaded with players from all of the teams west of us.

When I was a senior, we had a change of coaches. The other one left for greener pastures, and Superintendent Russell Eidsmoe took over the coaching duties. He was a complete gentleman, as he was all of the years I knew him. He and I always got along good together, even though some of the kids were afraid of him. As long as they behaved, there was no problem, but it was best not to get out of line – or else. Anyway, whether it was because we were friends or whether I had improved my ball handling skills, I got to play as a regular. I still didn't do too hot as a ball player, but did my best.

Ramona had a little gym with low ceilings and radiators hanging from the ceiling to heat the building. They had a pail hanging under one of the radiators that was leaking. The floor was asphalt and the crowd was back in the corner. The strangest set-up I saw. Gub Stangland hollered for the ball. I threw it to him and it was up so high it hit the pail of water. Down came the pail, water and all on the floor. They stopped the game for a while in order to get the mess cleaned up.

At that time we had a roaming guard and a standing guard. I was the standing guard because I didn't move much. I think I was to guard the basket so no one could shoot or steal it. The only time I was high point man was in Brookings when we played the Aggies and beat them 8 to 7. I scored two field goals. That was the most field goals I ever made in my life in one game. We stalled for three minutes with a one-point lead. If anybody shot the basketball with one hand he was out of the game for a while until he figured out he was supposed to use both hands. That is different than what it is today. After a shot was made we went back to center and had a jump ball.

We played at Bryant in their Auditorium. They had a heat register right in the middle of the floor. We were beating them pretty bad so they sent in Doc Larson's kid. He was just a little guy. They were playing man to man, so he wanted to know who his man was. They pointed out I was the one he was supposed to guard. He looked at me and said, "you mean that great big devil?"

At Erwin they played in the Assembly room – they didn't have any gym. Right above the basket was a hole in the ceiling. If they would hit the hole the ball would drop in the basket. We wouldn't play if they were going to do that, so we called the ceiling out of bounds. Didn't make any difference, we beat them anyway!

There was a full house at a basketball game one night. The four Andersen brothers, plus Kenny Anderson and another Anderson from north of town challenged the rest of the world to a basketball game. We had only six players, so couldn't afford to play dirty and foul out. It was comical when we told the ref, "Andersen out." He didn't know which one it was, but we knew who was to sit on the bench so the Andersens didn't get tired out. Don't remember the exact score, but I know we beat them even though the crooked time keeper stopped the clock for several minutes, hoping that the rest of the world could get some more points. We pulled the game out of the fire, but in order to get the game over, we had to go over to the time keeper en masse and twist his arm to blow the whistle, time was up. Guess he must have figured four Danes, one Norwegian and one mixed blood meant business, and the game was over at last. Lots of cheap fun, and the crowd enjoyed it as well as the players.

I played a lot of baseball and softball before we were married. After we were "hitched," I decided it was time to give up playing ball, as it wasn't fair for Eva to sit home while I was out with the boys playing ball, especially Sunday afternoons. My friends didn't think much of my decision to quit, but I never regretted it. Our family meant more to me than playing ball, even though I enjoyed the sport.

One day when our daughter, Myrna wasn't too old, she came into the house and told her mom that dad had insulted her, as I had been playing catch with her and told her she threw the ball like a girl. She decided that wasn't going to be. She got so she threw the ball harder than most boys and could hit the ball farther too. At school, when the kids chose up sides she was the first one chosen. At one of our school picnics, another school challenged Hetland to play softball. That was a mistake, as our kids were "Hetland" ball players. Myrna hammered two home runs over the center fielder's head. He said he had never seen anyone hit the ball like that. I tried to do the same, but must have been out of practice, as I couldn't do it. This was while the kids were still in the grades.

The Hetland High School teams were called the Broncos. Elden and I were in his truck loaded with cattle going to the Sioux Falls stockyards. When we went through Madison, Elden said, "Oh-oh, the Highway Patrol is pulling us over." The trooper looked us over and told Elden that he thought he was overloaded and we had better go back to town to get weighed. Elden was figuring and of course he said he was sure he was legal, but no use arguing with the cop. So I got into the act.

The cop used to referee some of the basketball games we played in, and we hated his guts! This was no time to dislike the guy, so I started talking about the games he had refereed. Then he took off, and I couldn't have done a better job of bragging than he did. "Boy, oh boy," he said. "Those Hetland Broncos, the Red and Black, were some ball teams - good players and good sports." He laid it on good and thick! When he let up for air, I would prod him on. Finally - it seemed like an endless time - he told Elden that he still figured he was overloaded, but told us to go on to Sioux Falls anyway. We took off, about 1,000 pounds overloaded. Elden said, "Boy, I'm glad that you were along and got him started on the Hetland Broncos, because we could have been pulled in." Guess I was at least good for something on that trip.

We had a school superintendent named Boegler who seemed to be more windy than others whom we had encountered. Seems as though he was the best performer in whatever endeavor he was in. It came time for the 17th of May celebration, when the Norwegians played kittenball against those who were not full of Norske blood. Tom Anderson, our manager, told us that he was going to let that "hot shot" superintendent pitch against the Norskes. He also informed us that this profound scholar was a real good pitcher. I asked him who told him that good news. The superintendent had told Tom that he was the best pitcher in college - so he must be extra good! The big night came and our star pitcher took the mound against the stalwarts who claimed Leif Erickson as one of their clan. By doing this, they left the Danes out on a limb, as for claiming old Leif had come from the Fatherland, Denmark. The umpires hollered "play ball," and play ball we did.

By the way, our pro pitcher for the Norwegian celebration was dressed for this festive occasion. He had on knickers and a foxy shirt, and even a ball cap. The rest of us ordinary players couldn't afford that kind of gear, so we were in our work clothes, and didn't even own a ball cap. Our hotshot pitcher wound up and started the ball for the catcher, and we knew it would definitely be a strike. Alas, the catcher never got to touch the ball, as that Norwegian was "dug in" and got a hit on the first pitch. We knew how to make a double play and wipe out the first runner. It didn't work out like that. The next Norske got a hit too, so no double play! It was a slaughter, as those Streels and Stavangers teed off on our pitcher like he was their cousin. The manager finally pulled his star pitcher out with one out and seven runs in the first inning. We got beat, of course, but we enjoyed it, as the lutefisk eaters had knocked the wind out of our pro pitcher. He never played again, as even our manager was down on him for feeding him such a line, only to have it fizzle out. If Boegler had been as good a pitcher as he pretended to be, maybe the score would have been in our favor. Who knows?

The 17th of May Norwegian celebration finally fizzled out when there were not enough full-blooded Norskies to field a team that was good enough to even come close to beating those of us who didn't have lutefisk-tainted blood flowing through our veins. We had some wonderful times celebrating the Norwegian Independence day, when the Danes gave them the "heave ho" and were independent at last, even though the Norskes had to import a Danish King to keep the country afloat!

We played softball one night in Brookings. We always paid John Cleveland a nickel apiece for the privilege of riding in the back of his cattle truck, and sometimes we could enjoy the aroma of pigs or cattle that had just gone to market. Boy oh boy, that would clean out your sinuses in a quick hurry. All of these extra treats were included at NO extra cost in the nickel fare. Wow, was that a bargain.

The game in Brookings was over, so John herded the truck west, toward the Promised Land # 2. When we came into Volga, we noticed that a ball game had just ended there, but the lights were still on. We pounded on the roof of the cab to get our Norwegian driver's attention, and we conned him into going over to the ball field. We hobnobbed with the Volga players and we asked them if they wanted to play another game. Why not? So play we did.

Skinny was the first windmill type pitcher in these parts, and we sicced him onto them. Boy, was that a disaster for Volga. Skinny mowed them down like a bowling ball heading for the pins, and the "strikes" had IT. Our manager finally took pity on the Volga team and put in one of our average pitchers so that they didn't get skunked, but when Skinny was pitching, it was just like leading lambs to the slaughter. This was just another day in the annals of history for the Hetland ball team, and we had a great time savoring it. Memories linger on, and time marches on, as well.

We always were taught that a game was a game, and if we got beat, just take it in stride. Either the other team was better than we were or else the referee was "crooked." Pa used to tell me that he could always tell if the Preston Legion baseball team got beat. There were seven of us kids that played on the Preston team, and they only had two from their own town on the team. Pa would tell me when I came from uptown, that if I was stepping right along, we had won. If I was dragging my bottom and looking dejected, that we were beat. He would ask how the game came out, and if we got beat, I'd tell him the umpire was crooked. The umpire had probably called it a ball when it should have been a strike, or vice versa.

Chapter 18
Fraternal Ties

Top left: Myrna, Vi, Dale and Virg at Dale's 60 year Masonic pin presentation, 2001

Top right: Easter Star Hawaiian Night, Dale and Eva

Middle: 50 year Masonic pin, Dale and Eva, 1991

Bottom: Cake honoring Dale and Everett Dill

Fraternal Ties

One of the nicest things that I ever joined, with the exception of the church, is the Masonic Lodge and its affiliates. I became a Mason in 1941 and have been an active member all of these years. I have really enjoyed the fellowship with my Brother Masons and Sisters in Eastern Star. I am sorry that I haven't been active in the Scottish Rite and Shrine, but there have been too many miles between their meeting places and my home. However, I have attended several reunions and enjoyed them.

Before Eva and I were married she taught school in a town in northern South Dakota, and was a good friend of Methodist minister Wendall Walton and his wife, Effie. He belonged to the Masons and both of them belonged to Star. They talked about the good times they had in their meetings, so Eva inquired how she could join Eastern Star. The man of God told her, "Marry a Mason." When we were married I wasn't a Mason but joined before long, so my dear wife was eligible to join Star, and join she did. I should have joined when she did, but didn't. I joined a few years later. Verlo Kjellsen and I joined Star together. After being initiated the Worthy Matron asked if we had any comments. After telling them how nice it was to be a member I told them how lucky Verlo and I were to be there. We had just bought a new ballot box, and we discovered that the white balls would go through the hole, but the black cubes were too big and wouldn't drop through. These were the so-called "black balls" that would have "knocked us in the head" and denied our membership. Of course some of the sisters, (not doubting Thomases) thought I was pulling their leg. After the meeting was closed, several of the female gender had to check it out, and they found out that there was NO leg-pulling going on, so I was cleared of that so-called tale.

Later on, we used a jack knife to enlarge the hole so the cubes would drop through too.

Eva and I both served several stations in Star, and she was Matron and I was Patron the same year. After that she was organist for umpteen years, until her health gave out, and she had to quit everything. She made the piano hop and everyone enjoyed the music, and it wasn't always the same pieces. Our good friend and sister, Gladys Zeller, was Worthy Grand Matron of Eastern Star for South Dakota, and appointed Eva Grand Representative to Illinois, representing South Dakota. We attended the Illinois Grand Session in Springfield, and later on visited a chapter in Peoria where the Illinois representative to South Dakota was a member. These were all memorable occasions, and we were always treated royally. We were both members for over 50 years.

When I was growing up in Hetland, I couldn't help but notice some of our prominent citizens who were active church members in the Hetland Congregational church and leaders in the good of the community. All of them, right to the last man, had ONE thing in common. They were ALL members of the Masonic Lodge in Arlington. Hmm, that got me to thinking. I admired these men for what they did, for their integrity and for what they stood for. So I asked my friend Jim Barber, a co-owner of the best hardware and IHC implement store in the country, and my friend Harry Starksen, our postmaster and general store operator a question. I asked them, "How do I join the Masonic Lodge?" NO problem. They got me a petition, and both Jim and Harry signed it, and recommended me for membership. I didn't get blackballed in the process, and I was on my way to over 66 years of enjoyable and rewarding fellowship with my Masonic Brothers, who are TOPS.

Back in days past when joining the Masonic Lodge it was necessary to learn and pass a proficiency test as to what transpired in the preceding degree, there being 3 degrees. Entered Apprentice, Fellow Craft, and Master Mason. Jim Barber was my teacher, and what a teacher he was. He spent many a day and many an hour with me after supper, seeing to it that I learned what I was supposed to learn, and to learn it RIGHT. I passed all 3 of the tests. Through the years I, too, have coached many a brother mason in the same manner, having them learn it RIGHT. Now days this test is not required, but for me, I am glad I learned what I did. It would seem to me that the newly-made Mason has missed out on something, not having to study and learn before passing on to the next higher degree like we did.

As the years flew by and age took its toll of Jim (as it does to all of us), he was not able, according to him, to come to Lodge. His memory was slipping and we all knew it. He was residing in the rest home in Arlington and I visited him quite often. On one of my visits I told him I was picking him up Thursday night to go to Lodge with me. NOPE, NOPE, No way was he going. I didn't take NO for an answer and told him I would be there Thursday night, and we would go to Lodge. I told some of his next of kin what I was going to do, and they all said it wouldn't work, as he wouldn't go out of that rest home with anybody, and he hadn't been out of the home since he came to live there.

Well the big night came, and I had gone out to Krueger's farm to pick up Jack. We motored over to Arlington to pick up Brother Jim. "Do you think that he will go?" asked Jack? "Yup," was my reply. As we went down the hallway we could see light shining from under Jim's door, and there he sat, ready to go to Lodge. To Lodge we went, a first time but not the last, as I took him to Lodge every time until he was so feeble that we had to help lift him up from the chair. The ice was broken and now he would go out of the home when others asked him out. Some of his relatives couldn't believe what they were seeing or hearing.

My brother Homer took him to church every Sunday after that. During one of our meetings we were short one of our officers, the Junior Warden to be exact. I told Jim to fill the station, and he balked. "Why I haven't done that in 40 years and I can't do it." "Get up there and do it," I told him. "You CAN do IT," and do it he did. There is quite a bit of memory work involved in this station, and Jim didn't miss a beat, done to perfection. What a feat, memory fading and after 40 years, word perfect. What more can I say? I had the honor of presiding at the Masonic gravesite service for my good friend and Masonic Brother Jim, in the Hetland cemetery. May our Brother Rest in Peace.

Once when Eva and I were in Sioux Falls, I went into a clothing store that was selling out to the bare walls. Eva was in another store looking around, too. They had suit coats on sale for two bucks. I tried some on and bought five of them. There was a guy standing up by the door with another coat on with the tag on the sleeve. I asked the clerk what that guy was doing. She told me he was waiting for his wife to see if he should buy it. Boy, he must have been henpecked if he couldn't spend two bucks for a coat! I went to the parking lot and put the five coats in the trunk and went to get Eva. When we got to the car, I told her I just bought five suit coats for $10.50. The 50 cents was for tax. Of course, my girl friend didn't believe such a far out tale, so I opened the trunk and showed her the five coats. That made a believer out of her!

When we went to the next Eastern Star meeting, I wore one of those coats. Dianne Pickering came over and told me how "sharp" I looked in that high priced coat. I couldn't resist telling her it cost $2.10. She couldn't believe it. The next Star meeting I wore a different coat, which also looked pretty sharp. Here came Dianne. "Boy, that is a sharp coat. How much did it cost?" I told her nothing, as Myrna had made the coat in Illinois, and sent it to me for a Christmas present. Didn't even get to try it on me, but it fit like a glove. Our girl did an excellent job making that coat from scratch, with no model to try it on. I still have the coat after all these years. I talked about wearing one of the $2.10 coats in the BS shop with a white shirt and tie, but my girl friend didn't dare me to do it. So, there wasn't any challenge, otherwise, who knows? A white-shirted blacksmith complete with tie! Glory be! What next?

Virgil and I both belong to the Masonic Lodge, Scottish Rite and the Shrine. Virg is also a 33rd degree Mason. We both belong to the Order of the Eastern Star, as do Myrna and Virg's wife Vi.

One night at our Star meeting in Arlington we had a program of identifying photos. I was meandering around looking at pictures and not having much luck identifying anyone. But, boy oh boy, luck was with me. There was Hulda Converse, admiring a cute, (at least I thought it was cute), picture, of four little stair step boys. Boy, did they look SHARP, all decked out in full dress. The youngest one stole the show, as he had on light colored pantaloons, and could have been the Crown Prince of the pack.

Dale joins Yankton Scottish Rite, May 1965

Virgil joins Yankton Scottish Rite, May 1965

Well, I stopped and looked over Hulda's shoulder, and made the comment, "Boy, those are some cute looking little Devils." She turned and looked at me with that knowing look, that women can give to men, and said, "THANK YOU." I asked, "What for?" Her reply, (and then she paid me an unearned compliment), "Why, that's YOU, because you would never say that about any one else." Boy, she must have had me mixed up with someone else, because the truth was surely being stretched on that compliment.

When we were younger and had a snapshot picture, Skinny was always the "dude" in the picture, as he would have a tie on to look sharp. The rest of us looked a little seedy compared to him. When he grew up, he grew out of the idea that he had to wear a tie, and had all kinds of excuses why he didn't need one.

When I was District Master I went to Brookings to present a 50-year medal to Prof Christy, as every one called him. He was a well-known band director at South Dakota State College. Before he was well known over there, he used to come to Hetland on the westbound passenger train at 7 PM, direct the Hetland band for a couple of hours, and ride back to Brookings on the 10 o'clock train. I don't think that our band did much as far as music, except to probably make a lot of noise.

There was a mob at Lodge that night, including the Grand Master, Roger Brown, and several "Big wigs" from around the state. Boy was I in luck, I would have the Grand Master present the medal, and I could just sit back and - relax. That was my way of thinking, but it didn't pan out that way. I asked Roger to present the medal, and that went over like a wet blanket. No way, that is YOUR job. OK, he pulled rank on me, but I did con him into pinning the medal on our distinguished band director, who I might add, was a full blooded Dane, and spelled Christensen with an ==EN. How about that?

Another time we had a 50-year medal for a brother who rode the train from Rapid City to Arlington for the big event. I was supposed to present him that evening. However that deal blew up, as the Master of the Lodge called me in the afternoon to say that he was sick with the flu, and would I take over for him? In the Masonic Lodge we very seldom say NO when asked to do something, so I had charge of the meeting. The District Master was a Brown but we called him Brownie. He was seated in the east beside me, when all at once he leaned over and asked, "What am I here for?" That about thew me for a loop, but I told him he was supposed to present a 50-year medal. "I am? What am I supposed to do? Do you have the medal?" He searched his pocket and no medal. Then he told me it must be at home on the dresser. All was not lost, as a member was present who liked to show off that he had 50 years of Masonry tucked under his belt, and was wearing his medal. I copped onto it, and presented it to our beaming brother, who later received his own jewel, sent in the mail.

I never used a book in these medal presentations so I luckily still had the procedure in my head. I was not immune from being absent-minded, just in case you may wonder. Howard Hewett went with me to Brookings one night, when I had a medal to present, or did I? All at once it dawned on me that the medal wasn't with me, but was back home on the table. I told Howard about it, and he volunteered to go and get it, but that wasn't so easy either. When he got here, Eva had gone to visit a neighbor and for some unknown reason had locked the house. Our dog Topsy was inside, barking like mad, when Howard was beating on the door, and no Eva. But our brother Howard found one of the windows in the porch that wasn't burglar proof, so he slid it open and Topsy let him in. Howard had the medal for me in time for the presentation, and no one knew what had transpired. Had our brother known it, there was a key on the key ring that would have opened the door. Well, all that is now "water under the bridge."

Ernie Nessan, a member of our Lodge, had moved back to his home town of Renner. He was a good friend of the Norwegian preacher and they were fishing buddies and good friends. Now out here, some of the Norwegian preachers think the members of the Masonic Lodges are in cahoots with the devil. But it is OK if the Norskes belong to the Norwegian Lodge, The Sons of Norway, which by the way, will even let Danes join. I had a lady ask me if I wanted to join the Sons of Norway. "Me, join the Sons of Norway?" I told her I wouldn't be caught dead joining them. We are still friends.

Well Ernie put the bite on his preacher friend and told him that when he died he wanted to be buried with a Masonic service. Ernie passed on to his Maker, and we were called on to do the service. Several of us motored to Renner for the funeral. When we came into the church I was amazed to see something up in the air above the parishioners that looked like a look out tower. When the preacher climbed up the stairs I realized it was the pulpit, high enough so that no one wanted to go to sleep during the service, or they would be caught sleeping.

We had our Masonic service for Brother Ernie and it went as good as could be expected, with me having charge of it. We had some good comments on it. This was probably the only Masonic service ever conducted from that church, and I would give pretty good odds on that, if betting were in order.

When gas rationing was on, gas was really scarce. Byron Foss, who lived in Minnesota at that time had died, and was buried in Clark, SD, quite a way north of here. I was to be a pallbearer, and didn't know how I would make it with not many gas ration cards. Jim Barber heard about it and told me not to worry about gas, as he would see to it that I had enough. They sold gas also, and that was pretty nice of one Masonic brother to let me go and help bury another Masonic brother.

When Virgil was growing up, I always hoped that he would join the Masonic Lodge, and that (the Lord willing) I could be there when he became a Master Mason. My hoping was not in vain, because when he was 21 years old his petition was all signed, and ready to be acted upon, and I was able to be present for the degree work. Boy, was I happy to be able to call him Virgil, our son, as well as Brother Virgil. Only a Masonic father could know the JOY of such an experience.

However never in my fondest dreams did the thought ever enter my mind that in 2005 he would be elected Right Worshipful Junior Grand Warden of the Masonic Grand Lodge of South Dakota. In 2008 he will be Grand Master of the state, with the title of Most Worshipful Grand Master. I have told him that I hope I will be around to see him installed as Grand Master. If not, his Mom and I will be floating around him, popping our buttons (if buttons were in vogue) in the place where we were residing. We are so proud of all of his accomplishments, he being a 33rd degree Mason, after years and years of dedicated service to Masonry and its appendant bodies, the Scottish and York Rites and the Mystic Shrine.

He, our son and my Brother, has earned his just reward. I need say no more except to say well done, Brother Virgil, and Best Wishes in all that you do. So Mote it be.

Chapter 19
Dale's E-mails

Email.... Dale's latest window to the world

Dale's E-mails

Internet access and E-mail have become a part of our lives. When one of Virg's friends built a new computer for Vi's office use in 2001, he took the old machine, added some parts and upgraded the software and suddenly Dale had an addition to his life – a computer of his own. Lawrence Kirwan, the friend who purchased the house where Dale was born, told us of Juno service which provided a free dial-up E-mail service, making electronic messaging available for the small cost of a long distance call to the nearest Juno server.

At first, friends were notified by mail that they could send him messages via E-mail. He enjoyed receiving them, but it was an incoming only existence. After some encouragement, he set out on the brave new world of technology, and started creating outgoing messages to the delight of an ever-broadening circle of friends. Many of them share Dale's stories and observations with co-workers and family members who eagerly wait to hear the news from the shores of Lake Ole. Woe unto those who don't reply or neglect to send an occasional message to him! They face banishment from his circle of E-mail buddies. A word to the wise should suffice.

There are issues in changing from touch typing learned in 1928 on a manual Remington typewriter, and using the keyboard of a Personal Computer. Dale's "hunt and peck" method of using one finger of each hand and looking at the keyboard has caused some complications. When his left pinky finger hits the "Control" key at the same time his index finger touches the "s" key, the Juno program sees it as a command to save the message. When he looks up at the screen, his beautifully crafted work is gone, and he is greeted with a blank screen, since the message has been dutifully sent to a "saved message" folder. Well-meaning friends sometimes send large files to him that just can't download to a dial-up connection, and block all of his incoming messages. You will see references to his frustration!

We have included just a few of his E-mail greetings and stories, loosely arranged in chronological order, and by topic. They range from reports of town and area events, weather reports and politics, church and cemetery and family updates. Likely as not, lutefisk and Norwegians play a prominent role, frequently in a printed representation of Norske dialect. Often he quotes or writes a few lines of verse, or relates his latest April fool joke. At times he refers to health issues or sinks into melancholy spirit. When the sun is shining, the days are getting longer, or there's mowing to be done or bread to bake to give to friends who might drop in, you can sense the joy in his heart and spring in his step. There's always solace in cuddling Snookie, one of the aging cats that Eva socialized. We hope you will enjoy this poignant glimpse into his daily life.

Technology? BAH, HUMBUG! —

December 21, 2002

Subject: Lost mail?

Greetings on the 21st, the first day of winter. We have had warm weather, but still my heat bill has been higher, than the last 2 months of last year. How come?? Oh yes, I had a letter nearly completed, yesterday, when I looked up from this fabulous hunt and peck system, and discovered that I had a blank page in front of me. Did everything, except throw this outfit out, and still haven't found where it went to. Oh well, win some and lose some. Maybe it was just as well, that it was lost.

Had good ol' smelly lutefisk for dinner, yesterday, and will try and run some through my system, today. Fish, butter and a half baked sweet spud, and a piece of apple pie, was the menu for yesterday. How's that for a well balanced diet?? No comment, please.

Cats are out, but would like to get back into the porch. It is only 20, so maybe I should take pity on them, and let them curl up in the chair, on the porch. Enough is enough, take care of yourselves, and don't do anything that I wouldn't. Diddler.

Saturday, May 17, 2003

I am MAD=== After spending several hours through the day, sending hundreds and maybe thousands of words to all of you after each mowing session, the whole she – bang is GONE. I thought that I was doing a pretty good job of filling you in on the last 2 days happenings, and now I am about ready to dismember this outfit. If it would only disappear when I first started to write that wouldn't be so bad. I was just ready to send it on when == Nothing. It doesn't even list the letter or the date when I try to bring it up. Any ideas?? Mory the Diddler, and he can't even send an E-mail with hunt and peck in slow motion. I had better give it up and do ??? NUTS. I hope that your day has been GOOD. Let's see if I can make this one go the way of the other one.

Thursday, October 7, 2004

Hi U 2: It is cloudy, dark, damp and breezy, but in spite of all of that, I LOVE YOU. Haven't heard anything as yet, from the computer guy, but maybe he will call this morning, when the joint opens for business. I have already told you what he said. Myrna said that she had a good time with you, as I knew she would. I hope that lodge went well. I started writing this this morning, but went over to DeSmet and voted against 4 more years. I hope that others can see the light, and do likewise. Dad

Incoming Mail

No incoming mail so I can just as well quit sending you the malarkey like I have been sending you, since you can't harangue me from the other end. That will probably be good news to most of U, so that you won't have to waste your time wearing out the Delete button. So now, after letting U NO that we have no sun, no more snow, but lots of blow, I will bid you = ADIOS, and pleasant dreams. Mory

If You Don't Like the Weather Right Now, Just Wait! —

February 2, 2003

Subject: snow–4-5 inches

WANTED, AT ONCE, OR SOONER. MALE OR FEMALE TO SHOVEL–SNOW. QUALIFICATIONS/// STRONG BACK- WEAK?? MIND, OPTIONAL. KNOWS WHICH END OF THE SHOVEL, GOES INTO THE SNOW.-

- READY TO WORK–CHEAP. SEND APPLICATION, ALONG WITH THE SCOOP SHOVEL, YOU INTEND TO USE–TO//OH WHAT THE HECK–FORGET IT ===DALE, MORY, DIDDLER

Saturday, May 31, 2003

Greetings, Salutations and Felicitations. Slight breeze, Sol is out, no rain, and that is it. Compared to yesterday, this is something good. I reported yesterday that we had 50 to 60 mile gale winds. The way that the dust and cornhusks were blowing around yesterday, for some strange reason I reverted back to my youth, while in school. The first thing that came to mind was poetry.

> *Listen my children and you shall hear, of the midnight, I mean- Daylight ride of NOT Paul Revere, but CORN HUSKS.*
> *Millions of corn husks to the right of them (Hetland),*
> *Millions of corn husks to the left of them,*
> *Millions of corn husks in front of them,*
> *Lying on the ground, the place of their birth.*
> *Just waiting to travel and see the world, especially == Hetland.*
> *The Big day came, with gale winds, out of the north,*
> *And away they went, heading south,*
> *Their wishes had come True.*
> *And amidst the dust and other flying objects,*
> *They left the land, the place of their birth,*
> *And took off, flying with the wind,*
> *Free of charge, to see the rest of the world.*
> *However, some of them, like me,*
> *Didn't want to venture too far from home,*
> *So many of them, like the sands of the sea, too numerous to mention,*
> *Settled down on the lush green grass,*
> *Near the Abode, which Dale and Eva Andersen, Call HOME.*
> *Mory the Diddler.*

Wednesday, September 15, 2004

> *In the good old summer time = BOOM BOOM.*
> *In the good old summer time = BOOM BOOM,*
> *There won't be any SNO=OH OH,*
> *In the good old summer time = BOOM BOOM.*

> *56 degrees, it is, by gum*
> *56 degrees, I say, by gum,*
> *Along with a half an inch of rain, by gum,*
> *Now, I tell you this, that we are going some,*
> *With a half an inch of rain, falling on us.*
> *And more of the wet stuff, coming down, by gum.*

> *But that ain't all, and I'll tell you why,*
> *There ain't any sun, either, by gum,*
> *And it is dark and cloudy,*
> *As you may have surmised,*
> *But that ain't all, and I'll tell you more.*

> *The wind, she's a-blowin' some,*
> *Maybe, even a gale, as some might say,*
> *And the tree leaves, they are a wiggling,*
> *As you may have guessed,*
> *Keeping in tune, with the breeze, I suppose,*

> *To the wind, that God in His Wisdom,*
> *Has sent us, to clear the air,*
> *Of dust and grime,*
> *And to make this a better place, and more sublime,*
> *For us to reside, and spend our time,*

> *While we are languishing here on earth,*
> *Enjoying another beautiful day, on planet earth.*
> *And that's the end of this, By GUM*
> *And so I'll close, with a Big and Hearty, = BOOM = BOOM.*
> *From me 2 U, at 11 AM on this, the 15th day of our Lord, in 2004*

Did You Hear the One About......??

Wednesday, May 4, 2004

Greetings, Salutations and Felicitations. Lend me your ears, I will give them back. Yesterday I gave you the boring and gory details of my dilemma trying to stuff a Big absentee voting ballot into a Little envelope. Today I will fill you in on another less trying situation.

Knute (Nutty) Knutson, a Norske of course, built a boat in the basement of his house, with the idea of going out on the big pond to snare some of those delicious Danish sardines that he had heard about. The boat was finished so he had several of his stalwart friends come over for a snack of coffee, with the idea of having them help get the boat out of the basement when they were well fortified with liquid caffeine. But they had a small problem, nothing like mine of course. The would-be ship, or boat, was Too big to go out through the door. Now what? After due and timely consideration, after several days of consultation with the more learned Norwegians, they decided to send an S.O.S. message to - Svenn (Skyhook) SwenSEN, over in Denmark to help them out, as they had finally decided that the only way to get the boat out of the basement was to either move the house or dismantle the boat.

The Norskes decided, all being in full agreement, that Skyhook could do the job easier than knocking down the boat and then having to rebuild it. Skyhook the Dane came with his outfit, wrapped the Skyhook around the house, lifted it up, and the boat lifting crew lifted the boat up on to "higher" ground. Then old Skyhook SvenSEN put the house down on the foundation and the trying situation was solved in the twinkling of an eye.

Now just in case some of you doubters might think that this old boy could be feeding you a line without a sinker about the Skyhook, let me inform you that many times (once) we chased around town looking for a Skyhook, as well as a left handed monkey wrench, doughnut stretcher and striped paint, vainly running from one place to the other looking for them at the request of our elders. As of now, these items have somehow eluded us.

As I size up the situation, Knute, the Nut, didn't have any problem with his boat, compared to me and my ballot. By the way, I CAN'T vouch or verify this, as I presume that Knute has departed this earth as his ancestors have, and are sitting around "shooting the breeze" on the wonders of Norske Land.

Tuesday, April 5, 2005

Dale was hospitalized in Brookings for a few days with blood clots in his legs. On his return, he sent an E-mail report to his friends, with the following postscript about his fun with the hospital staff on April 1.

PSS: Needless to say the nurses gave me a rough time while they were taking care of me but they did a good job of taking care of me. Even then I had to pull a few fast tricks on them. The first one was when the Doc and his helper came and I said, "How can a mouse get into this place." They said, "What do you mean a mouse?" I said "Yeah, the little devil was running along the baseboard back and forth and he was looking for a calendar to see if it was April Fools Day. What do you know? It was!" I got my laugh out of it and they about flipped. I also pulled it on some of the nurses, and when I mentioned a mouse they were ready to pull up their skirts, if they had any on. They were suckered into the same April Fool joke!

Come Sunday Morning..... —

January 19, 2003

Hi every one on this 30-degree Sunday. It is supposed to get way down below zero in the next few days. Had church this AM with a real nice service, but only 6 of us to take part in the service, sitting in front of the minister. However we know that there was a multitude of unseen host surrounding us, taking part in the service. I brought lunch to serve, afterwards. I was too busy getting every thing lined up that I forgot the paper plates and even didn't, or I should say, forgot to SHAVE. Nobody commented on it, so I told them. What a pity.

I had cooked up a smoked pork ham and then made ham salad sandwich spread to put on homemade bread. Then the menu consisted of lefse, courtesy of Virgil, olives, potato chips, cookies, bananas, chocolate covered peanut clusters, apple cider and orange juice. I think that was all that we had? Yesterday I made 3 loaves of bread so each family had part of a loaf of bread to take home with them. I came home to bake some for myself. While I was scurrying around getting lunch ready, I thought of one of my favorite poets, Longfellow, and the poem, "The Village Blacksmith." If you remember, part of the poem went thus –

"He goes on Sunday to the church, and sits among his boys. He hears the Parson pray and preach, he hears his daughter's voice, singing in the choir, and It makes his heart rejoice, as it sounds to him like her Mother's voice, singing in Paradise, and with a firm rough hand he wipes a tear out of his eyes."

I'm not ashamed of it, but I didn't wipe away a tear. I just sat and cried, thinking how our kids, Myrna and Virgil, were following in their Mom's foot steps, spreading God's Word here on earth, just as she did. I'm sure she is still doing God's will in that Wonderful Place where there is No sunset and No dawning, just as our Lord wants it to be. Love to all of you. Dale, Mory

Sunday, May 4, 2003

Hi in a nutshell. Cold, damp, cloudy, windy and had a dash of rain, and that is IT. Off to church, more later. Just back from church and I'm not hungry. The Lord said, "Where two or three are gathered in My name, there will I be also." That's the way it was today. Five in the pews, two couples back from the south, and me. Not many for numbers, but good on quality in spite of me. Am I Blue? Yes. Am I Discouraged? Yes. Am I ready to Cry? Yes. Dale

Sunday, January 18, 2004

Hi again: My (90th) birthday is over, but we are still celebrating. What I wasn't supposed to know was that my church friends were having a BIG splash for me after church. Even the church bulletins were decorated with a Happy Birthday slogan, as well as a picture of an anvil and a hammer depicting what I had been doing all of my working days. Then to top it off we had a delicious meal, complete with several kinds of sandwiches, relish dish, with pickles, carrots and all of the various and sundry things that go on such a dish. We had bugles, things for dip, birthday cake, ice cream, coffee, 2 different kinds of drinks, and you name it, we had IT. Boy what a blowout, just for another birthday of mine, and as far as I was concerned, Nothing that I deserved. But it was Great, with a Swell group of people preparing it with Loving hands. I had thought about bringing lunch, but decided to bake bread instead, so I baked 5 loaves and cut them in half so that each family had a sack of fresh bread to take home with them. Thanks to all of them and to all of you, we have really Celebrated in January. Love, Mory

Monday, April 11, 2005

Subject: kids are praying for your dad

Dear Virg, How's your dad today? I just wanted to tell you something about last night at confirmation. We always close confirmation with everyone offering prayers all around the circle. Ben Hardy and Colin Block prayed for your dad. I was touched that they both thought of him. I didn't even know that they knew he was taken to the hospital again. So if you have a chance, tell him that not only adults but also kids are praying for him to feel better!

–Marcia (Rev. Marcia Sietstra, Crestwood UCC, Sioux Falls)

Sunday night, December 31, 2006

Dear all 3 of U: Same 2 all. More ice and some snow, and I LOVE YOU. Myrna suggested that as long as we didn't have church I could get services on the TV. That I did. I ran the gauntlet from Mass in SF, then to Aberdeen for Baptist, and then back to SF for Lutheran. I am about pooped, as too much religion in one day gets tiresome. The Lutheran preacher said that they had 4000 members, and over half of them were C& E Lutherans (Christmas and Easter). We have a better average than that. So far I haven't ventured out to get the paper, even though I have salted down the deck and steps. 4 cats are in the porch, all except Skamper. Their outside dishes are frozen over, so they can enjoy eating without freezing their feet. Little Cutie was cavorting around on the chair and fell off on the side toward the kitchen, but that didn't slow her down. She jumped back up on the chair and went round and round in circles, enjoyed tearing up the coat as only girls can do. NO comments, please, from you Chicks. Stay warm. Dad

Final Resting Place –

Wednesday, May 19, 2004

Greetings, etc. Let 'er rain, let 'er snow, let 'er blow, who cares as long as we don't leave the ground and fly away on the wings of the wind. 60 above, cloudy and windy, with a good chance of storms tonight, according to Virgil's weather report from Sioux Falls. I haven't had time to size up the situation here as I have had the bread machine going, waiting for a call from Brookings to see if my belt is in for the busted down lawn mower. I was out to the cemetery, mowing in the rain the other day before Adeline Dutcher's funeral, to try and grind up the multitude of corn husks that were reposing there for their final resting place, without a hole in the ground to be deposited into.

When the rain finally got so heavy that it seemed useless even for a Dane to keep on mowing, I gave in to the elements and headed the Sherman tank toward Hetland, as fast as I was able to go. As I turned the corner a half mile north of town, the drive belt went " KAPUT," and there I was in a driving rain (2 inches of the wet stuff, to be exact), with the mower engine running and we were NOT moving. So being of Danish descent, this little problem didn't deter me. This problem was NOT insurmountable, as all I had to do was get off and push the crippled outfit to town. Boy was that quick thinking, and that was what transpired. I question whether a Norwegian could have figured that out that quickly without having to talk the situation over with some other Norskes.

But there was and is a GOOD side to the episode. Following me into town was Maurice Matson, a full-blooded, LEVEL headed Norske, with Shirley, his part German wife. They took pity upon me, ordering me, after a brisk argument of course, to get into the car while they took turns pushing the mower, as well as getting soaked in the deluge. It seemed as though they thought that I was too OLD to be pushing a lawn mower, especially in a blinding rainstorm. These two took turns getting soaked too, but finally got close enough to town where another Norwegian and part German friend of ours, seeing our predicament rushed out and got the "crippled" machine to the mower fixers door. Boy, what an escapade. Now I am waiting for a call from Brookings that they have a new belt. Now some of you can see what we do with our time when we live in a Small Town. This turned out to be an epistle, when I was just going to fill you in on the weather. Mory the Diddler

Thursday, May 10, 2007

HO HUMM: Yesterday was one of those days that you don't write home to Mom with any glee. Our cemetery mower man had called to let me know that he couldn't mow the Hetland cemetery this year. I called a young friend to see if he was interested in mowing the cemetery this year. He said that he would have done it but they were moving in a couple of weeks, but he could mow it for a couple of times. Hot Stuff, that was great.

My friend stopped to tell me that he had the cemetery mowed and I had fresh bread and cookies baked for him. Later on everything went to pot as it had done all day, when my friend called to tell me that he had mowed the WRONG ??? Cemetery. His Dad had filled him in on that. Two plots of land, two miles apart, and since all of the people residing there in were dead, there was NO living soul there to tell this young man, "You missed the boat, you are mowing the WRONG cemetery." But all is NOT lost. He will mow in the right place today. YIPPIEE. All done reporting. Mory

Say it in Verse —

February 15, 2003

Greetings:
Whatda you know, whatda you know?
Blizzard all gone, and so is the Blow.
Ground is all White, and covered with Snow,
Whatda you know, whatda you know?

Should have gone South, but too Dumb to know,
Now it's too late to open the gate, gotta stay home
And shovel da snow.
Whatda you know, whatda you know?

Shovel 's in da corner, and I'm eyeing it out,
Wondering–should I TAKE it OUT?
And give it some CLOUT, shoveling da snow, shoveling da snow
Whatda you know, whatda you know?
Let us go OUT, and SHOVEL da SNOW

NO, NO. PRAISE THE LORD, AND BLESS HIS HOLY NAME. I looked out the window,
after hearing a ROAR, and GOD with HIS wisdom, which NEVER FAILS, let me see
what HE HAD IN STORE - for little old ME.

Whatda you know, whatda you know? Out in da yard was a WONDERFUL SIGHT,
a great BIG TRACTOR, with a snow BLOWER TOO, MOVING da SNOW, MOVING DA SNOW and BLOWING IT HIGH INTO DA AIR,

what a BEAUTIFUL SIGHT, A BEAUTIFUL sight to BEHOLD. PRAISE THE LORD, AGAIN AND AGAIN, AMEN AND AMEN.

Thanks to my GOOD neighbor Fred Carey, I have taken off my winter coat, and da shovel is still eyeing me out, but I have news for it, NO shoveling here, now, but I wonder about the walk at the church???

Luckily, I had FRESH bread, a check and fresh BROWNIES too, so Fred and his son, James, can nibble and chew.

Brotherly Love —

Tuesday, June 03, 2003

Hi: What is so rare as a day in June?
If ever come perfect days
When Heaven tries the earth
To see if it be in tune
And over it softly her warm ear lies.

The poet that wrote that must not have been from SD, as it was down in the '40s last night. Finally ended up with a 1/2 inch of rain which was good, as we needed it. Today- nice and bright, cool and a slight wind, of course. I'm baking bread, what else is new? I'm taking it to Eastern Star tonight, and will give it away to some of my Sisters and Brothers, whoever has one of the lucky numbers enclosed with the bread. I don't call that gambling, just having the right number at the right time. In the Masonic lodge or Eastern Star we never gamble or have anything to drink that is stronger than Coffee, and that has too much clout for me. Maybe when I get older I might indulge?? I'm going to the clinic this PM.

Saturday, October 30, 2004

Brr: The temperature got up to 65 yesterday, and this morning it is 40 with a stiff northwest wind. No sun, no rain and no snow, although they had a foot or so out in the Black Hills. Virg is out trying his luck hunting for ducks and geese. So far his hunting has been only hunt, as he doesn't have anything as of now to take home to fill their larder. He has gotten a lot of much needed work done around here, for which I am deeply thankful. So far it has been too wet to chop up the leaves, so they have been blowing hither and yon, going north one day and coming back south the next day. The trouble with that is this. I mow on both sides of this abode, as there are no neighbors to help me work over the leaves, but on the other hand, when the mower gets in gear, "let ER rip."

Virg is going to Masonic table lodge in White tonight. I used to go for years and years, but now I don't dare to try it. He is Grand Orator for the Grand Lodge of SD, so he might have a seat reserved for him, with his name on the tag. White lodge has had this table lodge going on for 50 years, which is indeed a milestone for this small lodge. They know how to kill the fatted calf, when the grub is passed, family style, with all you can eat until the appetite has been fully appeased. Need I say more, as you lick your chops over the savory smell of prime beef, with ALL of the trimmings, cooked to perfection of course. Besides that, the Fellowship and Brotherly Love is = FANTASTIC. Mory

Days near Thanksgiving —

Friday in 2006,

Greetings, etc: 20 above this morning. Sol is out and there isn't much blow. Maybe that would be what is called the aftermath of a blow out. Virg is here and is hunting geese with an automatic shotgun that holds 9 shells. What do you old time hunters think of that? Anything is legal for spring goose hunting. Virg got me to Masonic lodge last night, for which I am very thankful. It was nice to hear him introduced as Right Worshipful Brother Virgil Andersen, Junior Grand Warden of the Grand Lodge of SD. My buttons were under a terrific strain. He just came into the house, with no evidence of any birds in sight, and he is heading back to Sioux Falls for a meeting this PM. Something like the story that went thus. Husband to wife: "Where have you been?" Wife, "Shopping." "What did you buy?" "Nothing." "How come you said you went shopping when you didn't buy anything?" The retort. "You go hunting and come home with NOTHING." I would suppose that would mean, what is sauce for the goose, is sauce for the gander. Need I say more? Mory

Tuesday, January 2, 2007

Dear Virg and Vi: Sol is out but it is still freezing, and I LOVE YOU. Spent the morning watching the funeral for Brother Ford. The teachings in Masonry really rubbed off on him. Stay warm. Shirley is furnishing dinner, as she sent over scalloped spuds and ham. Stay warm and collected. Dad

Ah-Vun und Ah-Two —

Occasionally, Dale has been struck with an inspiration to mimic some of the old Scandinavians he heard so often in his youth. These are only a few examples.

August 15, 2003

Hi, wid nuse frum up nort. Dis ol boy is eatin hi on de hog, von ere ov sveeet kornn, von our afterr 11 bels in de am, wid a coooky fer a folow upper. Den latter onn inn de pm, von our b- 4 - 7 at de nite, de samm ting, mor uv de sveeet korn, an den?? Las nitee it vas a pece uf pi, dat valked in de frunt dor, wid hellup frum dis ol buoy. Von uf mi frends mus hav thot dat eye vas inn nede uf som ting tooo sveten meee upp. It vas peche pi, an vas rell gut. Dat's al frumm yur Fadder, wid LUV frum de ol Geeezzer, whoo tinks dat ewe R, === GRATE.

May 4, 2005

Vot da ya NO, now U vill NO, dat fer de furst time since Hector had pups, it did KNOT freeze last nite. Hip Hip an Who=Ray. May B dat spring has dun sprung, att last? Ve vill vait an sea. De sun is out, an de vind, she is A blowin, sum, soo now U NO vat litle eye NO, frum mee 2 U. Toodle=oo an all uf dat stuff, vid sveet drems, 2. Alll uf dis iss frum, U gott it rite. –. Mory.

Monday, November 27, 2006

Goot knews. Eye findd itt, eye findd itt == LUTEFISK. De udder daay eye vent lookin fer de smelee stuf, an finded sum uff itt. Dun gott rid uff tventy buks all inn vun vad, B 4 dey vould lett me outt uff de stor. Eye hadd sum uff itt fer dinur yesturdayy aftr church. Lutefisk an lefse wid bred an buttr pikuls. A vel balunced meel?? Virg iss hear 2 dayy, out huntin, n ve vill haff sum uff dat brane foodd fer dinur. Ve mist out onn dee icee an sno, so ve iss lucke dat vey. Eye vondur iff de fish mite haff bin spiked bye de luks uff diss spellin?

Demoralizing the Grass —

Friday, June 22, 2007

A mowing we will go
a mowing we will go
hi ho the merry O
a mowing we will go.

The grass will shiver and shake
the grass will shiver and shake
when Mory and the Sherman tank
come roaring round the wake.

Around and around we go
at high speed, of course you know
and as long as there is grass to mow
the tank and I, will MOW and == MOW.

Dale mowing his lawn

Don't sing or hum this to the tune of Old Lang Syne. It WON'T jibe. But rather, the cat choose the rat. In this case, the Dane stands "Alone."

Nough said???

Monday in May 9, 2006

Greetings, etc: The other day I told you that at a later date I would fill you in on nearly a half century of a Joyous time I have had mowing the HETLAND CHURCH LAWN. This being a later date, I will try and fill you in on what it has been like, this day being cool and breezy, with very little sun peeking through the clouds, and I am in writeful mood to hunt and peck, so here goes????

If this bores you, I won't be offended if you delete this, as I won't know the difference. Let's see, where do we begin? Oh yes, we need a mower of course. 60 or more years ago, my Dad and I made whirlwind lawn mowers with a 24-inch blade residing under a 1 1/2 horse power gas engine. At first we used any kind of wheels that we could find, but finally we settled on 28-inch bicycle wheels, and boy could we make tracks like a rabbit. That is what I first used mowing the church lawn, pushing it as fast as my legs could travel. Those were uneventful times.

When I graduated to a riding mower the Lord and I had some harrowing times, but thanks to His expertise, we survived. I liked to think that I was sitting on the Lords lap, helping Him to run the mower at HIGH speed of course, with the throttle wide open. We needed to get the mowing done as soon as possible, as We had other things to do. In back of the church 2 of the trees were so close together that I really had to maneuver the mower at the right angle to mow between them. This went on for several years.

One year I miscalculated, or so I thought, and the mower wouldn't go through, so I backed up a few feet and took a run for it and that was a Bad mistake. I killed the engine and bent in the deck. I finally had to pull the outfit out, as the wheels kept spinning when I tried to back out. How was I to know, being a Dane, that those trees had grown a "pouch," and there wasn't room for the mower and me to go through? Even a Norwegian would have known that, I think. The mower that I had previous to this one (I have had 3 so far), and the first one was Bummer, and the second one was a close second. The old saying, 3 times and out, applied to that mower, all of which happened mowing the church lawn.

One time while heading for the church the tie rod busted, so no steering, but the Lord helped me to get it stopped before going to church. Another time the front axle busted in the middle, so no more mowing until I got it fixed. The third and final time was a "Joner." We were in road gear when KA-BOOM BANG BOOM, the engine BLEW up, literally. Smoke out the top, oil running out of the engine, and then all was = silent. Disaster had over taken Us, and the mowing wasn't finished. Now what? You guessed it, a new mower of course. Having seen a mower advertised in Madison, 40 miles away, that looked good, I got my mower friend Stricker with his trailer and we took off on a buying spree.

I bought the mower and gave the salesman my credit card to pay the 1,050 bucks to pay for it. He came back and told me that the card was NO GOOD. No money in the account, I told him that there was supposed to be money in there, but I said, "Well I'll give you a check THEN." Can you believe such audacity, give the guy a check for a thousand and fifty bucks when the credit card was no good? Do you know what? I gave him the check and he took it without asking any questions, if I was born, still living and where, and not even inquiring if Uncle Sam knew I was on this planet. Maybe he thought that I might not look like a crook, or maybe he saw my Masonic ring, as others have noted on previous occasions, or else he thought that I looked too dumb to beat him out of that tidy sum. We got the mower, but I think that Providence took care of it, as the churchyard wasn't finished mowing and needed to get finished in order to look "spick and span."

This is a long tale about an enjoyable time, talking things over with the Lord while herding a mower around the Congregational church lawn, and WE are still doing IT. Have a good day.. Mory

Monday, June 12, 2006

The Sherman tank is at a standstill as the grass, which heretofore grew like weeds, has slowed down to a crawl for lack of water. I miss demoralizing those innocent blades of grass, so maybe I will have to go out and rev up the tank just to keep in practice. You may wonder why I call the mower a tank. I have stripped off the whole front end, including the hood, so the engine and front end are in plain sight. That way I can tell if the engine is still running, and I can see better, if I might hit a tree or the side of a building. Only a Dane could think up something like that. And another thing, I don't even have to lift the hood to add gas or check the oil. Boy oh boy, what luxury. Dat's ittt. Mory

What's Up, Doc? –

HOME AT LAST!

Thank you for your prayers, letters, e-mail, calls, visits and anything else you did to help my stay in the hospital be better. The old Dane boat is still afloat, even though it has been leaking at the corners. So far it has shed water. I gained 8 pounds while I was in the hospital and then through the process of eliminating vitamin P it got back to normal.

Myrna brought me home today and I am not the best for wear and tear but I have a new walker with swivel wheels probably designed by a Dane because it is questionable if a Norske would know which way the wheels were supposed to turn. I also have a new walking cane, not fit for running, and some high priced socks to try to put over my swollen leg and to hopefully keep those nasty blood clots away.

I saw my ankle for the first time this morning. It has been a couple weeks since I was able to gaze on it. The leg had been swollen so big between the knee and the foot that when the swelling went down the leg looked like it had been in Custer's last stand. It was really washed out and reminded me of the 2 elderly gents sitting on a park bench gazing out into space when an elderly woman streaker went by them. One old boy said to the other "what was that?" The other responded knowingly "I don't know but it sure

Mory on his "Sherman Tank" mower

needed ironing." That's the way my leg looks so you now know what it looked like anyway.

This noon we had pork roast for dinner at the hospital and I put mine in a wrapper and brought it home so little Snookie the cat could have a treat. After all, when you have been away you are supposed to bring something home for the ones left behind. He looked cross eyed at me and pouted and then decided to come over and see if it was really me. Thankfully he decided it was me! Boy then did we have some loving! I broke up the pork roast into little pieces so he could handle them, as the vet says he has only 1 tooth left. Another one of my favorite yellow cats, Babe, was there to indulge also. The pork roast was better in their bellies than it was in mine.

I am supposed to keep my feet up in the air and not do a lot of chasing around. So that is the report I can give you from an old Dane who was nearly out but is still hanging in there. Maybe tomorrow I'll start the bread machine again, as the larder is empty. Myrna had a good supper tonight and we didn't need the bread. So that is it from the old Dane Diddler! With sincere thanks to all of you! Mory

Friday, April 22, 2005

Men, Women, Countrymen, lend me your ears: The old Diddler is back in his old abode, in the house by the side of the road where the two forks meet. I am not up to par, but still kicking, and as you can ascertain by this letter, still hunting and pecking. Thanks to all of you, my Dear Friends, for your Prayers, calls, cards and well wishes, while the Grim Reaper was breathing down my neck. I am so GLAD that the Reaper has given me another reprieve, as He has done in the past. At the present time, Myrna, as well as Virg and Vi, have been bestowing upon me all of the TLC that they so freely give to this old Duffer that they call=Dad. I am so Thankful for such Loving and caring kids, who take after their Dear Mom in so many ways. After spending 8 days in the Brookings hospital with blood clots in my leg and both lungs, and then home for 5 days, and then Myrna taking me to Sioux Valley hospital for another 5 days, with me having NO blood pressure on arrival. Then another 4 days with TLC from Myrna, Virg and Vi, at their home in Sioux Falls. Then home to the Promised Land #2 for a part of the day, and then back to Sioux Falls to the emergency room for more testing, as my stool was Black, indicating internal bleeding. The health nurse played it safe by telling the Dr in SF about it, and they in turn wanted to see what was going on. Some blood showed up in the test, but everything otherwise checked out OK, so we spent another night with Virg and Vi. I am back to baking bread, so hopefully I will get back in the "groove" and be useful again, the Lord willing. Again, my Thanks to all of you for being so Special to me. Mory

Furry Friends —

Feeding our Little Pals

It is time to feed our little pals, our cats, who are just waiting for me to come out with something to eat and in a LOUD voice proclaiming– "Here comes Grandpa, here comes Grandpa," and boy do they come, ready to eat. Even the birds, especially the robins, come on the fly and settle down next to the cats, waiting their turn to grab a bite, It is just comical to watch them. The cats eating out of one dish, and 6 inches away, the birds eating from the other one. Perhaps I should tell you, that I have told the cats not to bother the birds, and they have listened to me, as at No time have I seen them try to "nail" one of the birds. That is what I would call– well trained- cats. Live and let live. After all, the Bible says that the Lamb will lie down with the Lion, or the other way around, so here in Hetland our little ones are way ahead of the times. I almost believe that one of the robins would take food from my hand, as they are that tame and trusting. The oth-

Snookie likes cheese from Dale

er day after feeding them, I watched a robin take a piece of food from right beside one of the cats' legs. Will wonders never cease? It is too bad that the human race can't find it in their hearts to get along together as these little ones do. What a Better world it would be. Enough of this preaching? Mory the Diddler

Sunday, April 11, 2004

Dear kids: Happy Easter again: Great news. Snookie came home this afternoon, and was sitting on the railing, looking in for me. Boy, was he hungry, and then he wanted some High Class Loving, he being perched on my chair - - waiting, and neither of us were disappointed. He curled up on my shoulder and went Sound Asleep, and didn't mind how I petted him, as long as my hand was stroking him. When I took supper out to them, a few minutes ago he was not in sight, - ? Now, I intended to tell you this before I got sidetracked, I LOVE YOU, and think that you are GREAT. Dad

People Make The Difference! —

August 6, 2003

Hi to each of U: Another nice day out in the land South of North Dakota. It is still cool, but will warm up, if the weatherman knows what he is getting paid for. Yesterday I wrote about our plans for the day. Today, if you will bear with me, I will hunt and peck, and try and fill you in, detail by detail, on an enjoyable time spent with our two little friends, Tina and Jesse Drewes and their Mom, Louise. First we had dinner, which is at noon of course, at McDonald's. Big Macs for us and chicken for their Mom. When done, little Jesse let us know that he was FULL and couldn't eat any more. But when the greeter brought around animal cookies, he immediately found room somewhere for them, and then proceeded to get three more packages, which also went down the hatch. That was it, no ice cream to top it off.

The two kids – Tina, just barely a teenager and Jesse, a 6th grader, had been clothes shopping all by themselves, while their Mom kept another appointment. Mom wanted to help pay for the clothes, as she said it was too much for me to take care of. I let her know that there was no $ amount specified and that she had nothing to do with that. The kids were Bubbling with Joy over the clothes, and the feeling was Mutual. Little, tall, Tina wouldn't let me walk by myself with my cane, but held on to me to help keep me right side up. She opened and shut the car door for me, so what a little sweetheart she is, as is her little brother Jesse.

Then Mom and Tina left for home, and left Jesse with me, so we decided to go "out on the town," and boy did we ever do just That. We went shopping all by ourselves in the big city of Brookings, and did we shop. I had a 50 cent coupon for Parkay margarine, so we ambled into the store where the dope was on sale for 99 cents a pound. That is all we bought there, and they doubled the coupon so all that I had to dig up was 1/100 of a buck. I didn't think there was any use in arguing over that sizeable amount, as the tax man probably had to collect something in order to make the transaction worth while. Then we ventured out of the store and bought Fresh sweet corn so that both families could have something to nibble on.

OK, now what? Our little friend wondered out loud if we could go to Wal-Mart and get a list of things that he would need to get into grade 6? Fine with me, and I told him that we could just as well pick up the stuff as long as we were in the store. He thought that his Mom should get it, but age prevailed, and we went shopping. Wal-Mart had it figured out what was good for business; a dozen pencils, the same for pens, crayons etc, etc, etc. and stuff that I didn't have any idea that a 6th grader would Ever use. But it was good for sales, and our little friend was a Good shopper. We even ended up with 2 Large boxes of Kleenex as they too were on the list. When we went to school back in the good old days, we needed a pencil and paper and that was about it. We even had a nickel handkerchief in our pocket that was reusable after washing.

Oh Oh, the lights just went off, but came back without any loss of this epistle. Where was I? Oh yes, we were done shopping so our little friend and this old boy took off for home. It wasn't long before our little boy was conked out, sound asleep, probably dreaming of big Macs, French fries and animal cookies. I would steal a look at him and marvel what a Joy it was to have this little boy and his family as our Loving and Caring == FRIENDS. It was a JOYFUL day, and our Cup Still Runneth Over. Mory the Diddler, out in the Oasis of Hetland.

Monday, December 20, 2004

(to Doug Hansen, wagon maker in Letcher, SD)

Dear Doug: Thanks for keeping this old 90-year-old, ex-blacksmith on your mailing list. The catalog is Great and I do enjoy reading about your putting old time stuff, back into modern day perspective. It was only a couple of years ago when you and your friend were here, when our son Virgil and I met you across the street at the shop. It floors me when I look at the difference in prices that we got for the same thing that you are doing today. I recall asking you if you slept good at night, charging those prices, and you assured me that you did. The last buggy tire that we set, we got 75 cents for doing it, and the tightwad farmer thought that was TOO much. Now you get $43. Every fall we used to set dozens and dozens of wagon tires for a Buck apiece, and now I see that you get = $77. Wow: It is no wonder that us dumb blacksmiths went out of existence.

Dad and I never made much money, but we surely enjoyed what we did. I never really had much choice, and don't regret it, as to what I would be doing when I got out of school. My Dad, being right from Denmark, was from the old school, namely, that the first-born son followed in his father's footsteps. If I hadn't taken up the trade, my dad would have been devastated. Luckily for our son Virg that same old idea didn't rub off on me, as we both saw the light, and he took off for greener pastures. He would have been a better Blacksmith than I ever was, as he has more intuition and knowledge than I ever had. My wife, Eva, used to tell me that I was an unimaginative Dane, whatever she meant by that. Keep up the good work of bringing back old memories, and doing a beautiful job of doing it. Sincerely, Dale Andersen.

Monday, May 2, 2005

From: "Robin Prunty"

Subject: FW: The last day of April and the day before the first of May.

Hi Virg, I just had to send a copy of my dad's (Roger "Waja" Prunty) email to your dad. This is what they talk about. I think it is just great. I am going to kiss my dad the next time I see him. Robin

Hi Dale, My mother used to tell me that when I was 4 years old, I delivered a May Basket to my Sunday School Teacher in Hetland, I knocked on her door and hollered: "May Basket for Irene Nienamier" and then I would run away fast so she couldn't catch me and give me a kiss. I have now learned to run slower but I have not been caught for quite a while. Does Irene Nienamier ring a bell in your mind? Waja

Waja: It surely does. Mamie the mother was a sister of Anna Dutcher. They came here from Missouri, and Ivan the father had some odd sayings, as well as a southern accent. He used to say, "over yonda," instead of us Hetlandites saying, "over there." I presume that they both meant the same? Myrna just left for home in Galesburg Ill, so it is already lonesome around here. She is a Loving and Caring kid, just like her Mom, and has been here for 5 weeks, ever since I went into the hospitals. I seem to be getting better, but it seems to be slow. Today I am getting an emergency calling outfit so that I can call someone in case I need help. I hope that I don't ever need to use it, but it is good insurance. I called Del Barber the other day, when he turned 90 years old. They live in Omaha. We have had 8 nights of freezing weather, so that isn't good for crops. Hi to Betty.

Love, Mory

Monday, June 19, 2006

Greetings, Salutations and Felicitations, on a B= U= T= Ful day out in the Promised Land # 2. I don't know what key I hit to underline, so I can't hit it again to erase the line. With the old machine I could do it. Please bear with me. What a way to start the day. Uff Daa.

The weekend, to say the least, was out of this world. A beloved former minister, Chris Klug, and his wife Bev came to visit us on Saturday. Virg and Vi came from Masonic Grand Lodge, where he was elected Senior Grand Warden for the ensuing year. We all had supper together, and Virg and Vi did the cooking honors, so the meal was delicious.

Our friend Chris is partial to vanilla ice cream, so I scouted around and found 3 different kinds of the stuff so that he would have a choice, they being vanilla, white and plain, and the rest of us could have maple nut or tin roof sundae, served with fresh strawberries. Sunday we had a nice church service, and afterwards our good church cooks served a scrumptious meal so that our dear friends wouldn't start out being hungry on their 8 hour trip back to their home in Iowa. Father's Day weekend was, to say the least, WONDERFUL, I am still floating around on cloud 9. Thanks to family and friends. Mory

OH Lutefisk!! –

December 19, 2002

Cooking, etc.

Greetings on this cool blustery day. It is just above freezing, barely, but the wind is to be 30 or 40 miles per hour, Just a slight breeze. We don't have any gale warnings up. Got to thinking about lutefisk, yesterday. What a smelly thought. Well – my budget didn't have any place on the menu, for that hi-priced stuff. However, after due consideration and careful planning, I thought, just maybe, I could scrounge around and find enough cash to get some of that white soul food, as the Norskes like to call IT. Then I got to thinking, again. That is remarkable, twice in one day to tax my brain. A friend of mine had given me enough fresh fish to last for 4 meals. So for 4 days, I didn't have to shell out anything for meat, and I could apply that on the $9.00+ ? fish. That is what I finally did. Besides that, being a non-smoker, and non-hard-liquor drinker, that would help pay for my foolishness.

Monday, September 18, 2006

Differences

May Day, May Day, come all ye faithful to the aid of the Norskes. (SOL). (SAVE OUR LUTEFISK). Rumor has it that some of the "kooks" in Washington, of which there are many, have come up with the hair brained idea that if some of them were to eat lutefisk it might impair their capacity to = think??, and the fish might have some connection with terrorism, having migrated from across the pond. It seems as though they have zeroed in on Lake Ole to start their extermination process. We have had need for cops recently in our fair city, but this seems to this old Dane to be the last straw. It is Time for Action, and for us to do something about it. But what will be the best way to correct this brazen injustice? That is where I need your help and input. To me, it is time to put away petty differences and once and for all, the Danes, Norwegians and other offshoot nationalities get together, whether we like that smelly fish or not, and save the livelihood for our Norske friends, so that they don't starve to death, having no fish to sell, and thus end up in the poor house. Let us stand up and be COUNTED. Any suggestions would be welcomed. The need is Urgent. Mory

Wednesday, November 8, 2006

In fourteen hundred and ninety two, Christopher Columbus left Denmark,
To sail the ocean blue.

He didn't know where he was going, and being a Dane, he wouldn't know where he was, when he got to the place where he didn't know where he was going.

They sailed and sailed on the ocean blue, and finally old Chris decided, and rightfully so, that they were lost, completely lost, out some where, on the ocean blue.

He asked the Mate what shall we DO, for we are lost, and far from home? The good Mate pondered and then he said. my Captain, we should pray, for there isn't a single grasshopper in sight, to guide us on our way to any land.

So pray they did, through out the night, asking to see land, to get them out of their plight. And when daylight came, there was land in sight. So they high tailed it, to see what they had found. And lo and behold, here was Hetland, located on the shores of Lake Ole, which was abounding with, Lutefisk.

Old Christopher beamed with JOY, when he realized that he had found, the Promised Land # 2, not flowing with milk and honey, but with enough lutefisk, to feed the hungry crew.

Right then and there, he declared a day of Thanksgiving, and he and the Danish crew, stuffed themselves with lutefisk, but, sorrowfully, without any fresh Lefse.

And when done eating, the crew turned the boat around, and headed it back east, and they were ready to take a nap, while being stuffed, with ==== LUTEFISK

UFF DAA, What a Trip, on the ocean BLUE.

Tuesday, May 4, 2004

Greetings: Another nice day for a change. Nice and bright and warming up. I've been baking several loaves of bread, brownies, etc, as I serve Eastern Star tonight, so hopefully no one will go away hungry. Got by the bone cracker, yesterday, and went over to the courthouse, to vote absentee. Believe it or not, having voted in every election for 68 years, our "learned?" politicians in Pierre made me and others show identification that we are WE and Not some other "WE." In the instructions I, being too dumb to understand what it all meant started to ask questions, as some of us who are honored to be Danes have been known to do, not being too bright sometimes, according to some of our Norske friends. In the course of my ?'s, the girl wanted to know if I was Republican or a Democrat. Republican was my response, so she told me to mark the spot where it said Special. Whew, I never knew that before, and I didn't tell her that I was voting Democrat, as I register Republican so that I can vote against who I don't want to vote against in the general election. NO comments on that logic. So I went in to vote in a room all by myself, reserved for voters like me. More instructions as to what to do with getting the ballot to the right place at the right time. I figured most of that out all by myself, believe it or not? But there was a Big problem left that I don't think even a talented? Norwegian could solve all by himself. The ballot was Big, about a foot or so square, made out of heavy paper or cardboard, as the case may be. But the envelope that was to carry my secret vote was only about 4x8 inches or so, according to my old blacksmith eye, me not having a measuring stick with me. H-m-m, here was a BIG problem that even a Dane with what mentality that he had, would have to study on for a minute or so. The problem was this: At the bottom of the instruction sheet, in big bold letters, UNDERLINED, was this profound last instruction. DO NOT FOLD BALLOT. The Auditor must have deduced that I looked honest and took pity upon me, being so naive, let me fold it and stuff it into the secret envelope. Then I proceeded to go to the Treasurer and Register of deeds, big wigs, and let them know how bright the Republicans were, they all being of the Special group. My friends? didn't even offer to throw me out. My age may have protected me, having my cane in tow. Diddler.

Wednesday, June 28, 2006

Yi Yi Yippy Yi OOO: Stop the presses, hold the phone, Read all about it. Hetland's on the map, Hetland's on the map. Thanks to my good friend Greg Latza, expert photographer and excellent book writer from Sioux Falls. Another example of not what you know, but WHO you know, in this case, me knowing Greg Latza. Greg spent a considerable amount of time getting my picture taken in front of the blacksmith shop.

Perhaps because Greg is married to a Norwegian (and neither one of them eats lutefisk), the camera may have had to get used to having a lutefisk-eating Dane around the premises. Just a thought. If you want to get a copy of South Dakota's premier magazine with stories and pictures of the Sunshine state, especially the July and August issue, you can call 800-456-5117, or write South Dakota magazine, PO Box 175, Yankton, SD 57078. The picture on the front cover of the July and August issue is another example of Greg's artistic picture taking. Fantastic. Today is another really nice day out on the prairie in the Promised Land # 2. Mory

Wednesday, December 27, 2006

May Day, May Day hold the phone, stop the presses, Man the life boats, Disaster has Struck. 'Twas the night before Christmas, and all through the house. No No No. It was the day Before Christmas and all through the house there was clattering and banging and the noise was NOT made by a mouse. Bread machine # 9 was gasping for breath trying it's best to get the last loaf of bread baked before Christmas, and that it did, before giving up the "ghost." My oh my, what a fitting ending for the faithful bread machine, "conking" out after coughing up a lasting memento, a loaf of bread for Christmas Cheer to grace the table on Christmas day. Boy oh boy, that was SOMETHING SPECIAL.

But there is GOOD News to a go along with the bad. Our friend Hallie, who hails from Nebraska, was visiting us last summer, and being psychic or something like that, unbeknown to me, bought me a new bread machine. This Christmas Myrna put it under the tree, and so thanks to Hallie, we are back in business. I called Sunbeam and told them about the disaster, and lo and behold, they are sending me a new machine, free of charge. Besides that, a new Oster is on order to come in sometime after the first of the year. Retirement??? what a Challenge. If the flour mills quit making flour, I would be in Big trouble. Mory

PSS. Lutefisk is on the menu for today. Myrna told me that I had better eat it before it SPOILED. After all we throw out sour milk, and buy sour cream. I don't get ittt. Something must be "screwy?"?

Let's CELEBRATE!!! —

Friday, February 14, 2003

Warm greetings. Yesterday was a perfect day- today–ice is here now and snow on the way. Looks like Hetland is in the midst of it. What else is new? We seem to be in the north, south, east and central. So far nothing has been said about us being in the west. NOW.–Happy valentines day.

ROSES are RED,
VIOLETS are BLUE, SUGAR is SWEET,
And so are YOUUUU.
Come on over, and I'll treat you RIGHT,
Homemade BREAD and fresh BROWNIES TOO,
ORANGE JUICE to wash it DOWN,
And BESIDES that,
I LOVE YOU, Mory
P.S. THANKS for being My VALENTINE.

Monday, May 26, 2003

Greetings: A beautiful weekend with perfect weather. We had a nice church service yesterday with some visitors who are friends of ours. We are always happy to have them come to church and worship with us. Virg and Vi, our kids, were here and sang a nice duet to add to our church service. We very seldom get to have special numbers, so we are thankful when we can get a special number Volunteered with NO arm twisting.

Today we had a nice Memorial Day service at the Legion hall, and later at the Hetland Cemetery. Virg was the speaker, and of course his Father thought that he did a commendable job. But- there were others who thought the same, and they were Not all related to him. The Andersens took up most of the program, as Virg and Vi sang a duet, and then Virg sang a solo. After the trip to the cemetery we returned to the hall where we enjoyed a delicious pot luck dinner with scads of several kinds of food, all prepared with Loving hands by our Hetland ladies who Don't take the back seat for anyone, especially cooking. There was NO Lutefisk, as it is out of season. But we didn't need it. It has been an Enjoyable time in this household these past few days. My cup is RUNNING OVER and the Lord has really BLESSED me, even though I Don't deserve it. All for now. Mory

Friday, July 4, 2003

BANG BANG, BOOM BOOM & some more BOOMS, with a few Bang's mixed in. 60 degrees at 9 AM, a little breeze, no Sol and .3 or so of dew drops, with some hail mixed in for variety. Can U beat that?

A few years ago it would have been wild around here. The Melstad clan, mostly Norwegians, with a few Danes mixed in to put cream on the topping, would Celebrate the 4th, and I mean CELEBRATE. The clan would have a long line of tables which we would set up early in the morning so that they would become acclimated to the surroundings, as our tables were not used to their kind of terrain, which was a little bumpy. Obbie had a Big juice cooler which was run by electric current furnished by the power company. There were 2 large compartments in the outfit, which by the way came out of some vending eating place that sold soft drinks by the drink. He poured in the juice, one side always grape and the other one whichever kind he thought us sidewinders would indulge in. The kids had to sample it all day long, and as far as I know they never did decide which drink was the best until the hopper was empty. At 6 bells, it was time for chow. Hamburgers and wieners right off the grill, sometimes overcooked, but what the heck, they were good.

Now just in case that you get the cracked pot idea that we lived on this stuff, you have another guess coming. These women whose relatives came from the north countries from across the pond knew how to COOK, and still do. They had everything known to man, and very FEW women, to eat. Boy did we gobble it up, having waited patiently?? all day for Good food to fatten up on. I am pleased to say that no one, to the best of my knowledge went hungry. If they did that was their fault. Oh yeah, by the way. The clan and us had relatives from hither and yon that came to Hetland to have a safe and enjoyable 4th. They came from all over SD and even from the Twin Cities in Minn.

Virg and Vi and later their 2 young ones were also having a field day as he, Obbie and Leon were the chief fireworks operators. We always chipped in to get fireworks, and one year we had such big rockets that they had to be shot out of tubes buried into the ground. The only way these could be bought was to have some Wheel sign for them. Since I was on the town board, I had the distinct Honor? of signing for them. The other end didn't know how big a place we were, but we got the works, and the sellers got a signature. While we would be sitting around shooting the breeze. Obbie and I would have to tell all of the google-eyed Melstad kids about the dirty '30s. How the grasshoppers ate up the crops and chewed off the telephone poles and did a lot of other Nasty things. Needless to say, they lapped it up, and those of you who know Obbie and me know that we would NOT?? OVER DO IT???

Now U know what it was like in Hetland in the Good old days. If I survive long enough, I could tell you how we really Celebrated the 4th on one occasion. If I have taken up too much of your time, please excuse it, and finish it up–later. Mory the Diddler.

Friday, January 16, 2004

On his 90th Birthday

HI to one and all: Another day, and another year older. That is hard to believe that God in His Goodness has let me be a part of His world, here on earth for these many years. I don't deserve it but am thankful that I am still around, surrounded by all of you who are near and dear to me. Virg and Vi are bringing dinner today, even though I offered to take them out on the town. It is above freezing, so it is a nice day for this time of the year. I don't seem to remember what the day was like, a few short years ago when I first had a peek at what I was getting in to. I haven't been much of a "Nomad," as I was born across the street, so I haven't strayed far from the place where I first saw the light of day. From what I have been able to decipher, my folks must have started spoiling me at an early age. It seems as though I, being the first of four boys, received a lot of attention if I could make enough racket to get one of my folks' attention, that I received immediate service. When my younger brothers came to be a part of our family, I have been told that when one of them raised a ruckus to get some attention, Pa would remind Ma that the one making all of the noise might need some attention. Times must have changed, or she had gotten used to what the various sounds meant, and she would say, "He is all right," and she must have had it figured out right, as we all grew up sharing our lives with Loving parents who never had much in the form of worldly goods, but we were surrounded by LOVE. My celebration will be == low key. Mory.

Thursday, April 1, 2004

Rain - rain and more rain. If it keeps on pouring like this, old Noah would have to take the back seat for lack of water. It is a mess. The dam in Lake Ole, on the south edge of town is in danger of "busting." Not knowing what to do, we called the brain trust in Washington, DC as to what advice they could offer, knowing that the wheels there could solve any problem. After due and timely consideration the wheels? sent us some good? advice. The wheels that met together to get a handle on the situation thought that Bin Laden might be masterminding our problem, but they had devised a brilliant solution to our dilemma. Get all of the balloons that we could muster up, have them blown up by some folks with plenty of "Hot Air" to spare, and then carefully put the balloons up against the dam, on the side that as of now, didn't have any water pressing against it, in order to reinforce the dam. They offered to send some balloons out to us, as they had some to spare, and they also let us know that they had all kinds of "Hot Air" to share as well, but that they had a serious problem, as they were unable to find anyone who could figure out how to get air into the balloons. As time was of the essence, they wouldn't have time to appoint a commission to study the Air problem and report back on it.

So we took their sound? advice, and have an assembly line of Danes and Norskes blowing up balloons as fast as they can, while other people who are NOT so full of Air see to it that the air still stays where it is supposed to, and then they carefully put the balloons up against the dam to reinforce it. Boy was that ever a lifesaver. The only reason that I can think of for us not coming up with such a simple solution as this. We are paying those DC people big dough to think up ideas like this. Now you might begin to wonder who would be crazy enough to send something like this via the air waves, running the risk of the keeper of the flock, Ashcroft, getting his peepers on this. That would be the end of me, bread and water for the end of my days. OH=OH perish the thought.

All of this HOT AIR, only to discover that this is APRIL FOOL'S Day. What a waste of your time and mine. 3 guesses as to who this is from, and the first 2 don't count. Toodle- De -Ooo, and all of that Stuff. Enough, or Too much???

Monday, April 12 2004

Easter was a Great day, with a nice church service with folks from western and southern SD, Minnesota and Ohio, being with us. Not bad for a little spot on the map. I even conned a little 2 year old girl from Ohio to leave her Grandma, and having pointed at my lap, that cute little tyke forsook her Grandma, and came back to sit on my lap. It was surprising, as we had never met before, although I had shaken hands with her before church. Maybe my lap looked warmer? I helped her direct the singing, swinging her little arm, in tune of course, even though we were behind the singers. A little 10 year old from Minn played a flute solo and a former piano student of Eva's (probably one of her top students), one of our visitors, played the offertory as well as some lively hymns, after church. My Loved One's Heritage lives on even though she has gone "HOME."

I had dinner brought in by some of our friends, so I wasn't about to eat what I had lined up. Then in the afternoon, I took a loaf of bread to some of our friends in Lake Preston and came home loaded with more food, so my menu is all taken care of for this noon. Saturday was another Great day as I was at Virg and Vi's in Sioux Falls for a BIG dinner, with 15 or more family members sitting around the table, gobbling up lots of delicious food (non-fattening) as well as "shooting" the breeze, so my Cup is still "RUNNING OVER." Have a Great Day. Mory

Saturday, April 1, 2006

A day B 4 Sunday

Boy, is it ever nice to live in a town where the unexpected can be expected. That is what happened this morning in this little hamlet located on the shores of one of the Great Lakes, OLE.

This morning as I looked out of my window I just about did a double take, if that were possible for a FOF (Feeble Old Fart - ed.) like me. Out in the tree in front of the house were 2, yes I said 2, MONKEYS. Boy were they having a great time, cavorting around, jumping from tree to tree and branch to branch, hanging by their tails and doing flip flops and summersaults, and still staying above ground. What a sight to behold. Then I remembered, as Dane's sometimes do, that the TV stations were telling about 2 monkeys escaping from the zoo, and everyone should be on the lookout for them. I called the sheriff, and he called the zoo to tell them that the lost monkeys had been found and were languishing at Dale Andersen's in Hetland, where they were enjoying eating bananas and playing with the cats when they were not climbing trees.

Boy oh boy, it wasn't long before the streets were crowded with cars, cops, TV reporters and what-not. By this time the monkeys must have surmised that they were the center of attention and climbed up a little higher in the tree and proceeded to scratch and examine themselves, probably checking for lice or fleas that might inhabit a monkey's anatomy. The TV crews wanted to interview me, and they let me know that I would be on television. No big deal, as I told them that I had been on TV before and had even looked at my colon while the Dr. had examined it to see if it was "ticking."

By now, by conservative estimates, there were about a thousand people, give or take a couple, waiting for the Zoo crew to come and catch the above-mentioned monkeys. Finally, the zoo truck, accompanied by a fire truck with hook and ladders, drove into sight. The monkeys, seeing the zoo truck, must have known that something was brewing for them, and climbed up to the very top of the tree, for safety. One of the zoo crew came out with a big gun that looked like a Bazooka, aimed at the escapees and pulled the trigger. KA-BOOM! Out came a net which settled down over the monkeys, and the more they thrashed around to get out of the net, the more tangled up they got. Then the firemen hoisted the hook and ladder and grabbed the monkeys, and proceeded to deposit them in the zoo truck, ready to put them back in the pen where they came from. Boy oh boy, what an experience, all happening in our little town. To find out what time this old Duffer will be on TV, Scroll down the page, for the time.

APRIL FOOL. HO HO HO.

Week of Thanksgiving —

Thursday, November 22, 2004

HAPPY THANKSGIVING 2 all of U, from me 2 U. The weather is still B = E = U = T - Full out here in the Promised Land # 2, located on the shores of Lake Ole. I am going to Sioux Falls to Virg and Vi's for dinner tomorrow, and I have it on good authority, that there will NOT B, any of that savory lutefisk, to fill up on. However, I hasten to tell U, that there will B Lefse on the menu. WOW. 6 years ago on Thanksgiving day, when Eva went HOME we had snow "coming out of our ears." A lot different than 60 degree weather, as of now. Please don't over eat, especially if there is lutefisk on the agenda. A nap after eating, might be in order. Enjoy your day. Mory

Turkey Day

He'll be drivin' the old Red Mercury when he comes, Boom Boom,
He'll be drivin' the old Red Mercury when he comes, Boom Boom,
We'll have lutefisk and lefse, Boom Boom,
With plenty of butter and sugar, when he comes. Boom Boom.
And he'll be bringin' LOVE and KISSES,
He'll be bringin' LOVE and KISSES, when he comes. BOOM BOOM.
From your Dad.

Friday

Dear all 6 of U: Thank you, thank you and more thank yous for such a nice enjoyable time with you yesterday. It is a JOY to be a part of your Loving and Caring family. I wasn't going to eat any supper last night, as I was still Stuffed. But when I was putting away all of the goodies that you gave me, I could smell the aroma of == savory dressing, which I happened to know, was prepared with Loving hands, by a Master Chef.

Chapter 20
Epilogue

Josh, Dale, and Ben give a thumbs up!

Epilogue

I like to live in a little town
where the trees meet across the street
where you wave your hand and say, "Hello"
to everyone you meet.

I like to stand for a moment
outside the grocery store
and listen to the friendly gossip of
the folks that live next door

For life is interwoven
with the friends we learn to know
and we hear their joys and sorrows
as we daily come and go.

So I like to live in a little town;
I care no more to roam.
For every house in a little town
is more than a house – it's Home.
                    –Author Unknown

'Tis HETLAND, South Dakota
The land of Sunshine and Wind.

This unknown author's writing is taken from the last page of the Hetland Centennial book, HETLAND "MY HOME TOWN" and expresses the sentiment that I have had throughout my life, while residing here. As this book is brought to a close, I hope that you have caught some of the insight of friendship and caring that we who have lived here have enjoyed through out the years. Being now in the twilight years of my sojourn here on earth, I am reminded of some of the words of a song that we used to sing in church. "For I'm a Pilgrim, and I'm a Stranger, and I must travel on." My dear wife Eva sang this song, ever so sweetly, at the funeral of a young boy who lost his life in a traffic accident. It was such a comfort for the family, and for all of us who heard her sing.

Now as I think back over my life span, the years have flitted by so quickly. I am sorry for the things that I did, that I shouldn't have done. Sorry for the things that I should have done and didn't do. I have been so Blessed with a Loving and Caring family, and relatives who shared our Joys and our sorrows, and who were always ready to lend a Helping hand whenever needed. Friends! What would I have done without them? Without the love and concern of many friends, mine and ours, I could not have carried on living here by myself.

Now comes the BEST of all. I have a Loving and Caring Heavenly Father who has NEVER failed me, and His helping hand has been grasping mine, time and time again, guiding me on, even though I haven't deserved it. He has done it because of His LOVE, even as He sent His only Son, the Lord Jesus, who died on the cross for sinners like you and me. There have been Ups and Downs in our lives, but by the Grace of a Loving God, the UPS have far exceeded the downs. My cup still runs OVER. It has been a JOY living my life in Hetland, "MY HOME TOWN."

I hope that you have enjoyed reading this book as much as I have enjoyed "hunting and pecking" it out. THANK YOU kids – Myrna, Virgil and Vi, for your labor of LOVE, for prodding me, and for making this book a reality. Love from your Father and your Mom, who I am sure, has been looking over your shoulders from the "other side." She would say, as do I, "WELL DONE, KIDS."